A Viennese Waltz

Down Wall Street

To Nick Pardini

AEIOU!

Mark Shuster

2018

A Viennese Waltz Down Wall Street

Austrian Economics for Investors

By Mark Skousen

BOOKS BY MARK SKOUSEN

Economics

Economics of a Pure Gold Standard (1985)

The Structure of Production (1990)

Economics on Trial (1991)

Dissent on Keynes (editor, 1992)

Puzzles and Paradoxes in Economics
(co-authored with Kenna C. Taylor, 1993)

Economic Logic (2000, 2010)

The Making of Modern Economics (2001, 2009)

The Power of Economic Thinking (2002)

Finance

High Finance on a Low Budget (1981)
(co-authored with Jo Ann Skousen)

Tax Free (1982)

The Complete Guide to Financial Privacy (1983)

The Investor's Bible: Mark Skousen's Principles of Investment (1988)

Scrooge Investing (1993)

Investing in One Lesson (2007)

The Maxims of Wall Street (2011)

A Viennese Waltz Down Wall Street (2013)

ISBN: 978-1-6212909-2-6 (print)
ISBN: 978-1-6212909-3-3 (ebook)

18 17 16 15 14 13 1 2 3 4 5 6 7

Published by Laissez Faire Books, 808 St. Paul Street, Baltimore, Maryland
www.lfb.org

Cover Design: Mark O'Dell and Susanne Clark
Cover Illustration: Greg Houston
Layout Design: Kristen Duerling

To Jo Ann, my waltzing partner in life

CONTENTS

PART II
Essays on Austrian Financial Economics and History

PART III
Austrian Economics: Newsletters, Books, and Services

I INTRODUCTION TO WALL STREET: *A Random Walk or a Viennese Waltz?*

"Practical men, who believe themselves to be quite exempt from any intellectual influences, are usually the slaves of some defunct economist."

—John Maynard Keynes

Sit down and relax, and spend a quiet evening reading about the famous Austrian economists and how you can profit from their sound principles. While you're reading, why not listen to the sounds of the great classical composers? A little Mozart, Beethoven, or Strauss, perhaps. Afterward, why not have an elegant Viennese dessert, apple strudel, or Sacher-Torte. It will put you in the mood to make money!

I thought of writing this book after reading Burt Malkiel's classic work, *A Random Walk Down Wall Street*. As a student of Austrian economics and a practitioner of high finance, I never bought into the view that stock prices were random. Certainly, much of Malkiel's analysis of efficient market theory appears to be sound, but appearances can be deceiving. As Nassim Taleb says, we can be fooled by randomness, when, in fact, purposeful human action determines stock prices. The more we know about the motives of the buyers and sellers, the better we can analyze and profit from their actions.

In short, then, I see the stock market more as a dance, where the dancers—the buyers and the sellers—move freely up and down the dance floor within the set patterns or rules, not like some drunken sailors who stumble unpredictably along Broadway. Dancers engage in purposeful action and the rhythm and genre of the music guides them. They have the freedom to choose their direction on the dance floor, and which of the many patterns and steps they will take. They can even create a new step or direction.

But to be successful, dancers always have to match the rhythm of the music in the air around them. If they get out of step, they are likely to make mistakes and cause other dancers to falter, as well. Similarly, the rhythm of the markets controls investors. To be successful, they need to be alert to the atmosphere of the economy and the other investors around them.

Hence, the behavior of the stock market is more like a waltz, not a random walk. And, since this book is about applying the principles of Austrian economics to investing, I prefer to call it *A Viennese Waltz Down Wall Street*.

A Viennese waltz is not for everyone. Some may prefer a slower Tennessee waltz. A Viennese waltz is fast-paced and, when performed well, can be exhilarating. But it is also fraught with peril and can be exhausting. Dancers have to be in sync with the music and with each other, or they will falter. But when everything is in sync, it is glorious.

The efficient market theory and modern portfolio analysis have much to offer investors in reducing risk, avoiding the numerous pitfalls of investing, and increasing your chance of making money. But it also underestimates the ability of financial entrepreneurs and speculators to beat the market, to go contrary to the crowd, to incorporate gold and silver—real money—in one's portfolio, and to profit from a sound understanding of the effects of government intervention in the economy and the ups and downs of the business cycle.

Ludwig von Mises Goes to Wall Street

Enter the Austrian school of economics.

If you've ever read or listened to Peter Schiff, Harry Browne, Jim Blanchard, Gary North, Richard Band, Hans Sennholz, Doug Casey, Adrian Day, Larry Abraham, or a host of other famous financial gurus and brokers, you've probably heard references to the Austrian school of economics, and asked yourself these questions:

Who are Ludwig von Mises, Friedrich A. Hayek, Joseph Schumpeter, and Murray Rothbard? What is the Austrian school of economics? Why do financial writers and advisors such as myself pay attention to these academic wizards? And, most importantly, how can they make you a better investor?

This book seeks to provide answers. It is my opinion that the Austrian school of economics, along with other important schools, offers valuable insights into the exhilarating, volatile world of high finance.

It might seem strange that an investment counselor and forecaster such as myself would rely on the philosophy of Ludwig von Mises, Friedrich Hayek, Joseph Schumpeter, and other obscure academic scribblers from old Vienna who had virtually no experience in the investment markets. However, the Austrian economists provide a scientific method that helps investors make the right decisions and avoid traps and dangers. It is my judgment that Austrian economics can improve your market performance. Without this guidance, you may be at sea without a rudder and likely to commit many costly mistakes. Austrian economics won't satisfy all of your financial questions—I continue to rely on a variety of tools of analysis—but it is valuable in guiding you along the path of financial independence.

After studying in depth the works of these continental sages, I have found them beneficial in helping you satisfy your basic investment needs:

Can anyone predict the future price of stocks, gold, foreign currencies and other investments?

Are we headed for an economic boom, depression, or something in between?

Can you beat the market?

Is it possible for you to minimize risk and maximize return on your investment portfolio?

How can you profit from undervalued or overvalued situations?

What factors should you use to anticipate market moves?

Which investment theory is best—fundamental analysis, charting or technical analysis, cycle theory, geopolitical trends, or contrarian thinking?

What is the best mix of investment choices?

Are gold, silver, and foreign currencies good inflation hedges?

Can the government protect you from investment fraud and deception? If not, who or what will protect you?

The Austrian school of economics can provide valuable tools to answer many of these questions and make you a better investor.

I also address the risks and biases associated with Austrian economics, especially the doomsday "gold bug" mentality. These biases are considerable and may result in lost opportunities or bad investment choices (such as buying too much gold in a bear market). There are also risks in trying to time the market and in seeking ways to determine what stocks are overvalued and undervalued.

In this book, I start with the lives and ideas of each Austrian economist, from Menger to Rothbard, and explain how their contributions can be applied to personal investing strategies.

In Part II of the book, I have selected seven articles previously published in other works that will give you insights into Austrian finance:

- "Murray Rothbard as Investment Advisor" (1988)
- "What Every Investor Should Know About Austrian Economics and the Hard Money Movement" (1988)
- "The Economist As Investment Advisor" (1991)
- "Keynes As a Speculator" (1992)
- "Who Predicted the 1929 Crash?" (1993)
- "Financial Economics" (1994)
- "A Tale of Two Dollars" (2010)

A number of economists and financial writers have reviewed parts of the manuscript and have given me valuable feedback.

Milton Friedman read an early version of Part I of this book, prior to his passing in 2006.[1] His reaction was similar to what he told a group of Austrian economists at a meeting in 1974 at the now-defunct Royalton College in Vermont: "There is no Austrian economics—only good economics and bad economics."[2] He said he enjoyed reading it but felt that my application of Austrian economics was nothing more than "standard neo-classical economics." I think what he recognized is the fact that much of what we call Austrian economics, such as subjectivism, marginal pricing, and opportunity cost, has been integrated into mainstream economics now. However, there still remain many Austrian concepts that have not been integrated, especially the Austrian theory of the business cycle, the vital role of gold in monetary policy, and the less popular views that asset bubbles are important and that inflation creates substantial structural imbalances.

---

1. *Austrian Economics for Investors: Ludwig von Mises Goes to Washington* (London: Pickering and Chatto, 1995). I wrote this 48-page essay at the invitation of Bill Bonner, publisher of Agora, as an introduction to a three-volume collection of essays by Austrian economists. It is now out of print.
2. *The Foundations of Modern Austrian Economics*, ed. by Edwin G. Dolan (Kansas City: Sheed & Ward, 1976), 4.

A growing number of financial analysts, money managers, and investors are using Austrian concepts to make investment decisions, including Harry Veryser, chairman of the economics department at the University of Detroit-Mercy; Adrian Day, director of Adrian Day Asset Management; Bert Dohmen, publisher of the *Wellington Letter*; Nicholas Vardy, president of Hayek Capital Management in London; Frank Shostak, president of Applied Austrian Economics Ltd., a financial advisory service based in Australia; Jeff Berwick, editor of the *Dollar Vigilante*; Joseph Calandro, Jr., enterprise risk manager at ACE Group and author of *Applied Value Investing*; Ted Barnhart, manager of the Barnhart Investment Advisory, a Chicago-based fee-only investment firm; Thomas Aubrey, an investment analyst at Credit Capital Advisory in the U.K.; and Peter Schiff, president of Euro Pacific Capital in Westport, Conn.

There is also a whole host of investment writers, advisers, money managers, and investors who have formed social networks to study and discuss Austrian economics on Yahoo, LinkedIn, Facebook, etc., and I have enjoyed our discussions and debates on what works and what doesn't work in Austrian financial theory. I wish to thank Robert Blumen and others who have guided me in this direction and have provided insights into this book.

Finally, I thank my wife, Jo Ann, editor and English professor extraordinaire, for her reviewing and improving the manuscript. She is one of those unique editors who truly knows a participle from a predicate.

Yours for peace, prosperity, and liberty, AEIOU,

Mark Skousen
New York, New York

PART I

Austrian Economics and Investment Strategies

1 WHAT IS THE AUSTRIAN SCHOOL?

"Austrian economics provides one of the most fruitful scientific developments of our age."

—Lionel Robbins (1931)

"The Austrian school of economics is the most consistent and articulate advocate of the private property, free enterprise system."

—Hans Sennholz

The Austrian school is the foremost defender of free-market economics in the world. It started at the University ofVienna in the 1870s but has since spread throughout the world. It is relatively small, compared to other well-known schools of economics, such as the Keynesians (followers of John Maynard Keynes), the monetarists (followers of Milton Friedman or the Chicago school) or the Marxists (followers of Karl Marx). But it is growing in influence.

The Austrian school began with the work of Carl Menger, one of the three economists largely responsible for the marginalist revolution in economics in the 1870s. His students Eugen Böhm-Bawerk and Friedrich Wieser continued the tradition as professors at the University ofVienna. The third generation of Austrian economists—Ludwig von Mises, Friedrich Hayek, and Joseph Schumpeter—left Vienna prior to World War II and spread the principles of Austrian economists to England and the United States. There Austrian economists flourished under the direction of Murray Rothbard, Hans Sennholz, and Henry Hazlitt, among others. Today, you can find Austrian economists teaching and applying their principles around the world.

In the United States, economists with an Austrian orientation have teaching positions at George Mason University, New York University, Auburn University, University of Georgia, Hillsdale College, and other institutions of higher learning. In Latin America, Austrian economics is taught at the Universidad Francisco Marroquin in Guatemala and the ESEADE Graduate School in Argentina, among other places. In Europe, it is taught at the Universidad Rey Juan Carlos (Spain), the University of Geneva (Switzerland), University of Angers (France), and several universities in Germany. Austrian economics is taught at several colleges and universities in Japan, Korea, Hong Kong, and Singapore.

A number of conservative and libertarian think tanks are followers of the Austrian school, including the Cato Institute, the Foundation for Economic Education, the Manhattan Institute, the Mises Institute, and the Reason Foundation. International think tanks also have strong Austrian influence, including the Institute of Economic Affairs, the Adam Smith Institute, and the Cobden Centre in London.

And, of course, many investment advisors rely on the sound economic doctrines and theories of the Austrians, with their emphasis on entrepreneurship, subjectivism, individualism, and fundamental analysis.

To better understand this unique school of economics, let's now take a tour of old Vienna and see how valuable the Austrian economists can be.

The Hapsburgs and Old Vienna

The Austrian school has its roots in Vienna, the capital of the Austro-Hungarian empire prior to World War I. The empire's aristocratic leaders, the Hapsburgs, ruled Eastern Europe for more than 400 years. Many historians consider the Austro-Hungarian empire to be the greatest dynasty in modern history.

Friedrich III (1440–93) is considered the founder of the Hapsburg dynasty and was the first of his family to be anointed Holy Roman Emperor in Rome. His tomb bears the famous inscription, "A.E.I.O.U." At first these letters were interpreted in Latin to mean "II Austriae est imperare orbi universo," then later in (early modern) German, "Alles erderich ist Oesterreich untertan."Translated, these words mean "Austria is destined to rule the world." In English, the most common interpretation is "Austria's empire is overall universal." After World War I, Austria lost its position of political power and cynics suggested the following new meaning: "Austria's empire is ousted utterly!" The shifting meaning of Friedrich's cryptic motto mirrors the shifting understanding of how the world works.

Over the years, the Hapsburgs established Vienna as the political, cultural and intellectual center of Eastern Europe. Vienna, located on the beautiful Danube River, became the third-largest city in Europe, behind London and Paris. It was famous for its magnificent museums, palaces, parks, opera houses, and cafes.

For a century and a half, from the late 1700s until the early 1900s, there occurred an extraordinary intellectual flowering within the Austro-Hungarian empire. Vienna attracted some of the world's most creative musicians, scientists, philosophers, and economists. The world's greatest musicians lived there, including Mozart, Beethoven, Haydn, Schubert, Brahms, Mahler, and Strauss. One of the world's most revolutionary social scientists, Sigmund Freud, lived and worked in Vienna.

2 CARL MENGER: SUBJECTIVISM AND THE MARGINALIST REVOLUTION

"No book since Ricardo's *Principles* has had such a great influence on the development of economics as Menger's *Grundsätze*."

—Knut Wicksell

Another revolution took place at the University of Vienna through the work of Carl Menger (1840–1921), the founder of the Austrian school of economics. Menger was a lawyer, journalist, and civil servant and for two years was the tutor for Crown Prince Rudolf of Austria. At the young age of thirty-three, Menger was made Extraordinary Professor of Law and Political Science at the University of Vienna, based in part on the publication of a book written two years earlier, in 1871.

The book, *Grundsätze der Volkswirtschaftslehre*, later translated into English as *The Principles of Economics* (New York University Press, 1950), was a revolutionary work. What did his book accomplish?

The Principle of Subjectivism

First, Menger established the principle of subjectivism. He demonstrated that prices of goods and services are determined by the subjective demands of consumers, not the cost of production or labor theory of value, as Adam Smith and David Ricardo (of the Classical British School) had argued. Prices of all goods and services are never based on "intrinsic" value or cost. Value is always determined by the needs and desires of the ultimate user.

The principle of subjectivism has immediate relevance to the financial field. Prices of stocks, bonds, and other assets are sometimes bid up to extremely high levels, then bid down to depressed levels, often unrelated to their "intrinsic" value or cost of production. The financial markets are always subjective in nature, based on the attitudes and whims of investors.

According to Menger, there is no such thing as intrinsic value in goods, services or financial assets.

Buying Stocks Below Book Value

Example #1: Suppose a publicly-traded company is selling below its book value. By book value, we mean the company's stock "equity," which is equal to a company's total assets minus its liabilities, including goodwill. In practical terms, "book value" generally means how much is left over in assets if a company goes out of business and is sold.

"Value investors" are always searching for companies selling at relatively low prices, sometimes near or below book value. Is this not a sign that the firm is deeply undervalued and must eventually rise in price? This will happen only if the company turns around and recovers in sales and earnings. Then the stock price is likely to rise sharply, and it offers an excellent bargain opportunity. But there is high risk. Book value may be deceptive, especially when it includes vague assets such as "good will."

Many companies have sold below book, only to fall in price even further, as the company heads into bankruptcy. Remember, there is usually a good reason why a company's stock is selling for a low price. Sales may be lagging; debt may be rising. Buying cheap stocks works well only if the company turns around and recovers. And that's a big if.

Buying Commodities Below Their Cost of Production

Example #2: What if the price of a commodity falls below its cost of production? This has happened occasionally during a slump in gold, silver, aluminum, oil, and other natural resources.

During the 1980s, the price of copper dropped sharply, from $1.40 per pound to $0.60 per pound, at a time when most analysts estimated that the cost of producing copper was around $0.80 per pound. Since the price of copper was selling below its cost of production, they predicted that the price of copper had to rise. Why? Because copper producers in Chile, Zambia, and the United States could not have continued to stay in business selling copper below cost. It's simple economics. These companies would eventually have to shut down their mines, or somehow cut the cost of producing copper. With this theory in mind, investment advisors recommended buying copper futures contracts on the Chicago Board of Trade.

Was this a good recommendation?

Using Austrian economics, you would be very suspicious of this recommendation. Here's why: Prices could continue to fall, even though they are below their cost of production. Austrian economics tells us that the price consumers pay is not dependent on the cost of production. Prices are based solely on what customers are willing to pay for copper. All prices are subjective.

In addition, "costs" are also subjective and can change. There's nothing fixed about the cost of producing copper. When the price of copper is low and production is unprofitable, many copper companies will attempt to reduce costs by renegotiating their contracts with labor unions and suppliers. Maybe they can reduce costs so much that the company remains profitable, resulting in greater output of copper, while reducing prices further!

In short, investors should not view a commodity as a bargain-buying opportunity simply because it sells "below cost." It may continue to sell below cost for many months, if not years, before recovering.

In fact, the key to making money in commodities and commodity stocks is not to watch the cost of producing copper, but to watch the supply and demand factors affecting the retail price of copper.

Menger's law of imputation indicates that the retail price of a commodity ultimately determines the costs of the factors of production, not the other way around.

In his *Grundsätze*, Menger used the example of tobacco to demonstrate his law of imputed value. Suppose consumers decided to stop smoking. What would happen to the demand for and price of cigarettes? They would fall to zero. But what would happen to the price of land used in the production of tobacco? Would it fall to zero? No. The land would fall to its next best use—the tobacco farmers would switch to crops such as wheat or soybeans, or they would build homes or an industrial park.

What if people decided to smoke more cigarettes? Demand for tobacco and tobacco factors of production would rise—and so would the cost of producing tobacco. So we see that cost is a function of final consumer demand.

Granted, supply can change too, due to a technological breakthroughs or a temporary shortfall or famine, for example, causing retail prices to shift with the changing costs of production. In sum, we see that prices are determined by supply and demand, not necessarily by the cost of production. Investors need to be careful not to determine their investment decisions based on cost factors only.

Buying and Selling at the Margin

Second, Menger established the marginalist revolution in economics, explaining what determines prices. In his book, Menger broke away from the Classical School of Adam Smith and David Ricardo. Smith and Ricardo claimed that the exchange prices of goods and services are unrelated to their practical uses, but they were unable to explain adequately the value of those goods and services. They failed to resolve a popular paradox at the time, known as the "diamond-water" question: Why is the price of a diamond so much higher when water is essential to life?

Menger finally came up with the answer a hundred years after Smith raised the issue. He showed that the value of goods is determined by their marginal utility, rather than their by total utility. In other words, diamonds are more expensive than water because an extra diamond generally has greater utility than an extra cup of water. That is, the greater the quantity, the lesser the marginal value or price. Water is cheap because it is so plentiful; diamonds are expensive because their supply is so limited.

Again, the marginalist principle can be applied to investing. All prices on the stock exchange are created by a relatively small number of marginal buyers and sellers. On any given day, only a very small percentage of stockholders call their broker to buy or sell a stock. Even during a crash, only a minority of investors make trades. This is an important point to remember. It takes only a marginal shift in investor sentiment to change the direction of stock prices.

Only a Small Group of Traders Is Necessary to Move a Stock

Example #1: In 2007, the price of Yahoo, a high technology company, fell by 14 percent in one day, after missing its earnings estimate by only a penny. That penny was bad enough for shareholders to dump their shares and cause the stock price to plummet. Nearly seventy million shares traded that one day—and yet that represented less than 6 percent of outstanding Yahoo shares (1.18 billion). In sum, a marginal number of shareholders can make a huge difference.

On Oct. 19, 1987, the stock market crashed, falling 22 percent (I had quite a party on my fortieth birthday that might, especially as I had recommended selling "all stocks" six weeks earlier). I have since asked many groups of investors, "How many of you sold that day when the market crashed?" Never more than a handful raise their hands. It was the single biggest drop in the market, yet only a margin of investors made it happen.

Marginal Buying and Selling in Real Estate

Example #2: The marginalist principle applies equally to the real estate market. In normal times, perhaps only 5 percent percent of all houses may be up for sale in a given neighborhood. The average price level of the homes reflects this fact. But what would happen if the number of homes for sale suddenly doubled overnight? Assuming demand hasn't changed, the price of homes could fall precipitously. Remember, prices are determined by marginal buying and selling, not by the total number of homeowners.

How much is your home worth? Suppose you commission an appraisal and find out it is worth $250,000. But is it really worth that? You don't know until you sign the papers and you close on the deal. That $250,000 is based on the going price of comparable houses in your neighborhood, all things being equal. What do we mean by the phrase, "all things being equal" (a common term used by economists)? It means that the $250,000 price is a reasonable estimate of your house's value, as long as the same economic and financial conditions exist.

One of the assumptions is that only 5 percent of all homes are on the market at any given time. If 10 percent of homeowners suddenly wanted to sell, the value of your home would drop dramatically, perhaps to $200,000 or $150,000.

In short, prices of real estate (and other investment assets) can rise or fall, depending on how many buyers and sellers are interested. The larger the margin, the greater the volatility.

The Role of Time

Third, Carl Menger emphasized the critical role of *time* in economic activity. All consumer goods, from automobiles to food on the table, undergo many stages of production, from raw materials to final products. The process may take months or even years, depending on the product or service. It may also take months or years just to use up or consume a product.

This time structure forms the basis of a correct understanding of macroeconomics and how the economy operates.[1]

Time is, of course, critical in the investment markets, especially in determining the value of bonds, warrants, and other time-wasting assets. But time, as incorporated in the period of production and consumption, also has a great effect on the economics, financing, and pricing of companies.

Menger divided the economy into consumer goods (called "first order" or "lower order" goods) and producer goods (called "higher order" goods). He noted that the price and output of producer goods completely depend on the demand on final consumer goods (known as the "theory of imputation"). Menger's time-structural approach to the economy has significant importance to the financial markets, especially as developed by Mises, Hayek, and the next generation of Austrian economists.

Menger's theory of imputation also has significance in analyzing the financial markets. It implies greater price volatility in companies involved in creating "higher order" producer goods, such as in mining and manufacturing, than in companies involved in the production of "lower order" consumer goods. For example, crude oil prices tend to be more volatile than gasoline prices at the pump. Similarly, junior oil stocks are notoriously more volatile than the price of major oil companies.

---

1. For a more complete development of a macroeconomics model based on Menger's stages-of-production approach, see my book, *The Structure of Production* (New York University Press, 1990). It was updated with a new introduction in 2007.

The Inherent Volatility of Mining Stocks

Example: Several years ago, I was on a panel of gold bugs debating the outlook for gold. One of the panelists, representing a mining company, recommended that investors take a "buy-and-hold" strategy with gold stocks. "Just buy them and forget about them," he argued.

I disagreed, saying that because mining companies produce a raw commodity (gold) that is far from final consumer use, the profits and prices of mining companies must by nature be extremely volatile.

"I beg to differ," responded the mining spokesman. "Take Homestake, for example." Homestake is one of the oldest and largest gold mining companies in the United States. "You could have purchased Homestake for $4 in 1970, and today it sells for $20. That sounds like a pretty good 'buy-and-hold' strategy to me."

"Wait a minute," I jumped in. "Let's see what happened to the price of Homestake between 1970 and 1990. Over that twenty-year period, Homestake went from $4 to $20, dropped back to $5, and then bounced back up to $20. Now I ask the investors in the audience, how many of you would have stayed with Homestake through such a roller coaster ride? I doubt very many of you would have had the stomach to handle that kind of volatility!"

I made my point and won the debate. Austrian economics taught me that the further away a company is from final consumer use, the more volatile its profits, earnings, and prices will be. Such volatility is ideal for speculators who are on the right side of the market, or a disaster on the wrong side.

In my judgment, Carl Menger is the greatest economist who ever lived because he established the basis for a sound understanding of both microeconomics (marginal price theory) and macroeconomics (time structure of production). Most modern concepts in Austrian economics today come from Menger.

3 EUGEN BÖHM-BAWERK: SAVING, INTEREST RATES, AND THE THEORY OF CAPITAL

"Böhm-Bawerk was the best-known economist on the continent at the turn of the nineteenth century."

—Paul Samuelson

Eugen Böhm-Bawerk (1851–1914), a pupil of Carl Menger, made great contributions to the theory of capital, interest, and economic growth. Böhm-Bawerk is actually Menger's most famous student and, in fact, was probably the most famous economist on the European continent around 1900. He was the only Austrian economist well-known in his native country, having graced the front of the Austrian 100 schilling note until 2000, when Austria adopted the euro.

Böhm-Bawerk was Austria's finance minister three times in the 1890s. He helped restore Austria to the gold standard. (It was because of this success that his face appeared on the Austrian 100 schilling note.) After retiring from his government post, he became a professor at the University of Vienna. His theory of capital and interest has had a major impact on economic growth theory, and his critique of Marx's theory of exploitation is considered devastating. He is considered "the man who answered Marx," and left Marx's theory mortally wounded.

His most significant work is *The Positive Theory of Capital*, published in 1889 by Macmillan, and forms the basis of the modern theory of economic growth. Building on Menger's stages of production, Böhm-Bawerk argued that individuals and firms adopt more roundabout processes of production in order to achieve economic growth and a higher standard of living.

By "roundabout," Böhm-Bawerk means the sacrificing of current consumption to produce more capital goods, adopt new technology, and institute longer processes of production, which in turn lead to greater consumption in the future. For example, it may take two days for a worker to sew a dress by hand. But suppose she builds a sewing machine that could allow her to sew five dresses per day. The building of that sewing machine may take six months—a long roundabout process—but once manufactured, it would increase her productivity tremendously.

Böhm-Bawerk was the leading defender of savings and investment during a period of increasing antipathy toward the traditional virtue of thrift. He contended that increasing savings and postponing consumption does not hurt business, but that it was simply a more effective form of spending. It pays dividends indefinitely into the future if the funds are well spent on new businesses, technology, and capital formation. Thus, capital formation is *sine qua non* to economic growth.

Following Böhm-Bawerk's lead, the Austrian school has consistently argued that a high voluntary saving rate, both individually and nationally, is the key to rapid economic growth. Austrians are very critical of Keynesian economists who denigrate savings and promote a high-consumption society. They also criticize the monetarists, who emphasize the money supply as a key ingredient to economic growth. Austrians argue that more voluntary saving by individuals and firms, not more monetary inflation, more consumption, or more government, is essential to long-term prosperity.

By the same token, the Austrians have also criticized efforts by centralized governments to promote "forced saving" plans that artificially raise the investment rate. To be most efficient, all saving (and consumption) should be voluntary, based on the free desires of individuals to determine their own time preference.

The Importance of Saving

Austrian emphasis on saving and time preference can be helpful in personal economics, corporate finance and investment decision-making. For example, I am frequently asked at financial seminars, "Mr. Skousen, what is the key to financial success?" I answer, "It has two parts. If you do these two things, you will be eminently successful in life. The first is to save regularly; the second is to invest those savings productively."

You want to put aside as much money as you can without being a miser. Always spend less than you earn. "A part of all you earn is yours to keep," says Arkad in *The Richest Man in Babylon*. The old-fashioned virtue of thrift is just as vital today as it was in the past. I know individuals who are very well-off today simply because they consistently socked away 35 percent of their income over the years. Save at least 10 percent of your take-home pay, and you will be on the road to financial independence.

The second part is just as important as the first—put your savings to good use. Too many people squander their savings by being too conservative, placing their money in low-yielding bank certificates of deposit, passbook savings accounts, money market funds, and Treasury bills. If you make only 1–3 percent on your money, you'll never get excited about investing. You need to make 20 percent, 40 percent, even 100 percent on your money in a year. Then you'll have something to get excited about! But of course, you have to take greater risks to earn higher returns. You might lose your fortune if you are too risky. So you must be prudent and look for unusual "high-return/low-risk" opportunities.

The best place to earn money fast is in your own business. Almost every one of *Forbes'* 400 Richest People in America got there by doing just that. If you have the smarts to run a successful business, you'll make lots of money during your lifetime. Most entrepreneurs experience failure, but you should never give up. Eventually, you'll discover what you're good at, which will make up for all of the losses of the past.

Investing in Free Enterprise

Of course, if you don't have the stomach for running your own business, then do the next best thing: Invest in other people's successful businesses. And the best place to do that is the stock market. Invest in free enterprise, and you'll do well most of the time, assuming that the government doesn't ruin everything by over-regulating and overtaxing business.

Example #1: My favorite strategy is to buy successful, growing, and well-managed companies when they are relatively cheap. Avoid faltering or dying firms and industries or high-risk penny stocks. A better approach is to buy into companies and sectors that produce products and services that burgeon over time and to buy them after a correction in the market place. (Growth stocks tend to be overvalued by investors.) As J. Paul Getty, America's first billionaire, writes, "The seasoned investor buys his stocks when they are priced low, holds them for the long-pull rise, and takes in-between dips and slumps in his stride."[1]

To minimize risk, I recommend you consider buying into investment companies, private equity firms, and specialty finance companies that have a good long-term record of investing in successful businesses in their early stages. See my monthly investment newsletter, *Forecasts & Strategies* (www.markskousen.com), for the latest recommendations in this exciting area.

Example #2: What's true for an individual or a business is also true of a nation. Nations with high levels of voluntary savings and high levels of economic liberty will, other things being equal, achieve higher rates of growth. Investing in stock markets of market-friendly nations with a high savings rate, for example, should offer superior returns.

Today, there is a great new way to invest in free enterprise around the globe: Buy country funds! These mutual funds invest in a well-diversified group of stocks all located in a single country or region. But which country funds should you buy? Austrian economics helps you decide: Look into countries that encourage free markets and free trade, that have a high rate of saving, and whose governments exhibit self-control when it comes to limiting spending and inflation. Sell country funds that impose regulations, taxes, inflation, and low savings rates. This is a simple but powerful way to make global investment decisions. Nevertheless, you would be surprised at how often investors, brokers, and security analysts violate this principle and try to trade country funds on the basis of technical or cyclical analysis. My advice: Check out the economic fundamentals of a country first, then look at the technical patterns.

John Templeton, the father of foreign stock market investing in the 20th century and a devotee of Austrian economics, said it best: "Avoid investing in those countries with a high level of socialism or government regulation of business. Business growth depends on a strong free-enterprise system and a lack of socialism." In the 1970s, he decided against investing in India and instead invested in Hong Kong. "The Indian government regulates nearly everything, so there's very little progress;

1. J. Paul Getty, *How to Be Rich* (Jove Books, 1965), 154. I highly recommend this book to all of my students, especially his chapter on "The Wall Street Investor." It is the best 16 pages ever written on investing in the stock market.

whereas in Hong Kong, the government keeps its hands off." The Hong Kong stock index has done extremely well since then, while the Indian stock market has only recently begun to increase in value—thanks to a government that has finally opened its markets to the world and reduced its taxes and regulations.

4 FRIEDRICH VON WIESER: THE "GREAT MAN" THEORY

"Many students considered Wieser the best teacher and the unquestioned authority in general economic theory in Vienna."

—Jörg Guido Hülsmann

Friedrich von Wieser (1851–1926) was Eugen Böhm-Bawerk's brother-in-law (Böhm-Bawerk married Wieser's sister), and they did everything together. He was appointed a professor at the University of Vienna in 1884 and in 1903 succeeded Menger as chair of economic theory. Böhm-Bawerk, Menger, and Wieser served as members of the Austrian House of Lords. In 1917, Wieser became the minister of commerce. He died in 1926, outliving both Böhm-Bawerk and Menger.

The Theory of Social Economy (1918), written by Wieser, was the standard Austrian textbook for many years. His main contribution to the study of economics was the invention of terms such as "marginal utility," "economic planning," and "opportunity cost." The last of these, opportunity cost, is an extremely important concept in economics. The price you pay for something is equal to what you give up to obtain it.

If you choose to go into the legal profession, you give up your next best alternative, which may be medicine or accounting. If you go to Europe on vacation, you lose the opportunity to go to California. If you marry Beth, you can't marry Sue. In finance, if you have $10,000 to invest, and you buy IBM, you miss out on other stocks that you may find almost as appealing. In short, there is a cost to all actions in the marketplace.

But the most important concept that Professor Wieser focused on is the importance of the creative individual in all walks of life—commerce, industry, education, religion, and government. He was especially impressed by the contributions of inventors, pioneers, capitalists, and entrepreneurs—individuals who were willing to take risks, sometimes big risks, to achieve their goals.

In the world of finance, who are the creative individuals? They are the superior money manager, the independent investment advisor who can beat the market, the chief executive officer who single-handedly turns a company around, and the political leader who adopts sound economic policies. If you want to make money in the markets, look to the great leaders in finance, industry, and politics.

The Creative Entrepreneur

Example #1: Steve Jobs, the founding CEO of Apple, had an "Austrian" streak in him. Walter Isaacson calls him "the greatest business executive of our era," equal in stature to Thomas Edison and Henry Ford. His was the classic Horatio Alger story, starting a computer business in his parents' garage that became the world's most valuable company (Apple). He was responsible for major advances in six industries: personal computers, animated movies, music storage, phones, tablet computing, and digital publishing.

Jobs is a good business example of Wieser's great man theory. He was very independent minded and notorious for his "bad boy" behavior. But he has a lot to teach us when it comes to business and investing.

Jobs showed that consumers don't drive the economy; entrepreneurs, business innovators, and visionaries do. Jobs made a point of creating products that customers didn't know they wanted—the Mac, the iPhone, the iPad. When asked whether he did marketing research, he replied, "No, because consumers don't know what they want until we've shown them."

The Marginal Revolution of Thatcher and Reagan

Example #2: Why did the supply-side revolution of the Reagan and

Thatcher era in the 1980s create such a strong bull market in stocks and bonds? After all, the amount of government spending wasn't reduced, and the federal deficit actually worsened. The reason is that these great political leaders made marginal changes for the better in government policy.

Average tax rates stayed about the same, but marginal tax rates were reduced—and that made all the difference. Inflation wasn't eliminated, but the marginal rate of inflation declined sufficiently to reduce interest rates, igniting a bull market in stocks and bonds. Thatcher didn't eliminate government in Britain, but she began a program of privatizing wasteful government services, one at a time. And that change in policy caused a revolution in the way political leaders think and act.

The revolution of "one" reminds us of the marginalist revolution of Carl Menger. Values are determined at the margin. Thus, a marginal victory experienced by a new politician can make a huge difference in your investments, favorably or unfavorably.

When General Augusto Pinochet took over Chile in the mid-1970s, the previous leader (the Marxist Salvadore Allende) had left it in shambles. But Pinochet adopted the economic policy recommendations of free-market economists (followers of Milton Friedman) and turned the country around. Today, everyone talks about the "quiet revolution" in Chile, and a few other Latin American countries are trying to imitate its success.

When Narasimha Rao was elected president of India, he did not revamp the country completely. India still has its problems of poverty, bureaucracy, and provincialism. But his government reduced tariffs, sliced marginal tax rates, and privatized some national industries. The result? India is growing as never before, and the Indian stock market is on the rise.

One of the best examples of the "great man" theory is Lee Kuan Yew, known affectionately as Harry Lee. As prime minister of Singapore since its independence in 1965, Yew led the republic on the road to becoming one of the fastest growing economic "tigers" of Southeast Asia. The authoritarian leader almost single-handedly directed Singapore's economic miracle by emphasizing high rates of saving (shades of Böhm-Bawerk!), free trade, technical education, infrastructure, and law and order.

Of course, not every political leader moves in the right direction. In 2000, Marxist Hugo Chavez was elected in Venezuela and moved in the opposite direction—nationalizing the oil industry, depreciating the currency, taxing the rich, and corrupting the poor with handouts. Consequently, Venezuela has suffered, despite its rich oil reserves. Americans should watch out, and free marketers should become more vocal.

One leader can make a difference! The right kind of leader can be bullish, and the wrong kind of leader can be bearish.

In sum, marginal changes in government policies regarding inflation, interest rates, taxes and spending can make a huge difference in your investment decisions.

5 LUDWIG VON MISES: HUMAN ACTION

"Mises and Hayek articulated and vastly enriched the principles of Adam Smith at a crucial time in this [20th] century."

—Vernon L. Smith

Ludwig von Mises (1881–1973) represents the third generation of Austrians. He brought Austrian economics into the twentieth century and is regarded as the father of the modern Austrian school. Mises taught economics at the University of Vienna and was chief economist at the Vienna Chamber of Commerce. With his book, *The Theory of Money and Credit* (1912), Mises became the first Austrian to develop a comprehensive theory of subjective economics. In addition, he wrote the first economic critique of socialist central planning in his book, *Socialism* (1922), which argues that central planning can never work efficiently and will eventually collapse.

Mises' magnum opus, *Human Action: A Treatise on Economics*, was published in 1949 by Yale University Press and later revised in 1966. *Human Action* is not always easy reading. A novice might do better to begin with *Planning for Freedom*, a series of speeches and articles written by Mises for a general audience, or *Economic Policy*, a series of lectures he gave in Argentina in late 1950s. Nevertheless, *Human Action* establishes many key principles of economic activity that can be applied to the financial markets.

Cause and Effect

One of Ludwig von Mises' major points is that human action is always purposeful and rational. Therefore, for every cause, there is an effect; and if any economist is sufficiently knowledgeable about the actors and their motivations, he may be able to accurately predict the future in some cases. The rational buying and selling by individuals establishes the price of every stock or commodity. Therefore, prices are never random, even though price patterns may appear to be.

Example: When Carlos Salinas was elected president of Mexico in 1988, his supply-side revolution suggested a high probability that the Mexican economy would turn around and start growing rapidly. In addition to reducing taxes and encouraging foreign investment, his party eliminated the capital gains tax. The seasoned investor asked: Is this bullish or bearish for the Mexican bolsa? Clearly, he could forecast with some reliability that the Mexican stock market would rise, perhaps sharply, as a result of the policy decisions of the Salinas regime (1988–1994).

And indeed that is exactly what happened. Adrian Day, editor of *Global Analyst*, foresaw the rise in Mexican stocks and recommended the Mexico Fund (NYSE: MXF) at less than $5 per share. I recommended the fund a little later, at $15 per share, and still the Mexico Fund rose to more than $30 per share before topping out.

People Are Different

Another Misesian concept is methodological dualism: the idea that social science (the science of human action or praxeology) is distinct from the physical and biological sciences. According to Mises, human beings think, adopt values, make choices, are conscious, make mistakes, and learn from the past. In short, they act purposefully. On the other hand, the actions of animals and matter are essentially mechanical.

They are acted upon. Mises states, "Reason and experience show us two separate realisms: the external world of physical, chemical, and physiological phenomena; and the internal world of thought, feeling, valuation, and purposeful action. No bridge connects—as far as we can see today—these two spheres."[1]

In scientific experiments with animals, plants and physical elements,

1. Ludwig von Mises, *Human Action*, 3rd ed. (Regnery, 1966, 1949), 18.

the results are often exact and repeatable. Not so with human action, which is often unpredictable and unreliable. In essence, Mises argues that human beings have free will; animals and things do not.

The philosophy of dualism is extremely valuable in the current debate over the true nature of the financial markets, to what degree they reflect "random" behavior or purposeful behavior, and to what extent market action can be forecast.

Mises is critical of quantitative and mathematical economics because it's so mechanical. For the Austrians, economic and financial behavior is by nature qualitative and subjective, not quantitative and objective. The financial pages may be full of numbers indicating prices, ratios, and percentages, but the Austrian-oriented financial analyst looks beyond the obvious. What's behind the numbers? The Austrian sees human decision making, involving emotions, thinking, and calculating.

Austrian economists are also suspicious of technical trading systems that rely on cycles, trends, and other mechanical devices linked to the past. Constant, objective standards are impossible in economics as well as finance. Unreliable financial theories include the Kondratieff cycle theory, the Elliott wave theory, the Dow theory, and the gold-silver ratio.

Many analysts were rightly suspicious of the mechanical financial models. These models, developed by Myron Scholes and Robert Merton, both Nobel Prize winners for their work in derivative markets, were used by Long-Term Capital Management to leverage its position in the futures markets. Systems that depend exclusively on past patterns are bound to fail sooner or later, and sure enough, Long-Term Capital Management blew up in 1988. These forecasting systems depend on an objective standard that is inconsistent with subjective expectations.

Example: In the 1990s, at the end of each calendar year, Louis Rukeyser would ask a group of panelists on *Wall Street Week* to answer the question, "Where will the Dow Jones Industrial Average be a year from now?" According to Mises and the Austrian school, the correct answer is, "I don't know." Any answer is, to some extent, guesswork. No one can know precisely what the Dow Average will be at any time in the future because there are so many variables—changes in government policy and actions by millions of individual investors and money managers—that no one can know for sure what those decisions will be. Investors are not lemmings. They are not totally predictable. Investors should be wary of any financial advisor or economist who predicts exact dates or sets precise price targets.

Does that mean that the future is completely unpredictable? Can investors and analysts make an educated guess about the direction of the economy and the markets? This is a hotly debated topic in the academic world. Some economists argue that the future of the stock market is unknown and no one can beat the market over the long run. They are known as followers of the "efficient market" theory.

Even some of the Austrian economists, such as the South African economist Ludwig Lachmann, fit into this camp. They are known as "radical subjectivists." They argue that the markets are in such constant change and are so complex that it is virtually impossible to predict their direction. Roger Garrison (Auburn University), on the other hand, takes a more sanguine approach. Garrison has written extensively on Austrian macroeconomics, business cycle theory, and the degree of uncertainty in the economy. He has focused on the relationship between money and the economy, asking the fundamental question, "What is the causal connection between monetary policy and economic activity?" He differs with Lachmann, contending that the connection is loose, but not disjointed, using a Hayekian symbol. His work is helpful in determining to what degree the markets are predictable.[2]

There are times in the financial markets when uncertainty is extremely high and times when it is extremely low. When it's low, and you can see cause and effect and specific trends in place, take advantage of the situation. When the situation is extremely uncertain, it's best to stand aside. That's what Austrian economics teaches.

Mises and the Socialist Calculation Debate

Mises was also famous for his uncompromising attack on socialism and central planning by Communist regimes such as that in the Soviet Union. As early as 1920, the Austrian professor argued that without prices and competitive bidding, a centrally planned totalitarian regime could not operate an efficient, progressive economy. Mises rightly predicted that socialist regimes would eventually collapse.

The economics profession, led by Keynesian economist Paul Samuelson of Massachusetts Institute of Technology and socialist Robert

2. Roger Garrison, *Time and Money: The Macroeconomics of Capital Structure* (Routledge, 2000).

Heilbroner, scoffed at Mises. Years later, when the Soviet centrally planned model collapsed in the early 1990s, Mises was proven correct. In fact, Heilbroner admitted in the early 1990s, after the fall of the Soviet Union, that the fifty-year-old debate was over: Mises was right; capitalism had won over socialism. "Capitalism organized the material affairs of humankind more satisfactorily than socialism.[3]"

What does the collapse of socialist economic theory mean for investors? Expect to see more and more countries rejecting socialist slogans and adopting free-market solutions to their problems—privatization, denationalization, tax cutting, and monetary and fiscal restraint. Long live capitalism! Long live bull markets!

---

3. Robert Heilbroner, "The Triumph of Capitalism," *The New Yorker* (January 23, 1989), 98; and Robert Heilbroner, "Reflections After Communism," *New Yorker* (September 10, 1990).

6 FRIEDRICH HAYEK: THE AUSTRIAN THEORY OF THE BUSINESS CYCLE

"Fortunately, a correct theory of depression and of the business cycle *does* exist, even though it is universally neglected in present-day economics . . . [It is] known as the 'Austrian' theory of the business cycle."

—Murray N. Rothbard, 1969

Mises' most famous colleague was Friedrich A. Hayek (1899–1992), who received two doctorates at the University of Vienna and worked under Mises as director of the Austrian Institute of Economic Research. In 1974, Hayek received the Nobel Prize in Economics for his work in the business cycle theory, among other things. He is the only Austrian economist to receive the Nobel Prize. His paper, "The Use of Knowledge in Society," published in the September 1945 issue of the *American Economic Review*, is one of the top-20 most cited papers in economics.

Attention was drawn to the pair's work when Mises and Hayek predicted the cataclysmic events of the 1930s. The 1929 stock market crash and subsequent worldwide depression took the economics profession by surprise. Neither Irving Fisher (the monetarist of the day) nor John Maynard Keynes foresaw the collapse in the world economy. But Mises and Hayek did.

Austrian economics began to flourish in the early 1930s. Many scholars came to Mises' famous private seminar in Vienna to seek the two out. And Lionel Robbins, chairman of the economics department at the London School of Economics, invited Friedrich Hayek to lecture there.

Hayek's explanation of the depression in *Prices and Production* (1931), which was based on Mises' earlier work, *The Theory of Money and Credit* (1912) was well-received at first in the early '30s.[1]

Together, they developed the Mises-Hayek theory of the trade cycle, known today as the Austrian theory of the business cycle. It is based on Menger's theory of marginal utility, Böhm-Bawerk's capital theory, and Swedish economist Knut Wicksell's natural interest rate hypothesis. This Austrian theory of the business cycle emphasizes how monetary and credit inflation by central banks artificially distorts the structure of the economy.

Mises and Hayek demonstrated the non-neutral impact of money and credit on relative prices, income, and business activity. That is, when the government inflates the money supply or artificially lowers interest rates, certain individuals and organizations benefit while others are hurt. Easy money does not simply raise prices, but disrupts the economy and creates winners and losers.

According to Mises-Hayek, increasing the money supply and credit (through the fractional reserve banking system) and reducing interest rates below the natural rate misdirects resources into "higher order" producer goods. However, this capital boom cannot last and eventually must collapse into a bust when the money supply and credit stop growing or interest rates rise. According to the Austrians, the government's monetary policy, not free-market capitalism, is primarily responsible for the boom-bust cycle and market instability.

Clearly, the Austrian theory of the business cycle is extremely useful in forecasting movements in stocks, bonds, and other financial assets. Many security analysts rely on this theory to anticipate the ups and downs of the economy. I use it myself to make forecasts in my monthly investment letter, *Forecasts & Strategies*.

How the Austrian Business Cycle Theory Works

The Austrian theory is basically as follows: Suppose the economy is growing steadily and long-term interest rates for blue-chip corporate bonds are stable at around 6 percent. The government decides that the

1. I have recently written a lengthy introduction to a new reprinting of Hayek's *Prices and Production* (1931) and *Monetary Theory of the Trade Cycle* (1935) in a new work entitled *Hayek's Triangles: Two Essays in the Business Cycle*, published by Laissez Faire Books (www.lfb.org).

economy isn't growing fast enough, so the central bank expands the money supply and reduces interest rates to 4 percent, below the natural rate of interest. Lower interest rates encourage business borrowing and expansion, especially in manufacturing, housing, student loans, and capital-intensive industries, which are more sensitive to interest rates than the rest of the economy. The economic boom spreads to the investment markets as the stock market skyrockets.

Mises and Hayek warned that such an inflationary boom is artificial, created with fiat money, and cannot last. The boom must end in a bust. How? As the economy booms, prices rise and eventually interest rates stop falling and start rising. The rise in interest rates cuts the boom short and many capital-intensive industries, such as housing and manufacturing, collapse. The economy enters a recession, or worse, a depression, and the stock market falls, sometimes sharply.

In short, the Austrians argue that there is no free lunch in the monetary sphere. An expansion of the money supply and credit markets cannot create a genuine boom, but rather a boom-bust business cycle. Monetary inflation doesn't just raise prices; it also distorts the structure of the economy, creating sizable malinvestments that must eventually be liquidated.

The Austrians Versus the Keynesians in the 1930s

How did the Great Depression of the 1930s occur? Essentially, Mises and Hayek argued that the Great Depression had its origin in the cheap money policies the Federal Reserve created in the 1920s, which caused an artificial boom in industrial production and in the stock market. Both Viennese economists contended that a crash on Wall Street was inevitable once the Federal Reserve began lowering the discount rate in the 1920s.

It was only a matter of time, especially given the international gold standard that was in place at the time. However, Mises and Hayek never specified a date for the crash (remember the principle of uncertainty?). Finally, the Federal Reserve was forced to raise interest rates in 1929, and it wasn't long before Wall Street fell and the world headed into recession.

But what turned a recession into a worldwide depression? According to both the Austrian and Chicago school economists, it was government bungling, not laissez-faire capitalism. The Federal Reserve raised interest rates and failed to act as a lender of last resort, forcing thousands of banks to close their doors. Congress increased taxes and tariffs, the Hoover administration promoted a high-wage policy, and the Roosevelt administration discouraged business investment. The result was persistent and widespread unemployment, and a loss of faith in the capitalist system, which took a full generation to restore.[2]

As the Depression wore on in the 1930s, economists and government leaders failed to see their own blunders and became disenchanted with Hayek, Mises, and the other laissezfaire economists. They searched for alternatives. Marxism and other radical solutions gained support during this dark period in world history, but gradually the Western world adopted a middle-of-the-road philosophy under the guidance of Cambridge economist John Maynard Keynes.[3]

Keynes introduced a new model emphasizing spending rather than saving as the key to economic recovery. According to Keynes, it wasn't necessary to adopt full-scale government control of the economy, as the Marxists and socialists advocated. In a downturn, all the government need do is deliberately run deficits and expand government spending and the money supply. World War II, more than any other event, convinced economists and government leaders of the efficacy of Keynes' theories. Meanwhile, the theories of Mises and Hayek fell into obscurity.

It was not until Hayek won the Nobel Prize for economics in 1974 that interest in Austrian economics resurged. It is important to note that the co-winner of the Nobel Prize in 1974 was Swedish economist Gunnar Myrdal. While the two were on opposite ends of the political spectrum, they shared a strong interest in Wicksell's monetary theory of the cumulative process and the natural interest rate hypothesis. In that year, the world was also in the midst of major economic turmoil, with commodity shortages, double-digit inflation, and an energy crisis. Stocks and bonds fell sharply, while unorthodox investments such as real estate, gold, silver, and Swiss francs skyrocketed in price.

There was also a major paradigm shift in economic thinking. The world was suffering from its first major "inflationary recession," an event

---

2. For a list of six causes of the 1930s depression, see my article, "The Great Depression," *The Elgar Companion to Austrian Economics*, ed. by Peter Boettke (Edward Elgar Publishing, 1994), 431–39. The differences between the Austrian and Chicago schools regarding the Great Depression are discussed in chapter 6 of my book *Vienna and Chicago, Friends or Foes?* (Capital Press, 2005).

3. See chapters 13 and 14 of my *Making of Modern Economics*, 2nd ed. (M.E. Sharpe, 2009).

that the Keynesian economics establishment could not readily explain. The Austrian school offered an alternative point of view.

How to Use Austrian Business-Cycle Theory in Your Investment Decisions

How can the Austrian business cycle theory help investors today? Changes in monetary policy—the money supply and interest rates—can have a dramatic impact on stocks, bonds, currencies, real estate, precious metals, and other investments. Most schools of economics (monetarist, Keynesian, and Austrian) would agree that an "easy money" policy (expanding the money supply and lowering interest rates), especially at the bottom of a recession, would be highly favorable toward the stock market.

However, the Austrians go further in suggesting that "easy money" is inherently unstable, that an inflationary boom will cause a bull market in stocks, but it can't last. Eventually, at some point, the bull market will become grossly overvalued and will turn into a bear market. The clear sign is seen when a credit crunch occurs, with sharply higher interest rates.

Of course, monetary policy isn't the only guideline of where the stock market is headed; technological advances, taxes, foreign trade, and private capital also affect the market. But the work of Mises and Hayek teaches us that, most importantly, we cannot ignore the machinations of the central bankers. They can have a deep impact on the cycle of the markets.

The Reagan Bull Market and the Stock Market Crash of 1987

Example #1: By 1982, the U.S. economy had been under a "tight money/tax cut" policy for several years (one recommended by Robert Mundell, Art Laffer, and other supply-siders). The prime rate had skyrocketed to 21 percent. Recession was everywhere, with collapsing prices in oil, stocks, bonds, real estate, gold, and silver. Inflationary expectations had been broken, but there was fear of a banking crisis, beginning in Mexico.

Suddenly, in the summer of 1982, the Federal Reserve bailed out Mexico, injected reserves into the monetary system, and lowered the discount rate. The stock market exploded upward from around 700 on the Dow Industrials. This turned out to be the beginning of the Reagan

Bull Market of the 1980s. A smart investor was a buyer at this time.

But the Austrian trade theory teaches us a very important principle—a central bank's reinflation policy creates an inflationary boom in certain sectors that cannot last. Eventually, interest rates must rise, causing the economy to slow down and the stock market to fall. When will it happen? Nobody knows for sure. The bull market in stocks lasted for five years. Then in late summer 1987, stock prices peaked as interest rates rose and the Federal Reserve tightened money. The reaction caught most investors off guard, and the stock market crashed on Black Monday, Oct. 19, 1987, with the DJIA falling 508 points, more than 20 percent in one day.

Federal Reserve Chairman Alan Greenspan acted swiftly, injecting reserves into the banking system and issuing a statement of confidence. The market rebounded and since then moved to new highs.

"Irrational Exuberance" and the High-Tech Bubble of the 1990s

Example #2: The 1990s witnessed one of the most powerful bull markets in history. Both genuine technological advances and easy money fueled this surge. The economy and the financial markets boomed with the advent of cell phones, personal computers, and the Internet. A huge number of companies went public, and the Nasdaq Composite hit a record high of 5,000 in early 2000. In the mid-1990s, I predicted the Nasdaq would "double and then double again." At the same time, Federal Reserve Chairman Alan Greenspan characterized the high-tech boom as "irrational exuberance."

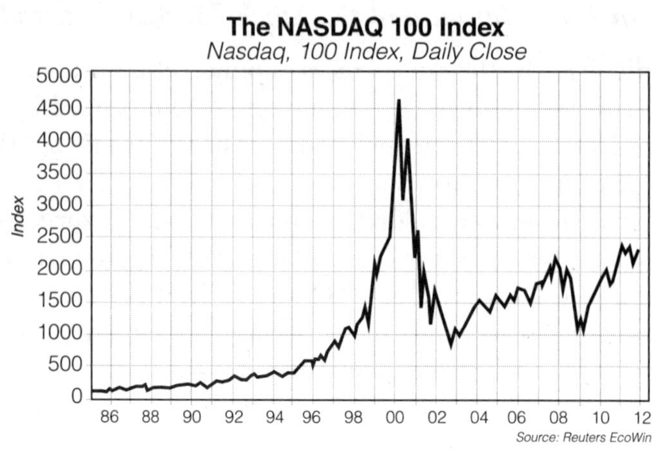

The Federal Reserve encouraged this "irrational exuberance" by reducing interest rates and expanding the money stock during the mid-1990s in response to three crises: the Asian financial crisis of 1997; the collapse of the hedge fund Long Term Capital Management; and the sovereign debt crisis in Russia in 1998. The Fed's intervention prevented these crises from reaching American shores but extended the bull market to excessive heights.

When the Fed raised rates sharply in 1999, the bull market entered unchartered territory. The yield curve went negative, and leveraged margins were squeezed. At this time, I visited Burt Malkiel, professor of economics at Princeton University and famous for his classic work, *A Random Walk Down Wall Street.* He is a lead defender of the efficient market theory, the belief that you can't predict the future of stock prices. Yet even he couldn't ignore the obvious. He showed me a chart of the stock market and noted that the tech-laden Nasdaq Index and other market indexes had gone hyperbolic. He and I came to the same conclusion: This bull market couldn't last.

Sure enough, a few months later, the stock market—both the Dow and the Nasdaq—fell sharply and continued to fall for the next two years. *(See chart to the left).*

The Real Estate Boom-Bust Cycle of 2000s

Example #3: My third example involves a complex combination of government intervention, tax policy, entrepreneurial finance, and easy money, all developing quickly around the turn of the twenty-first century into the worst financial disaster since the Great Depression.

The federal government aggressively encouraged home ownership, especially by minorities, in the early 1990s. This program accelerated in the 2000s with the advent of "no doc" and "subprime" mortgages—an imprudent banking practice that many traditional banks rejected. (It was never permitted in Canada and most other Anglo-Saxon countries). Bankers went along with this dangerous policy once they realized that they could sell most of these mortgages to Fannie Mae and Freddie Mac, two reckless government-guaranteed corporations.

At the same time, investors enjoyed special tax and financial benefits from home ownership and rental properties. For example, investors could postpone paying taxes on capital gains by investing in real estate, and after the 9/11 terrorist attacks and the closing of the New York Stock Exchange for a week in 2001, many investors feared investing in stocks and switched to real estate.

Wall Street was also in a creative mood and imitated Fannie Mae and Freddie Mac by bundling mortgages into "risk-free" packaged financial instruments. In fact, Moody's and Standard & Poors, the rating agencies on Wall Street, made the fatal decision to give these mortgage packaged deals a AAA rating because of the government guarantees.

In a deregulatory environment, Wall Street investment banks such as Lehman Brothers, Bear Sterns, and Goldman Sachs created and sold so-called "collateralized debt obligations" (CDOs), investment-grade securities backed by a pool of bonds, loans, and other assets. They also organized real estate investment trusts (REITs) that invested in pools of mortgaged securities, which, when leveraged, offered temptingly high monthly income to investors.

Last but not least, Fed Chairman Alan Greenspan feared that America was facing deflation similar to Japan and convinced the Federal Reserve Board to reduce short-term interest rates to 1 percent in 2004. This easy money policy only added fuel to the real-estate boom, which by 2006–07 reached the point of "irrational exuberance" characterized by a buying frenzy in many areas of the country, especially in Florida, Nevada, Arizona, and California.

The Fed, recognizing an asset bubble, reversed its course and raised rates in 2006, creating an inverted yield curve for the first time since 2000.

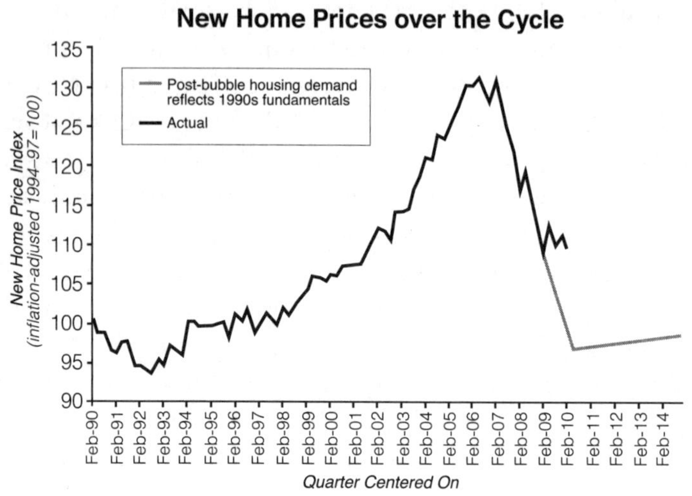

It was the beginning of the end for the real estate boom. Profit margins declined, REITs cut dividends, and mortgage securities and property prices began a downward trend. Leveraged positions started unraveling, and the mortgage market quickly became illiquid, forcing financial giants such as Bear Sterns, Lehman Brothers, and the big banks (Citibank and Bank of America, especially) to raise capital by selling off assets.

The results were the collapse of these institutions, a major bear market on Wall Street and global stock markets, and a financial crisis that required massive bailouts by the Federal Reserve and the federal government (TARP). The money supply ballooned and the deficit ran up to 17 percent of the federal budget.

How to Recognize a Top in the Stock Market

One of the most difficult dilemmas facing investors is to determine when a major sell-off is going to occur on Wall Street. When stock prices start falling, investors must decide, "is this a bull market correction or the beginning of major bear market?" There is no easy predictor. Mises was of the opinion that nobody could know for sure when the top is reached. Many a financial guru has had his reputation damaged by making false forecasts about an impending stock market crash. Bull markets can often last longer than anticipated. For example, Federal Reserve Chairman Alan Greenspan made his famous "irrational exuberance" comment about the stock market in 1996, four years before it topped out.

The Inverted Yield Curve

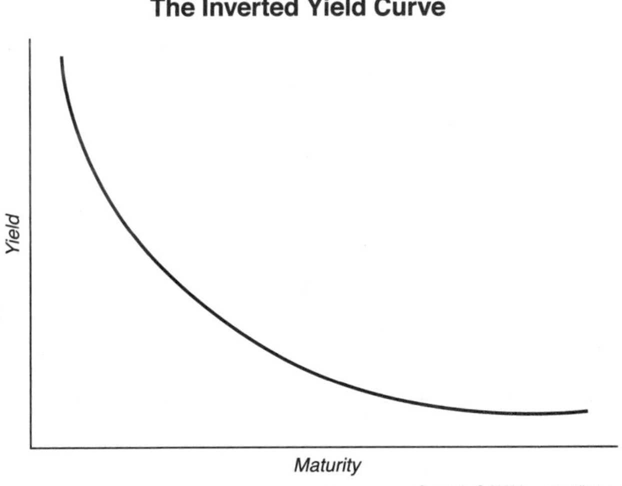

Astute "Austrian" financial analysts use several indicators to predict a major top in the markets. One is a "tight" money policy, when the Fed finally decides to withdraw liquidity from the market place and raise interest rates. A timely indicator of a top in the market is the inverted yield curve, when short-term rates are suddenly higher than long-term rates. See chart on previous page.

Hayek noted this fact in 1929, right before the stock market crashed, and Harry Veryser, who teaches Austrian economics at University of Detroit-Mercy and is a seasoned investor, saw the inverted yield curve as a key factor in predicting a bear market in 2000 and again in 2008. He recently wrote:

> For the trade cycle the inversion of the yield curve is a danger sign—a sign that the turning point is coming. A yield curve inversion has preceded every recession and depression since World War II . . . . The yield curve can invert for several reasons—the tightening of credit by the central bank, the cash crunch that results during a scramble for liquidity, and the downward effect on long-term rates that occurs as long-term projects are canceled. Beyond those reasons, short-term rates can rise because monetary expansion weakens the value of the currency on foreign exchange markets and the prices of imports begins to rise . . . . Finally, the perception of inflation can put pressure on the central bank to raise interest rates.[4]

A Wicksellian Contribution to the Business Cycle

In a fascinating new work, *Profiting From Monetary Policy: Investing Through the Business Cycle* (Palgrave Macmillan, 2013), investment analyst Thomas Aubrey has developed a strategy to anticipate the top and bottom of the stock market using Knut Wicksell's cumulative process and natural rate of interest theory. In his classic work, *Interest and Prices* (1936), Wicksell contended that macroeconomic equilibrium could be achieved only when the return on capital (profits of businesses, including opportunity costs) should equal the cost of capital (their borrowing costs).

4. Harry C.Veryser, *It Didn't Have to Be This Way: Why Boom and Bust is Unnecessary—and How the Austrian School of Economics Breaks the Cycle* (ISI Books, 2013), 244–5.

Wicksell dubbed the return on capital the "natural" rate of interest; the cost of capital the "money" rate of interest. If the money rate of interest is artificially reduced to a point below the natural rate, there will be an increase in demand for credit and an economic boom. And when the money rate increases above the natural rate, the boom will be cut short, causing a slump.

Aubrey has come up with a way to estimate the two rates. He uses the return on corporate investment capital (both debt and equity) for the return of capital (natural rate of interest), and the five-year moving average of five-year government-bond yields for the cost of capital (money rate of interest).

Using these two figures, he created a figure he dubs "the Wicksellian Differential" (WD). When WD widens, Aubrey is bullish; when WD narrows, he's bearish. Historically, he found that using this model between 1986 and 2011, switching into equities when WD rises, and into government bonds when WD falls, his portfolio earned an 8.7% average real return on U.S. stocks during this twenty-five year period, an above-average return.

His WD model was especially useful in getting out of the market in 2007, missing the entire collapse, and in which his portfolio actually made money by being fully invested in government bonds. However, Aubrey's technique was less useful during the tech boom-bust cycle of 1996–2001. According to his model, WD started to decline in 1996, just as Alan Greenspan warned of an "irrational exuberance" on Wall Street. He switched from stocks to bonds prematurely, as the Nasdaq doubled and then doubled again, and then recommended getting back into stocks in late 1999, just before the precipitous fall in 2000!

Finding the Bottom of a Market

What about a bottom? Austrian analysts might look at the Fed's cutting rates and injecting liquidity as a sign of a bottom, but experience shows that it can be months before the market recovers. Milton Friedman was always keen on demonstrating a lag of six months or longer between a change in Fed policy and a commensurate change in the economy or the stock market. For example, the Fed cut rates and engaged in a series of "quantitative easing" in late 2008, but the market didn't bottom out until March 2009.

One useful indicator may be long-term trend lines in stock market indexes. Jeremy Siegel, a professor of finance at the Wharton School and author of *Stocks for the Long Run*, came very close to predicting the bottom of the bear market in early 2009 based on his 200-year chart of the U.S. stock market. He found that major bear markets in the United States usually end after a 50 percent decline. The only exception was the 1929–32 bear market. I well remember visiting his home in February 2009 when he showed me his long-term charts and said he felt the market had reached a bottom. I wrote up his findings in the March 2009 issue of *Forecasts & Strategies*, quoting him saying that the stock market was a "screaming buy." It turned out to be quite accurate.

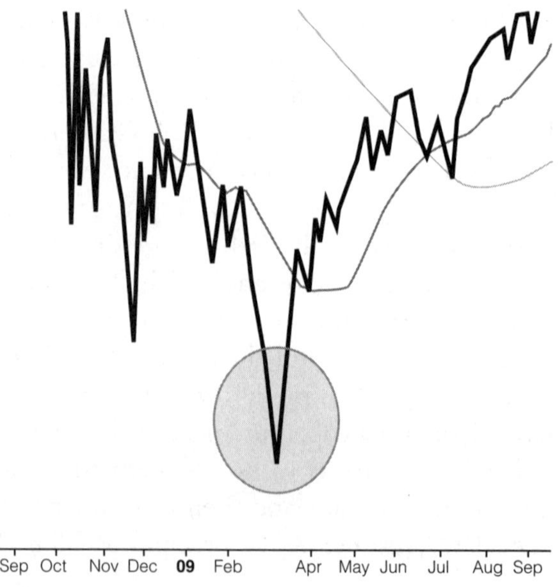

Bear in mind that Professor Siegel, as all of us, do not have anywhere near a perfect record in calling market turns. For example, Siegel failed to call the top of the bull market in 2008. Neither did I, although I recognized many signs of a top (See the February 2008 issue of *Forecasts & Strategies*).

In sum, predicting the ups and downs of the stock market is easier said than done; it is more an art than a science. Accurate forecasting often depends on an entrepreneurial ability to understand correctly the underlying fundamentals and to sense the psychology of investment crowds.

It has challenged the most astute of investment analysts and speculators. As Sir Isaac Newton once said, "I can calculate the motion of heavenly bodies but not the madness of people."

The Downside to Austrian Economics: The Permabear Syndrome

While Austrian business-cycle theory can be useful in playing the trends in the stock market, it also has its built-in biases that can lead investors astray. Both "Austrian"-style academic economists and financial advisors tend to be bearish, in contrast to the Chicago economists such as Milton Friedman and George Stigler whose writings are generally more upbeat.

Ludwig von Mises and Friedrich Hayek experienced the ravages of world war, runaway inflation, and the Great Depression in the first half of the twentieth century and were undyingly pessimistic about the future. Felix Somary, an economist who became a Swiss banker, forecast the 1929 crash, the Great Depression, and World War II, turned decidedly bearish in the mid-1950s, predicting another great depression right before his death.[5]

Ludwig von Mises was incurably gloomy about the future. Peter Drucker, the management guru who grew up in Vienna and had contact with Mises at New York University, expressed dismay about Mises. "He was the most depressing person I ever met," he told me. Mises's despair is clearly noticeable in his searing intellectual memoir, *Notes and Recollections* (1978). Mises was downhearted about many things—the world wars, the rise of socialism and Keynesianism, and his failure to receive a full-time teaching position at a major university.

Joseph Schumpeter, the *enfant terrible* of the Austrian school, was deeply depressed about the prospects for capitalism and entrepreneurship. He predicted that big business would gradually become more bureaucratic and less entrepreneurial, destroying individuality and initiative. At the same time, socialist central planning would engulf the world. He famously remarked, "Can capitalism survive? No, I do not think it can . . . . Can socialism work? Of course it can."[6]

Gold bugs and hard-money investors are often bearish in their outlook and constantly expect a crash or bear market around the corner.

5. Felix Somary, *The Raven of Zurich* (St. Martin's Press, 1986), 293–302.
6. Joseph A. Schumpeter, *Capitalism, Socialism and Democracy* (Harper & Row, 1942, 1947), 61, 67.

When the financial markets went into a tailspin in late October 1997, my doomsday colleagues appeared gleeful. "The bear market has begun," predicted Gary North. "It isn't going to end for about ten years." Adrian Day told me at the time that the market was probably 70 percent overvalued and was delighted to see some air come out of the "bubble." Doug Casey had been forecasting the "Greater Depression" for more than a decade. "It could be worse than even I imagine," he told me.

Of course, Wall Street continued its meteoric rise until topping out in early 2000.

The 1990s was perhaps the most profitable decade in modern Wall Street history, yet most of the Austrian-friendly investment writers were bearish. Richard Russell, editor of the *Dow Theory Letters* and long-time gold bug, is famous for publishing in each issue of his monthly newsletter a box showing either a bull or a bear. For most of the 1990s, the bear was in the box.

Over the years, I've been collecting books written by the "permabears," and the number is so high that I may need another shelf. Some of them have become #1 bestsellers: Howard Ruff, *How to Prosper During the Coming Bad Years* (1979); Doug Casey, *Crisis Investing: Your Profits and Opportunities in the Coming Great Depression* (1979); Jerome Smith, *The Coming Currency Collapse* (1980); Harry D. Schultz, *Panics and Crashes* (1982); Dr. Ravi Batra, *The Depression of 1990* (1987); James Dale Davidson and Lord William Rees-Mogg, *The Great Reckoning: How the World Will Change in the Depression of the 1990s* (1991); Harry Figgie, Jr., *Bankruptcy 1995: The Coming Collapse of America and How to Stop It* (1992); Robert Prechter, Jr., *At the Crest of the Tidal Wave: A Forecast for the Great Bear Market* (1995). James Grant, *The Trouble With Prosperity: A Contrarian's Tale of Boom, Bust, and Speculation* (1998). Harry Browne wrote a series of negative titles: *You Can Profit from a Monetary Crisis* (1974), *Why the Best-Laid Investment Plans Usually Go Wrong* (1987), and *The Economic Time Bomb* (1989). So has Peter Schiff: *Crash Proof: How to Profit From the Coming Economic Collapse* (2007) and *The Real Crash: America's Coming Bankruptcy* (2012).

A whole cottage industry of doomsday financial newsletters has developed since the turbulent 1970s. Self-styled investment gurus such as Martin Weiss and Porter Stansberry have sent out promotional copy warning investors of impending natural disasters, bear markets, panics, and crashes. Apparently bad news sells better than good news, and fear sells even better than greed.

Of course, few of the doomsayers' dire omens have come true so far, yet their resolve in forecasting new crises is only strengthened.

The Root of Pessimism

What is at the root of this deep-seated pessimism about the global economy? Part of it may be Christian theology, which includes an apocalyptic vision of the future (Matthew 24). But since many of the doomsayers are not Christians. An alternative source may be the Austrian school of economics, some of whose leading figures feared for the future and whose theories suggest financial and monetary trouble down the road.

But pessimism about the future goes beyond world events and personal tragedy. It is also inherent in the theory of Austrian economics—especially with regard to the world monetary system and the theory of business cycles.

Austrians are deeply suspicious of the current fiat money system, which they regard as unstable and prone to crisis. Today's monetary system of unbacked inflated currencies is inherently unstable. Floating (or sinking) exchange rates may postpone, but cannot escape, the day of reckoning. Someday, a monetary, economic, or financial crisis will arise that will cause a run on the dollar, a collapse of the fractional reserve banking system, and the re-establishment of gold and silver as real money. Not surprisingly, sound-money advocates recommend the accumulation of precious metals as a hedge against such an impending crisis.

The Mises-Hayek theory of the business cycle suggests inherent instability in the financial and economic worlds. An increase in the fiat money supply will not only raise prices but it will also create an imbalance in the structure of the economy, a boom-bust cycle. The economic and financial boom cannot last but will cause prices and interest rates to rise, which eventually will cause a recession and a collapse in stocks, real estate, and other assets. As Murray Rothbard puts it, "The boom requires a bust."[7]

7. Murray N. Rothbard, *America's Great Depression*, 4th ed. (Richardson & Snyder, 1983), 20. An excellent related booklet is *The Austrian Theory of the Trade Cycle and Other Essays*, ed. by Richard Ebeling with an introduction by Roger Garrison (The Ludwig von Mises Institute, 1996 [1983]).

The Missing Ingredient

Sometimes, I feel like a lone bull among Austrian economists and financial analysts. I have generally been more optimistic about the global economy and stock prices (though not always). While the Austrian bears make a valid point about the inevitable dangers of monetary inflation and a fiat money system, they overlook another key element: Free markets lead to long-term economic growth, rising standards of living, and hence bull markets.

Genuine Versus Artificial Prosperity

One of the flaws in most Austrian-type investment writers is their tendency to ignore the bullish phrase of the market place before the crash or bear market comes.

It reminds me of the Parable of the Wheat and the Tares in Matthew 13:24–30. Jesus tells the story of a wheat farmer whose crop comes under attack by an unknown assailant. In the middle of the night, this enemy sows tares (weeds) in his wheat fields. Soon the farmer's servants discover that the farmer's crop appears to be twice the normal size. Yet the master realizes that half the crop is real and the other half is fake—weeds instead of wheat. But he warns his hired hands not to tear out the weeds for fear of uprooting the good shoots; they must wait and let the wheat and the tares grow up together until harvest time. Months later, the wheat produces good grain, while the tares are merely weeds that provide no fruit. The servants pull out the weeds and burn them and store the grain in the barn.

The parable is applicable to the markets. In today's robust global economy, the wheat represents genuine prosperity—the new products, technologies, and productivity generated by capitalists, inventors, and entrepreneurs. It represents real economic growth and, when harvested, a true higher standard of living. Under such conditions, stock prices are likely to rise.

On the other hand, the tares represent artificial prosperity that bears no fruit in the end and must be burned at harvest time. Where does this artificial growth come from? The central bank's easy-money policies. The Fed pushes interest rates below their natural rate and creates new money. This new money, like regular savings, is invested in the economy and stimulates more growth and higher stock prices—higher than sustainable over the long run.

Who is this enemy who sows the seeds of artificial prosperity? The Fed chairman. The central bank controls the flow of the money supply and short-term interest rates.

There is no free lunch, even in the monetary sphere. At some point, the harvest time comes and the wheat must be separated from the tares. This is the crisis stage, in which the boom turns into a bust. Harvest time in agricultural products is fairly easy to predict but not the topping out of the economy or the stock market. At some point, a "burning" of excessive asset values must occur. As Ludwig von Mises stated, "If a brake is thus put on the boom, it will quickly be seen that the false impression of 'profitability' created by the credit expansion has led to unjustified investments."[8]

The smart investor realizes that the business cycle can be played on both sides of the cycle—the inflationary boom phase and the deflationary bust phase.

The Turning Point in 1980

I well remember 1980, a turning point in the investment climate in the United States and the world. The 1970s had been rocked by inflation, energy crises, and skyrocketing commodity prices, including gold and silver. The inflationary seventies gave birth to the hard-money movement, of which I was a part. In fact, my first investment in the early 1970s was not a stock or bond, but a silver dollar, purchased after reading Harry Browne's bestseller, *You Can Profit from a Monetary Crisis.* "Buy gold, buy silver, buy Swiss francs" was the rallying cry of the era.

But then Ronald Reagan had been elected president, and Federal Reserve Chairman Paul Volker was determined to fight inflation. The New Orleans Investment Conference, the unofficial conference of the gold bugs, was held a week after the election, and the turnout was the largest ever, with more than 3,000 attendees. Everyone was abuzz about the significance of the Reagan election. Gary North and I held private meetings in a suite in the Hilton Riverside Hotel, where we repeated the meetings several times late into the night to accommodate everyone lined up to enter the room.

I came to the conclusion that the Reagan election had been a watershed event. It sent a signal to the world that Reaganomics—lower taxes,

8. Ludwig von Mises, "The 'Austrian' Theory of the Trade Cycle," in *The Austrian Theory of the Trade Cycle and Other Essays*, compiled by Richard Ebeling (Mises Institute, 1996), 30.

lower inflation, fewer government regulations, etc.—would reverse the trends of the 1970s. In fact, I wrote a package for my new newsletter, *Forecasts & Strategies*, which began right after Reagan was elected. The outside of the envelope said, "The financial shock of 1981." Inside the envelope, the headline read, "Reaganomics will work! Sell your gold and silver and buy stocks and bonds!"

It turned out to be a minority point of view. Jim Blanchard, producer of the New Orleans conference and editor of the *Gold Newsletter*, told the large audience that nothing had changed, that Reagan would not be able to reverse the inflationary trends. My views were considered heretical, and I felt like I was excommunicated from the hard-money movement.

The promotional copy failed miserably. Nobody believed me. We had to go back to writing bearish copy about the economy collapsing and the markets failing to get anyone to subscribe in those early years.

But I was proven right. It took a couple of years, but starting in 1982, the stock and bond markets rallied sharply, and gold and silver descended into a long bear market.

I learned an important lesson: Government policy in a country can make a big difference in one's investment portfolio. Bad policies can hurt traditional stock and bond markets, while good policies can help them. It pays to know the signs of the times. Anticipating changes in government policy can offer huge opportunities for profit.[9]

We can constantly focus on the short term and play on the fears of a bear market, or we can take a long-term view. During the twentieth century, bull markets lasted a lot longer than bear markets, and almost 70 percent of the time, stocks were rising in price. Why? Because in spite of wars, recessions, taxes, regulations, and inflation, the U.S. economy has remained largely favorable toward free enterprise. As the optimist Adam Smith once wrote, "The effort of every man to better his condition is frequently powerful enough to maintain progress, in spite of the greatest errors of administration."[10]

Financial Advice in the Hard-Money Movement

From my experience in the financial world and having participated

9. See chapter five of my book, *Investing in One Lesson* (Regnery, 2007). The lesson is "Wall Street exaggerates everything," offering tremendous speculative opportunities.
10. Adam Smith, *The Wealth of Nations* (Modern Library, 1965 [1776]), 326.

in hard-money conferences (such as the New Orleans Investment Conference) over the years, I became convinced that the overemphasis on the coming collapse and bear markets has introduced a fatal flaw in the gold bug/Austrian camp. The investment advice of many of these permabears has been less than stellar. It has caused them frequently to underperformed the markets, especially when gold was in a secular bear market (1980–2000).

In fact, Harry Browne, one of the financial advisors in the hard-money movement, was so frustrated in attempting to time the market that he gave up and created the Permanent Portfolio Fund, a well-diversified mutual fund that could, he said, do well in any investment climate. "A permanent portfolio should let you watch the evening news or read investment publications in total serenity. No actual or threatened event should trouble you, because you'll know that your portfolio is protected against it, whether it be inflation, deflation, recession, or war."

Browne created the permanent portfolio concept in the late 1970s, arguing that a balanced portfolio of stocks, bonds, cash, and gold would hold up well no matter what happened. "Stocks, bonds, gold, and cash combine to provide balance and safety, one that will do well in any economic environment," he stated.

Browne's strategy is to invest equally—25 percent in each category—into four investments: growth stocks during the good times; bonds during times of deflation; precious metals during times of crisis and inflation; and cash (T-bills or money market funds) during a credit crunch or bear markets. However, the bias of his permanent portfolio is heavily weighted to hard assets, such as gold and silver, which have been volatile.

The Permanent Portfolio Fund (symbol PRPFX), created originally by Harry Browne, has a similar investment mix: 25 percent precious metals (20 percent gold bullion, 5 percent silver bullion); 10 percent Swiss franc bonds (yielding less than 2 percent); 15 percent real estate and natural resource stocks, foreign and domestic; 15 percent aggressive growth stocks; and 35 percent in government securities, including T-bills.

How has the Permanent Portfolio Fund done? Since its inception in 1982, it has enjoyed an average return of around 7 percent, with few down years, and in the past ten years, when precious metals were in a major bull market, 10 percent annualized return. It has a five star Morningstar rating. There's much to commend in this approach for investors who are not interested in timing the market. It does appear to allow an investor to read the newspaper and sleep relatively well at night. Some folks prefer the sedate Tennessee waltz to the hectic whirl of the Viennese waltz.

In sum, the Austrian bears have wisely recognized that crashes and bear markets are inevitable in today's inflationary world, but they must not ignore the bull markets that result in economic recovery and in countries that are built upon free enterprise. The smart investor develops a strategy to play both bull and bear markets.

7 SCHUMPETER AND CREATIVE DESTRUCTION

"Of these two greatest economists of this century [Keynes and Schumpeter] . . . it is Schumpeter who will shape the thinking . . . on economic theory and economic policy for the rest of this century, if not for the next thirty or fifty years."

—Peter Drucker

The Austrian economist who maintained his status throughout the twentieth century is Joseph Schumpeter (1883–1950). After leaving Vienna in 1932, he remained a professor at Harvard University until his death in 1950. Although his predictions that capitalism would fail and socialism would succeed were off base, his dynamic view of capitalism and entrepreneurship applies to today's global economy. Schumpeter rejected the perfect competition/perfect knowledge model of new-classical economics. Instead, he focused on the entrepreneur as the vital figure in all economic activity, the capitalist who constantly searches for innovative ideas and improvements in a process called "creative destruction."[1]

Schumpeter's emphasis on the entrepreneur is reminiscent of Wieser's "great man" theory.

Clearly, Schumpeter's term is apropos of today's topsy-turvy financial markets. The financial pages are constantly telling of mergers, takeovers, and hot markets. New issues stream forth from the major underwriters, while old line companies go bankrupt. Some companies may have a string

1. Joseph Schumpeter, *Capitalism, Socialism and Democracy*, 3rd ed. (New York: Harper & Row, 1950 [1942]), 81–6.

of sharply higher quarterly earnings, while others have a string of losses. Non-performing corporations may suddenly be taken over by a creative CEO, who turns the company around.

Example: International Business Machines (IBM) is a classic case of Schumpeterian entrepreneurship and "creative destruction." In the early days, IBM was run by Thomas J. Watson, a real entrepreneur who turned IBM into the world's biggest computer company. But then bureaucratic management crowded out IBM's competitive advantage, and by the 1970s, IBM became a stodgy, oversized company. Meanwhile, upstarts such as Microsoft and Apple entered the market.

IBM had also adopted a "Keynesian" management approach, refusing to fire anyone during downturns. Unlike Jack Welch, whose philosophy was to fire the bottom 10 percent every year, IBM kept everyone working. But guaranteed lifetime employment made IBM less responsive to the changing marketplace. Its share of the growing computer industry shrunk, and its stock price deteriorated.

By the early 1990s, the writing was on the wall; IBM needed to make a change. IBM hired Louis Gerstner, an outside manager, who changed its long-standing employment policies. Big Blue, like many other large companies, engaged in downsizing and the introduction of better management techniques. One of those changes was a gradual shift from a defined-benefit retirement plan to a defined-contribution (401k) plan, thus saving billions and potential bankruptcy, as future employees and consumers would no longer be burdened by a growing retirement population.

As a result IBM, made a significant turnaround in 1994, and its outlook is bright once again. The stock has more than tripled from those dark days in mid-1990s. Gerstner wrote a classic management book on the subject, *Who Says Elephants Can't Dance?* (Harper Business, 2003).

One other observation can be made about Schumpeterian economics. The conventional wisdom of the ivory tower argues that no one can beat the market consistently, yet a few smart investors are proving the academicians wrong. Investors are entrepreneurs. They are constantly searching for undiscovered opportunities in the stock market. Some attempt to beat the market. Examples in the past include John Templeton, Warren Buffett, Peter Lynch, and Arnold Bernhard, founder of Value Line Investment Survey. Not everyone can beat the market, but a small number of investors manage to do so, especially when they have superior knowledge of how the markets and economies operate.

8 KIRZNER AND THE DISCOVERY PROCESS

"Israel Kirzner brilliantly and rigorously developed the modern Austrian theory of market process and the role of the entrepreneur."

—Peter Boettke

An American "Austrian" economist who has focused his professional career on the role of the entrepreneur is Israel Kirzner (1930–), an ordained rabbi who taught economics at New York University for many years. His book, *Competition and Entrepreneurship* (University of Chicago Press, 1973) is considered a classic in the field.

Kirzner emphasized the "discovery process" in the marketplace. Given the uncertainty that constantly exists in the economy, it's always a surprise to learn which products sell and which don't, why some countries go to war, or why one actor suddenly becomes more popular than another.

Example #1: During the financial crisis of 2008, almost everyone was shocked by how extensive the mortgage security business had spread throughout the world. Nobody really knew how vast and big the collateralized debt obligation (CDO) market had become until Lehman Brothers was allowed to fail. Prior to the 2008 crisis, most economists thought that asset bubbles could be contained and would not have macroeconomic impact. They were wrong. As Ludwig von Mises states, "In retrospect, all fools become wise."

His approach differs from Schumpeter's view. Schumpeter saw the entrepreneur as a troublemaker, one who disturbs the current marketplace with new products and marketing techniques. Kirzner's entrepreneur, on the other hand, engages in a "discovery process" to find profitable situations in the marketplace that no one else has noticed.

Example #2: Kirzner's approach has great application in the financial markets, where arbitrage is constantly taking place. Speculators are always searching for undiscovered discrepancies between prices in one market and prices in another.

Contrarians also try to find profitable situations before others notice the undervalued or overvalued condition. There is no set technique, but many investors have made big profits acting before the public finds out what is happening. The entrepreneur-investor is always alert to undervalued or overvalued situations.

Example #3: Steve Jobs always emphasized the uncertainty of what customers want until they see it. It's a discovery process. Jobs made a point of creating products that customers didn't know they wanted, and he opposed most forms of market research.

In an age when the media constantly promotes the Keynesian myth that "consumer spending is the largest single driver of the U. S. economy" (to quote a recent issue of the *Wall Street Journal*), Steve Jobs set the record straight. "Some people say, 'Give the customers what they want.' But that's not my approach," he said. "Henry Ford once said, 'If I'd asked customers what they wanted, they would have told me, "A faster horse!' People don't know what they want until you show it to them. That's why I never rely on market research." All of Apple's major products—the Mac, iTunes, iPhone, iPad—were "whole new devices and services that consumers did not yet know they needed."

As the Austrian economists have repeatedly emphasized, it's entrepreneurship, productive investment, and creative innovation that create a higher standard of living. Consumption is the effect, not the cause, of prosperity.[1]

1. This is known as Say's law, named after J. B. Say. Say's law ("supply creates demand") stresses that economic growth depends on productivity, capital, savings, technology, and entrepreneurship a term Say invented—all on the supply side of the economy. See chapter 17 in my book, *Economic Logic* (Capital Press, 2010), and http://www.thefreemanonline.org/columns/consumer-spending/

9 MURRAY ROTHBARD AND THE "HARD-MONEY MOVEMENT"

"Rothbard's role in the hard-money movement has been to teach solid economic theory, illuminate historical examples like the Great Depression, and inspire with a vision of the free society."

—Lew Rockwell and Walter Block

"Blessed paper credit! Last and best supply! That leads corruption lighter wings to fly."

—Alexander Pope

Murray N. Rothbard (1925–1995), who was a professor of economics at Polytech Institute of Brooklyn and the University of Las Vegas at Nevada, was in the forefront of reviving Austrian economics during the post-World War II period. His magnum opus is *Man, Economy, and State*, a 1,000-page economic treatise published in 1962. He was editor of the quarterly *Review of Austrian Economics*, published by the Mises Institute.

Another highly influential book, Rothbard's *America's Great Depression*, published originally in 1963, argued that the government, not free-enterprise capitalism, was responsible for the Great Depression. It went through four editions during his lifetime. His work was in many ways an "Austrian" alternative to Milton Friedman's *Monetary History* that was published at the same time.

In his typically refreshing readable style, Rothbard introduced the Austrian theory of the business cycle to explain why business economy-wide would suddenly experience a "cluster of errors" and a slowdown or recession/depression. Then he applied his theory specifically to the Roaring Twenties and the Great Depression, arguing that the seeds of collapse were sown in the inflationary 1920s. In contrast, Friedman claimed that the 1920s were relatively stable and non-inflationary; a garden-variety recession turned into the Great Depression because of the inept deflationary policies of the Federal Reserve in the early 1930s.[1]

The Cause of Stagflation

The second edition of *America's Great Depression* came out during the early 1970s. At this time, no one in the established economics community had a sophisticated model to explain "stagflation," characterized by rising prices and falling output. Austrian economists, on the other hand, did have a theory, although they didn't recognize it at first.

In the second edition, Rothbard argued that Austrian theory

> not only explains [inflationary recession], but demonstrates that it is a general and universal tendency in recessions . . . [that] the prices of consumer goods always tend to rise relative to the price of producer goods. The reason that this phenomenon has not been noted before is that, in past recessions, prices have generally fallen . . . . The result of the government's abolition of deflation, however, is that general prices no longer fall, even in recessions. Consequently, the adjustment between consumer goods and capital goods that must take place during recessions must now proceed without the merciful veil of deflation. Hence, the prices of consumer goods still rise relatively, but now, shorn of general deflation, they must rise absolutely and visibly as well.[2]

The Origin of Money and Banking

Probably his most influential work among investors and financial advisors is his sixty-page essay, "What Has the Government Done to Our

1. See my Vienna and *Chicago, Friends or Foes?*, chapter 6, for a detailed discussion of this debate.
2. Murray N. Rothbard, *America's Great Depression*, 2nd ed. (Los Angeles: Nash Publishing, 1972 [1963]), Introduction.

Money?" Originally published in 1964, it probably had the greatest impact of any other short work on the subject. What *The Communist Manifesto* was to Marxists, Rothbard's "What Has Government Done . . . . ?" was to the hard-money movement. It was my first introduction to Austrian economics, and I found it electrifying.

This essay was highly influential because, for the first time, simple and understandable terms were used to explain what money is all about. His straightforward prose takes way the mystique of the dollar and foreign currencies. It explains the creation of money all the way from barter to the modern fiat money system. It shows the ill effects of government's meddling with money, why central banking was inflationary, and the reasons for the monetary breakdown of the West. Finally, it demonstrates that the only stable monetary system would be one that returns to the classic gold standard.

Rothbard's Influence

Although Rothbard was an academic economist, he has been the ideological mentor of most of the major investment advisors and writers in the non-academic "hard-money" camp, including Harry Browne, Adrian Day, Gary North, Jerome F. Smith, John Pugsley, James Dines, James U. Blanchard III, and Richard Band. His popular works provide the theoretical foundation for investing in precious metals, foreign currencies, and other potential hedges against inflation or monetary crises.[3]

Example: Rothbard's principal works appeared right before the first monetary crisis in the United States occurred in the post-war period, i.e., the silver shortage of the 1960s. Many gold bugs note the influence of Rothbard's books on their decision to invest in silver coins. Gary North wrote that, after reading Rothbard in the summer of 1963, "I knew that silver, dimes, and quarters would gradually become scarce, and I started hoarding the coins."

In the 1930s, the U.S. Mint had established a controlled price for silver at $1.29 per ounce, based on how much silver there was in dimes and quarters. Yet the government continued to inflate the money supply, which meant that the silver content in the quarter would eventually

3. See my article, "Murray Rothbard As Investment Advisor," in *Man, Economy, and Liberty: Essays in Honor of Murray N. Rothbard*, ed. by Walter Block and Llewellyn H. Rockwell Jr. (Auburn, Alabama: Mises Institute, 1988), 151–74. Reprinted in this book.

be worth more than a quarter. At that point, it paid to hoard all dimes and quarters, which could be melted down and sold for more than their face value. That's exactly what happened in 1963–64, when silver coins disappeared in the United States and were replaced by "clad" coins.

Harry Browne acknowledged the impact of Rothbard's economics in his forecasting the devaluation of the dollar in the early 1970s.[4] He also recommended investing in inflation hedges such as gold, silver, and Swiss francs. Such is the way that Austrian economics can make you a better investor—it can help you anticipate dramatic events.

The Value and Role of Gold

The Austrian school is one of the few schools supporting an old-fashioned gold standard and free banking. Gold bugs have long been fans of Mises, Rothbard, Steve Forbes, and other theoretical defenders of gold. They reject the Wall Street view that "gold is just another commodity." Their response: Gold is not just another commodity like wheat or pork bellies—it has a long history of serving as money. Therefore, gold remains the best reserve currency, a hedge against monetary upheaval and inflation.

For hard-money investors, gold represents an asset independent of government intervention. The gold standard was established precisely as a method of controlling the state's penchant for depreciating the currency. Citizens who have studied world history are highly suspicious of government. Government is a force that can abuse its privileges through taxation, confiscation, inflation, and war. Investors must always be vigilant in protecting their hard-earned assets by purchasing gold and silver coins as a hedge against a moneyhungry government.

Austrian economics can be useful in creating an appropriate investment portfolio. It makes one more aware of the effects of government policies on various markets. Gold should be a key ingredients in anyone's portfolio. Why? Because it is the ultimate hedge against bad government, a monetary crisis, currency depreciation, or inflation. Even an investor who is extremely bullish on the traditional markets of stocks and bonds should have a small gold position as a hedge against an uncertain future. In fact, since the world went off the gold standard in 1970, gold and silver

4. Harry Browne, *How You Can Profit from the Coming Devaluation* (New Rochelle, New York: Arlington House, 1970), Acknowledgements.

have become superior inflation hedges.[5]

A Word of Warning to Gold Investors

But one word of caution: Often investors, driven by sound-money ideology and Austrian economics, get caught up in what I call "gold bug" fever and devote too much of their investment portfolio to precious metals and mining stocks. I've even met gold bugs who have completely sold out of stocks, bonds, and traditional investments and invested their entire life savings in gold and silver. When precious metals are moving up, everything looks good. But what happens when gold and silver enter a bear market during disinflationary times, as they did for twenty years in 1980–2000? They can lose half their value.

I recommend that everyone have a position in gold and silver in their portfolio, but be prudent. Investing in hard assets should be an insurance policy against bad times. It should typically represent 5–10 percent of your portfolio, and it should be held for the long term. The majority of investment funds, however, should be invested in successful businesses via the stock market.

5. See the introduction to the 4th edition of my book, *Economics of a Pure Gold Standard* (Foundation for Economic Education, 2010).

10 THE 2008 FINANCIAL CRISIS: AUSTRIAN RESPONSE TO THE CHICAGO SCHOOL OF MILTON FRIEDMAN

"A renewed belief in the superiority of markets reflects the eventual victory of this viewpoint, a tale of two cities—*Vienna and Chicago*."

—Daniel Yergin and Joseph Stanislaw

Finally, after years of economic turmoil, of boom and bust in the global economy, the Austrian school is making an impact as the premier challenger of Keynesian policies of easy money, stimulus, and big government.

The real estate boom-bust cycle and the financial crisis of 2008 caused the academic world, government officials, and Wall Street to search for a theory that explains asset bubbles and structural imbalances in the global economy, and the Austrian theory of the business cycle has suddenly come back into vogue. Articles in the *Financial Times*, *The Economist*, and the *Wall Street Journal* have highlighted the Austrian explanation that asset bubbles have a macroeconomic impact. Even the mainstream CFA Institute recently featured Austrian economics in its study materials for the Level 1 exam for would-be Chartered Financial Analysts. It has published several Austrian-friendly articles.

China has taken notice. Economists there are raising the specter of the "Hayekian risk" of wasted investment (what fellow Austrian Ludwig von Mises called "malinvestment") over the "Keynesian risk" of inadequate demand and weak growth. As *The Economist* states, "Malinvestment . . . squanders the hard-earned saving of China's citizens, leaving them with empty malls rather than much-needed clinics; vacant villas alongside overcrowded dormitories; sewers that cannot cope with downpours; and buildings that collapse like tofu."[1]

In the Oct. 13–14, 2012, issue of the *Wall Street Journal*, a reporter interviewed Zhang Weiying, the top economist at Peking University and former government official in charge of Chinese economic policy. In the interview, Dr. Zhang invoked Hayek's business cycle theory to warn against further Keynesian-style government spending and easy-money policies to keep the Chinese economy propped up. "The current economy is like a drug addict, and the prescription from the doctor is morphine, so the final result will be much worse," he said. The reporter noted, "He [Zhang] invoked the ideas of Nobel laureate Friedrich Hayek and the Austrian School of Economics to argue that if the economy weren't allowed to adjust on its own, China's minor bust would be followed by a bigger one." Zhang even wrote an article praising the libertarian Austrian economist Murray Rothbard.

Hayek's economics has reached the pinnacle of pop culture among economics students with the release of two rap videos, "Fear the Boom and the Bust" in 2010, and "The Fight of the Century" in 2011. Both are available on YouTube and have been seen by more than 3,000,000 viewers. Developed by director John Papola and George Mason University economist Russ Roberts, the lyrics pit Hayek—not Friedman or Mises—against Keynes in the battle of ideas over how to cure economic depressions.

The fight has spilled over into the academic world with the 2012 publication of *Keynes Hayek: The Clash that Defined Modern Economics* by British journalist Nicholas Wapshott. The author states:

> As the stock market crash of 1929 plunged the world into turmoil, two men emerged with competing claims on how to restore balance to economies gone awry. John Maynard Keynes, the mercurial Cambridge economist, believed that government had a duty to spend when others would not. He met his opposite in a little-known Austrian economics professor, Freidrich Hayek, who considered attempts to intervene both pointless and potentially dangerous. The battle lines thus drawn, Keynesian economics would dominate for decades and coincide with an era of unprecedented prosperity, but conservative

1. "Hayek on the Standing Committee," Free Exchange, *Economist*: September 15, 2012, 73.

economists and political leaders would eventually embrace and execute Hayek's contrary vision.

Chicago's Milton Friedman: Watch the Money Supply!

But there is another rival to the Austrian school besides Keynesian economics: The Chicago school of Milton Friedman. Milton Friedman (1912–2006) was the most famous and influential free-market economist of the twentieth century, the author of several classics, including *Capitalism and Freedom* (1962) and *Free to Choose* (1980).

As long-time subscribers know, I frequently refer to both the great Austrian and Chicago schools of free-market economics to understand the mega trends in the world and how they might affect your investments. The Austrians have much in common with the Chicago school of Milton Friedman, known as monetarists. They both agree that monetary policy and central banking are critically important to understanding the ups and downs of the economy. I rely on both schools to make investment decisions and the direction of the economy.

However, there are significant differences that investors should be aware of.[2] Let's review each school's perspective.

First, I learned from Milton Friedman the importance of Fed policy, especially watching the money supply and interest rates. Friedman became famous for his studies on monetary policy at the University of Chicago in the 1960s and 1970s, having written with Anna Schwartz the monetarist bible, *A Monetary History of the United States, 1869–1960.*

In his work, Friedman proved that the Great Depression of the 1930s was <u>not</u> caused by any inherent weakness in the free enterprise system, but rather by the government, especially an inept Federal Reserve that allowed the nation's money supply to collapse by one-third. He concluded, "The fact is that the Great Depression, like most other periods of severe unemployment, was produced by government mismanagement rather than by any inherent instability of the private economy."[3] His empirical findings shocked the economics profession and created a monetary counterrevolution to Keynesian economics.

Friedman demonstrated that labor unions or big government do not cause price inflation, but "inflation is always and everywhere a monetary

2. See my book, *Vienna and Chicago, Friends or Foes?* (Capital Press, 2005).
3. Milton Friedman, *Capitalism and Freedom* (University of Chicago Press, 1962), 38.

phenomenon," produced by excessive expansion of the money supply by the Federal Reserve. He showed that the Fed causes the boom-bust cycle: An easy-money policy causes an economic expansion, and a tight-money policy causes an economic contraction.

Based on Friedman's work, I always watch the money supply figures very carefully. Monetary aggregates do matter.

Friedman and the Financial Crisis of 2008

Since I wrote *Vienna and Chicago, Friends or Foes?* in 2005, we've suffered another monetary crisis, this one so serious that it undermined the very foundation of our monetary and economic system. It is known as "The Great Recession."

How do the Austrian and Chicago economists differ when it comes to these questions?

1. What caused the financial crisis of 2007–09?
2. What is the best way out of the crisis and Great Recession?

Let's start with the Chicago school and Milton Friedman's famous article, "Why the American Economy Is Depression Proof."

Is the U.S. Economy Depression Proof?

In late 2009, I was in Stockholm, Sweden, for the Mont Pelerin Society meetings, where 300 top experts gathered from around the world. At this meeting, I organized a special ad hoc session reassessing Milton Friedman's famous lecture "Why the American Economy Is Depression-Proof."[4] Friedman gave this optimistic lecture in Sweden in 1954, at a time when some prominent economists and financial advisors were predicting another crash on Wall Street and a collapse in the economy.

A little over fifty years later, in the face of the worst financial crisis since the Great Depression, everyone at the meeting wanted to know if Friedman, one of the founders of the international society, would change his mind. Nobody knows for sure how Friedman would have

4. Milton Friedman, "Why the American Economy is Depression-Proof," lecture delivered in Stockholm in April, 1954, and reprinted in *Dollars and Deficits* (Prentice-Hall, 1968), 72–96. Friedman's controversial lecture is still not available online, although my response, "Why the U. S. Economy Is Not Depression-Proof" is: http://mises.org/journals/rae/pdf/RAE3_1_5.pdf

responded, since he died in late 2006. I do know that until his death, he always defended his bold prediction. From 1954 until his death in 2006, the United States suffered numerous contractions in the economy, a savings and loan crisis, a major terrorist attack, and even a few stock market crashes, and still it avoided the "big one," a massive 1930s-style Depression characterized by an unemployment rate of 15 percent or more, which was Friedman's definition of a depression.

In his lecture in 1954, Friedman pointed to four major institutional changes that would keep another Great Depression from happening: federal bank deposit insurance; abandonment of the international gold standard; the growth in the size of government, including welfare payments, unemployment insurance, and other "built-in stabilizers"; and most importantly, the Federal Reserve's determination to avoid a monetary collapse at all costs. Because the public and officials are petrified by the possibility of another depression, Friedman predicted that any signs of trouble would lead the Federal Reserve to take "drastic action" and shift "rapidly and completely to an easy money policy." Consequently, according to Friedman, rising inflation would be far more of a threat to post-war America than another Great Depression.

So far so good. But now, following the financial crisis of 2008, I suspect Friedman would be forced to revise his views if he were alive. Admittedly, Friedman is still technically correct. There has still been no Great Depression, according to government statistics at least. The official unemployment rate rose to 10 percent in 2009, far below the 15 percent rate necessary to qualify as a "depression."

However, it's important to note that the official unemployment rate does not include discouraged workers who have stopped looking, and those numbers apparently are in the millions. According to economist John Williams, editor of *Shadow Government Statistics* (www.shadowstats.com), if you count discouraged workers, plus stay-at-home welfare recipients, the real unemployment rate exceeds 20 percent.

The Fed and the federal government appear to have averted disaster once again, at least in the short term. Yet they were able to do so only by putting millions of Americans on unemployment insurance, taking on unprecedented powers, and adding trillions of dollars in debt through TARP and Quantitative Easing. These measures may so weaken the government and the public's trust in its financial capacity that a deflationary collapse, hyperinflation, or centrally planned economy sometime in the future is a serious risk.

Clearly, bank failures are not a phenomenon of the past. There have been runs on commercial banks and other financial institutions, such as money market funds, although Friedman is right that most failing banks are now either taken over by the FDIC or the Treasury, or forced to merge with a bigger, safer bank. Still, major institutions like Bank of America and Citibank would not have survived had it not been for government bailouts.

Friedman stated in his 1954 lecture, "There has been no major depression that has not been associated with and accompanied by a monetary collapse . . . . Monetary contraction or collapse is an essential conditioning factor for the occurrence of a major depression."

Yet a monetary expansion provides no guarantee that a crisis can be avoided. In fact, the U.S. came awfully close to an economic collapse in late 2008 without any monetary contraction. *During 2008, the money supply (M2) grew every month, and it grew 9 percent for the year.* Clearly, monetary contraction isn't the only source of instability in the economy. Economic disaster can also be precipitated by too much monetary inflation, irresponsible banking practices, or perverse tax and regulatory policies. One of the weaknesses of the Friedman/Chicago school approach is their belief that inflationary asset bubbles have only micro effects on the economy and can be defused without having a debilitating macroeconomic impact. The real estate crisis of 2007–09 demonstrated otherwise, and that's why most Chicago economists failed to predict the 2008 crisis.

Interestingly, Friedman's famous chapter, "The Great Contraction, 1929–1933," taken from his magnum opus, *A Monetary History of the United States, 1869–1960* (Princeton University Press, 1963), was reprinted in 2007, with a new introduction by his co-author, Anna J. Schwartz. The short book had long been out of print and was brought back just before the real estate crisis started and after Milton Friedman died. It was perfect timing, as we were about to witness the worst economic debacle since the Great Depression. Yet Professor Schwartz was oblivious to any evidence of a collapse in writing her introduction. She wrote, "As the federal funds rate moves in a low and narrow range in response to low and stable inflation, volatility of the business cycle and real economy has moderated."[5]

5. Anna Jacobson Schwartz, "New Preface," *The Great Contraction, 1929–1933* (Princeton University Press, 2007), xi.

The Austrians' Response

The Austrians, on the other hand, knew full well that the Fed's artificially low interest rate policy and the government's meddling with banks and mortgage companies to encourage excessive home ownership was about to blow up in their faces. American "Austrian" financial economists such as Peter Schiff, Bert Dohmen, and Fred Foldvary, anticipated the crisis (each warned of the impending crisis at the 2007 FreedomFest conference). That is why I concluded "Advantage, Vienna" in the debate between the Austrian and Chicago schools on the business cycle in chapter 6 of *Vienna and Chicago.*

Based on the Mises-Hayek theory of the business cycle, the Austrians proposed their fundamental thesis that monetary inflation is never neutral, and that asset bubbles cause unsustainable structural imbalances on a macro level. Inflation has many negative unintended consequences. The Austrians knew that eventually a collapse was inevitable. As Ludwig von Mises once said, "We have outlived the short run and are suffering from the long-run consequences of [inflationary] policies."

At the end of our special session, I asked members of the Mont Pelerin Society how many of them still agreed with Friedman, that the American economy is "depression proof." Only a handful raised their hands, and they were all American economists. The rest of the crowd, mostly from abroad, pointed out that most other countries did not suffer a banking crisis in 2008–10. The financial crisis was largely Anglo-American induced. They agreed that until the United States adopts a stable monetary and banking system, it can no longer be considered depression proof.

Government Response to the Crisis

What should the government do in response to the crisis, if anything? The United States and many other countries followed the standard Keynesian prescription; the government ran massive deficits, and the central banks cut interest rates. In short, they engaged in easy money policies at all levels: They injected liquidity and adopted activist fiscal and monetary policy.

The 2007 reprint of *The Great Contraction* published Fed Chairman Ben Bernanke's remarks given at a 2002 conference in Chicago honoring Milton Friedman on his ninetieth birthday. At the end, Bernanke said, "I would like to say to Milton and Anna: Regarding the Great Depression. You're right, we did it. We're very sorry. But thanks to you, we won't do it again."[6] Bernanke said he had learned the Friedman lesson well. The Fed would not allow the banking system to collapse and cause another Great Depression. Indeed, he lived up to his word during the 2008 financial crisis by injecting massive amounts of liquidity through printing more fiat money.

Unfortunately, Bernanke failed to recognize the other lesson found in Friedman's scholarly works: Activist fiscal policy doesn't work and is unnecessary. In Friedman's testing of Keynesian policy prescription, he found that the deficit spending multiplier was extremely low—not four or five as taught in the textbooks, but zero to one, in its impact on the economy. Recently Robert Barro (Harvard) concluded it was close to zero, offering no positive impact at all. The increase in government spending was largely offset by a decline in private spending, due to crowding out or uncertainty.

Friedman and the Chicago economists argued that the money multiplier in the banking system was much higher, as much as three or four. Accordingly, Friedman advocated that the Fed should be the primary source of new stimulus to get the economy going again, and fiscal policy should remain stable by focusing primarily on its fundamental role.

In short, it was unnecessary and maybe even downright harmful for Ben Bernanke to have called Treasury Secretary Henry Paulson in September 2008 and encourage Congress to get involved. According to this view, the trillion-dollar deficits and TARP monies were completely unnecessary. Monetary policy could do all of the heavy lifting. After TARP became law, I asked Glenn Hubbard, former president of the Council for Economic Policy under Bush and the dean of Columbia Business School, if the Fed had all of the emergency powers necessary to buy any asset—Treasuries, mortgages, even stocks—to avert a meltdown, and he said emphatically, "Yes." It was not necessary to get Congress involved.

The most extreme response to the financial crisis is the recommendation by some Austrians to "do nothing," that is, for the government to let the malinvestments collapse under their own weight. According to these economists, government should not increase spending (the Keynesian

6. Ben S. Bernanke, "Remarks," *The Great Depression, 1929–1933* (Princeton University Press, 2008), 247.

prescription), nor should the Fed engage in easy-money policies and inject liquidity (the monetarist solution). If anything, the government should retrench like everyone else. This was known as the classical economic policy. Thomas E. Woods, Jr., Austrian economist with the Mises Institute, wrote about the 1920–21 period in American history as an example:

> The conventional wisdom holds that in the absence of government countercyclical policy, whether fiscal or monetary (or both), we cannot expect economic recovery—at least, not without an intolerably long delay. Yet the very opposite policies were followed during the depression of 1920–1921, and recovery was in fact not long in coming. The economic situation in 1920 was grim. By that year, unemployment had jumped from 4 percent to nearly 12 percent, and GNP declined 17 percent. No wonder, then, that Secretary of Commerce Herbert Hoover—falsely characterized as a supporter of laissez-faire economics—urged President Harding to consider an array of interventions to turn the economy around. Hoover was ignored. Instead of "fiscal stimulus," Harding cut the government's budget nearly in half between 1920 and 1922. The rest of Harding's approach was equally laissez-faire. Tax rates were slashed for all income groups. The national debt was reduced by one-third. The Federal Reserve's activity, moreover, was hardly noticeable. As one economic historian puts it, 'Despite the severity of the contraction, the Fed did not move to use its powers to turn the money supply around and fight the contraction.' By the late summer of 1921, signs of recovery were already visible. The following year, unemployment was back down to 6.7 percent and it was only 2.4 percent by 1923.[7]

It takes a great deal of faith in capitalism to adopt this laissez-faire policy in today's world.

The Austrian Alternative to Keynes and Friedman

The Austrian economists Ludwig von Mises and Friedrich Hayek

---

7. Thomas E. Woods, Jr., "The Forgotten Depression of 1920" (Mises Institute, November 27, 2009): http://mises.org/daily/3788

have developed a more sophisticated model to predict the boom-bust business cycle, compared to the monetarist "disequilibrium" model. Pumping up the money supply and lowering interest rates below the natural rate does more than stimulate the economy; it also creates artificial imbalances in the economy, especially in the capital markets like stocks and real estate.

Like the Chicago school, the Austrian school of economics places a high value on the impact of monetary aggregates on the structure of the economy. Both interest rates and the money supply are important in understanding how the economy works and how structural imbalances occur.

In *America's Great Depression*, Rothbard showed how important interest rates and the money supply were in causing the boom-bust cycle of the 1920s and early 1930s. Rothbard showed that the Federal Reserve adopted an easy-money policy at various times during the 1920s to support the British pound, and this, in turn, led to the asset bubbles in real estate, manufacturing, and the stock market. Then, worried about excessive speculation on Wall Street, the Federal Reserve raised the discount rate, creating an inverted yield curve, and the stock market crashed in October 1929.

An Austrian Approach to Monetary Aggregates

Responding to Rothbard's *America's Great Depression*, Austrian economists such as Joseph Salerno and Frank Shostak have tried to get an accurate measure of the "true" money supply.

This has been a difficult task, even for monetarists at Chicago, because in the early 1980s, the financial markets were deregulated and M1 became a misleading monetary aggregate. In the mid-1980s, I asked Milton Friedman about M1, a narrow definition of the money supply that includes cash and bank account deposits. I pointed out to him that M1 had declined sharply. "Doesn't this mean a slowdown, if not a recession, in the economy?" I asked. Friedman demurred. He pointed out that after financial deregulation, M1 was no longer an accurate predictor of economic activity, and that a broader definition, M2, which includes money market funds, should be used. According to M2, monetary policy was still accommodating, and therefore no recession was in sight. He proved to be right.

Shostak has argued that only true money used to make transactions directly should be considered the "money supply." Credit, money market funds, short-term certificates of deposit, and other interest-bearing financial assets, no matter how liquid, should not be considered a part of this narrow definition. Only money used as a direct medium of exchange should qualify as the "money supply." This definition has come to be called the "Austrian Money Supply" (AMS), which appears awfully close to M1 (cash and demand deposits).[8] This is much more narrow than Murray Rothbard used in his book *America's Great Depression*, wherein he included cash balances in whole-life insurance policies as part of the money supply.[9]

Friedman's Wall Street: Never Overvalued?

Milton Friedman and other monetarists make one claim that seems as bizarre as Murray Rothbard's oversized monetary aggregates: They don't seem to think that the stock market can ever be overvalued, or that the economy can ever be overheated.

In the April 1993 issue of *Economic Inquiry*, Friedman published a paper introducing his "plucking model" of business fluctuations. Essentially, he contends that the economy reaches a full employment range of steady economic growth, but then pulls back from the long-term trend line. See the figure on the next page that illustrates Friedman's plucking model.

Thus we see in Friedman's business cycle model that there never is an unsustainable boom, only an undervalued bust. Essentially, Friedman denies the Austrian view that "what goes up must come down," but rather "what goes down must come back up."[10] According to Friedman, there's fully employed GDP and underemployed GDP, but never overemployed GDP.

---

8. See Murray N. Rothbard, "Austrian Definitions of the Supply of Money," in *The Logic of Action One: Method, Money, and the Austrian School* (Edward Elgar Publishing, 1997) 337–49; Joseph T. Salerno, "The 'True' Money Supply: A Measure of the Supply of the Medium of Exchange in the U.S. Economy," *Austrian Economics Newsletter* 6 (Spring 1987): 1–6; and Frank Shostak, "The Mystery of the Money Supply Definition," *Quarterly Journal of Austrian Economics* 3:4 (Winter 2000), 69–76. I prefer to use broader monetary aggregates (such as M2 or M3) as a reflection of monetary policy.
9. See Murray Rothbard, *America's Great Depression* (Richardson and Snyder, 1983), 85. Milton Friedman called Rothbard's monetary aggregates "pure chicanery." He said Rothbard was artificially expanding the monetary aggregates to prove that the Fed was excessively inflationary. Friedman argued quite the opposite: the 1920s was the "high tide" of Federal Reserve policy; the chief mischief occurred in the 1930s, when the Fed ineptly adopted a deflationary policy. See *Vienna and Chicago*, 172–174.
10. For more discussion, including Austrian economist Roger Garrison's critique, see *Vienna and Chicago, Friends or Foes?*, 176–8.

Friedman's Plucking Model

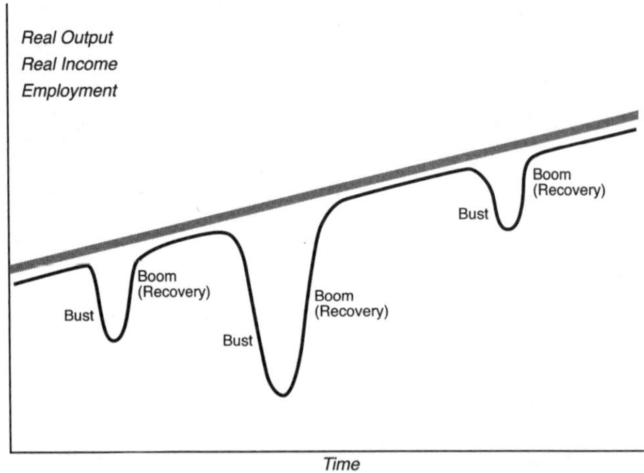

Friedman's plucking model also implies that there never is an overvalued bull market, only an undervalued bear market. Stocks can reach the upper limit of a trend line or fall below it, but never above it in an overvalued situation. Anna Schwartz, Friedman's colleague in *A Monetary History*, makes this argument with regard to the speculative boom in Wall Street in the Roaring Twenties. Most financial analysts are convinced that the 1920s experienced a speculative orgy. The Dow Industrials climbed from a cyclical low of 66 to a high of 300 by mid-1929, more than quadruple its earlier value, much faster than industrial production had experienced. Yet Schwartz opines that Irving Fisher was right in believing that stock prices in late 1929 were not generally overvalued. "Had employment and economic growth continued," Schwartz states, "prices in the stock market could have been maintained."[11]

In recent times, there have been several episodes that contradict the plucking model in the stock market: the Asian asset bubble of mid-1990s, ending in the Asian currency crisis of 1997; the high-tech dot-com speculative bubble of the late 1990s; and the real estate bubble in 2001–07. Milton Friedman did not live long enough to witness the collapse of the real estate bubble, but he did live through the speculative orgy of the late 1990s and once told me that he thought stocks were indeed overvalued.

11. Anna J. Schwartz, "Understanding 1929–1933," *Money in Historical Perspective* (University of Chicago Press, 1987), 130. Schwartz based her denial of a speculative stock market boom based on a "reasonable" price-earnings ratio of 15 for stocks at the time. For my critique, see the article, "Who Predicted the 1929 Crash?" in this volume.

PART II

Essays on Austrian Financial Economics and History

11 MURRAY ROTHBARD AS INVESTMENT ADVISOR

"Practical men, who believe themselves to be quite exempt from any intellectual influences, are usually the slaves of some defunct economist."

—John Maynard Keynes

It may seem inappropriate to cast Murray Rothbard as an investment advisor, since by profession he is an academic economist who is largely disinterested in personal investment strategies. Nevertheless, Professor Rothbard has been the ideological mentor of most of the major investment advisors, writers and entrepreneurs in the hard-money movement, including Harry Browne, Gary North, Jerome F. Smith, John Pugsley, Julian Snyder, James U. Blanchard, III, Richard Band, and myself.

Others, such as Howard Ruff and Douglas R. Casey, have been influenced by Rothbard indirectly through the writings of Harry Browne. Rothbard's writings, especially those published in the early 1960s, greatly affected their way of looking at the effects of government economic policy on the financial world. His popular works provided the theoretical foundation for investing in precious metals, foreign currencies, and other "hedges" against inflation or monetary crises.[1]

There are, of course, other "free market" economists who also greatly contributed to the hard-money movement. Alexander P. Paris mentions

---

Reprinted from *Man, Economy, and Liberty: Essays in Honor of Murray N. Rothbard*, ed. by Walter Block and Llewellyn H. Rockwell (Ludwig von Mises Institute, 1988), 151–174.

1. Sources, unless otherwise indicated, are based on private interviews with individuals in the hard-money movement. Each has had the opportunity to review references to them, but only I am responsible for any conclusions reached in this paper. I also wish to thank Robert D. Kephart for the use of his extensive library in preparation of this paper.

Friedrich A. Hayek, current leader of the "Austrian" school of economics.[2] James Dines credits the French economist Jacques Rueff.[3] Donald J. Hoppe says he was influenced by E. C. Harwood, who founded the American Institute for Economic Research in Great Barrington, Mass., and Dr. Elgin Groseclose, author of *Money and Man*, a book that Hoppe considered a "classic."[4]

In addition to Rothbard, Gary North credits Ludwig von Mises, F. A. Hayek, and Hans Sennholz.[5] Hans Sennholz, both an academic economist and avid speculator, was influenced by Wilhelm Röpke and Ludwig von Mises. John Pugsley praises, in addition to Rothbard, the works of Henry Hazlitt, especially his *Economics in One Lesson*; "I probably would never have written this book [*Common Sense Economics*] but for his inspiration."[6] Harry Browne acknowledges the influence of several other economists besides Rothbard, including Hazlitt, Mises, and Milton Friedman.[7]

But it is apparent from hard-money books and articles that Rothbard has had the broadest appeal and is the chief intellectual architect of the hard-money movement. Harry Browne says, "Rothbard has had far greater influence than Mises on the popular hard-money investment community, although some writers have read only Rothbard's popular pamphlets and pay him lip service." Undoubtedly, it was Rothbard's ability to write to laymen in a lucid, practical fashion that made him so influential. As one of the members of the hard-money movement, Larry Abraham, states, "Murray Rothbard is the best popularizer of the Austrian school of economics who has ever lived."

Are Economists Superior Investors?

While Professor Rothbard's theoretical and historical writings have had a significant impact on hard-money investment advisors, this fact does not mean that he considers himself an investment counselor or

2. Alexander P. Paris, *The Coming Credit Collapse* (New York: Arlington House, [1974] 1980), x.
3. James Dines, *The Invisible Crash* (New York: Random House, 1975), xiv.
4. Donald J. Hoppe, *How to Buy Gold Coins* (New York: Arlington House, 1970), 17, 19–20.
5. Gary North, *How You Can Profit From the Coming Price Controls* (Durham, N.C.: American Bureau of Economic Research, 1978). See also his *Introduction to ChristianEconomics* (Nutley, N.J.: The Craig Press, 1973), 107–23.
6. John A. Pugsley, *Common Sense Economics* (Costa Mesa, Calif.: Common Sense Press, [1974] 1976), v–vi.
7. Harry Browne, *How You Can Profit from the Coming Devaluation* (New York: Macmillan, 1974); *Inflation-Proofing Your Investments* (New York: William Morrow &. Co., 1981), co-authored with Terry Coxon, is dedicated to Rothbard, Mises, Hazlitt, and Friedman.

even a gifted speculator. Rothbard freely admits that his investment advice, which he occasionally proffers, has been wrong from time to time. Moreover, he has suffered incredibly bad luck in the stock market, according to his own account.

For example, in 1956, he bought shares in Shell Oil, only to see the value of the stock plummet when Egypt nationalized the Suez Canal the very next day. On another occasion, he bought some cheap "junk" bonds, only to see them delisted the following week. Investment advisor Douglas R. Casey says that he once called Rothbard in the mid-1970s and tried to talk him into buying South African gold shares, which at the time were selling at bargain prices, but he wasn't interested. Rothbard says he has primarily lost money based on "inside tips" from brokers. He has since then become much more conservative, putting most of his savings into money market funds and a few gold coins.

Of course, some economists have done well as investors. The British economist John Maynard Keynes was considered an astute foreign currency speculator, "dealing in rupees, the dollar, the French franc, the German mark, and the Dutch florin."

He made several highly profitable trades, often while "still in bed in the morning."[8] However, the belief that Keynes was a consistent profiteer taking advantage of sources inside government is probably mistaken. Like most speculators, he also lost money frequently. He almost went bankrupt in 1920, when he shorted the German mark and took severe losses in the 1929 and 1937 stock market collapses.[9] Still, Keynes became well-to-do and considered financial success a sign of a "versatile genius." In his *Essays in Biography*, Keynes praised Sir Isaac Newton as not only a preeminent scientist but also as a successful investor who survived the South Sea Bubble fiasco and died a rich man.[10]

There is no evidence to indicate that the financial performance of economists is any better than other professions. Some contemporary economists, such as Paul A. Samuelson and Milton Friedman, have become wealthy, but they have done so primarily because of their business—through teaching, writing, and lecturing—not from their investments. Indeed, if one evaluates Rothbard's financial performance in terms of

8. Charles H. Hession, *John Maynard Keynes* (New York: Macmillan, 1984), 174–75, 212.

9. Ibid., 174–75, 305.

10. John Maynard Keynes, *Essays in Biography*, in *The Collected Writings of John Maynard Keynes*, vol. X, A. Robinson and D. Moggridge, eds. (London: Macmillan and Cambridge University Press, 1951).

his own business, which also comes from teaching, writing, and lecturing, he would be rated highly successful compared to the average income level of academic economists.

One might think, initially, that sound economic theory should lead to correct economic predictions, which, in turn, should result in superior personal moneymaking strategies. Certainly, that is the implication of the hard-money investment advisors. Jerome Smith, for example, writes on the value of using sound economic principles:

> Its application permits us to determine where we are, approximately, in any given cycle and, more importantly for investment decisions, what the next stage of the cycle is, approximately when it will begin, and its probable impact on various investment categories . . . . Austrian economists have developed techniques of economic analysis which allow them to understand these secondary effects of government intervention and, based on micro-economic analysis of the impact of these interventions on acting individuals, to forecast the range of distorting and damaging consequences that follow the obvious immediate impact.[11]

Economists' Ability to Forecast

However, there are many reasons why economic analysis may not lead to correct economic forecasts or sound investment advice. There could be a sizeable slip twixt the "theoretical" cup and the "investment" lip.

Making predictions and investment decisions depend on a complex set of factors. Hayek has written:

> The value of business forecasting depends upon correct theoretical concepts . . . . Every economic theory . . . aims exclusively at foretelling the necessary consequences of a given situation, event, or measure. The subject matter of trade cycle theory being what it is, it follows that ideally it should result in a collective forecast showing the total development resulting from a given

11. Jerome F. Smith, "Charter Issue: Understanding the Business Cycle," *Jerome Smith's Investment Perspectives* (October 1983): 1–2.

> situation under given conditions. In practice, such forecasts are attempted in too unconditional a form, and on an inadmissibly oversimplified basis: and, consequently, the very possibility of scientific judgments about future economic trends today appears problematical, and cautious thinkers are apt to disparage any attempt at such forecasting.[12]

Forecasting is extremely difficult because financial data, such as interest rates, the inflation rate, and the prices of commodities, stocks and other investments, are determined by a myriad of supply and demand factors, both major and minor, which are constantly undergoing change. The markets are in continual disequilibrium, and, in fact, as Ludwig Lachmann states, "Relative prices change every day . . . a price system implying a uniform rate of profit and wage cannot exist. The forces tending to bring it about will always be weaker than the forces of change."[13]

Take interest rates as an example. Why is the movement of interest rates difficult to predict? Because they depend on both the supply and demand for money. Suppose, for instance, that the Federal Reserve starts a massive inflation. If the government has not previously been inflationary, interest rates may drop as the supply of money increases. However, the drop in interest rates is only temporary. As nominal incomes increase, the demand for money rises, which pushes interest rates up. This is the general scheme of events.

Economics may properly determine the *direction* that interest rates may take, but it is extremely difficult to determine *when* interest rates will start changing direction and *by how much*. As Rothbard notes, such decisions are "quantitative" in nature, while economics can properly deal only with "qualitative" changes. "There are no constant numerical relations in human action, and therefore there are no coefficients that can be included . . . that are not simply arbitrary and erroneous. Economic theory is and can only be qualitative—not quantitative."[14] It's up to professional speculators and entrepreneurs to try to predict and profit from "quantitative" changes.

12. Friedrich A. Hayek, *Monetary Theory and the Trade Cycle* (London: Jonathan Cape, 1933), 41, 36n.

13. Ludwig M. Lachmann, *Capital, Expectations, and the Market Process* (Kansas City, Kans.: Sheed Andrews and McMeel, 1977). 31–32.

14. Murray N. Rothbard, "Foreword," in James B. Ramsey, *Economic Forecasting—Models or Markets?* (San Francisco: Cato Institute, 1977), x.

The whole scenario can change radically, too, if the government has inflated in the past and the general public starts to anticipate the effects of high prices. The result may be an immediate rise in interest rates when the government starts inflating again. Inflationary expectations play a major role in determining interest rates, both long- and short-term.[15]

The outlook for inflation is another case in point. Rothbard, in the various introductions to his book, *America's Great Depression*, has consistently pointed out the inflationary nature of government policies. In the perennial "inflation-deflation" debates that go on at investment seminars, Rothbard has consistently been on the inflationist side, arguing that higher consumer prices are practically inevitable: "As long as the Federal Reserve has the unlimited power to inflate, and the will to inflate, it will not stop inflating. It's inevitable. Even in the deep recession of '82, we still had inflation. Sometimes more inflation, sometimes less. But always inflation."[16]

But Rothbard has not pretended to know the rate of inflation, nor by how much it will vary from year to year. One of the principal reasons why the rate of inflation is difficult to predict, as Rothbard clearly demonstrates, is that the central bank's fiat monetary system affects both relative prices and the production of various goods and services. There can be no scientific way to measure a "general price level." One can only look at "relative" prices as they relate to the structure of production, from capital goods to final consumer products.

The monetarists' quantity theory of money and alleged long-run neutrality of money is rejected.[17] Monetary inflation, no matter how large or small, causes a business cycle and malinvestments, particularly in the capital goods markets. Because of malinvestments, it's possible to have both a "recession" and an "inflation" at the same time. Rothbard was the first economist to offer a practical explanation of the phenomenon of "inflationary recession." As Rothbard states:

> . . . the prices of consumer goods always tend to rise, relative to the prices of producer goods, during recessions. The reason that this phenomenon has not been noted before is that, in past recessions, prices have generally fallen . . . . But, in the last

15. Interview with Murray N. Rothbard, *Predictions* (April 1985), 6–7.
16. Murray N. Rothbard, "The Inflation-Deflation Debate," *World Market Perspective* (January 1985), 2.
17. Murray N. Rothbard, *Man, Economy, and State* (Los Angeles: Nash Publishing, [1962] 1970), 727–37.

> few decades, monetary deflation has been strictly prevented by government expansion of credit and bank reserves . . . . The result of the government's abolition of deflation, however, is that general prices no longer fall, even in recessions . . . . Hence, the prices of consumer goods still rise relatively, but now, shorn of general deflation, they must rise absolutely and visibly as well.[18]

The Importance of Timing

Timing is critical in making investment decisions. Rothbard's outlook for continued inflation might suggest investing in gold and other inflation hedges, yet a fall in the rate of inflation can have an adverse effect on "inflation hedges" for many years. For example, when inflation was generally rising in the 1970s, gold rose to nearly $850 per ounce by January 1980, only to fall back to less than $300 per ounce when the rate of inflation significantly dropped during the first half of the 1980s.

In short, investing is an art, not a science. It requires unusual skill, keen interest, and the ability to forecast accurately based on assessing a myriad of supply and demand factors and investment psychology.

Given the complexity of the economic and financial world, it is not surprising that economists have made serious blunders in their predictions and investment advice. Perhaps the most egregious prediction was made by Yale economist Irving Fisher, when he stated, "stock prices have reached what looks like a permanently high plateau . . . . I expect to see the stock market a good deal higher than it is today within a few months" on October 16, 1929, a few days prior to the stock market crash.[19]

Even in recent times, sophisticated econometric programs developed by economists in conjunction with high-speed computers have not fared well. The record of most of them in predicting the future of the economy has been dismal.[20]

How about the "Austrian" economists? It's difficult to assess their

---

18. See Murray N. Rothbard, "Introduction to Second Edition," *America's Great Depression* (New York: Richardson and Snyder, [1963] 1983), xxv–xxxviii.
19. Irving Fisher, *New York Times*, 16 October 1929. Quoted in *Oh Yeah?*, compiled by Edward Angly (New York: Viking Press, 1931), an amusing compilation of predictions about the economy and the stock market during the 1929–1931 depression.
20. Ramsey, *Economic Forecasting*.

ability to make predictions. Early in his career, Ludwig von Mises was offered a high position at the Credit Anstalt, the largest bank in Austria, but he refused because he expected a great "crash" to be coming and he didn't want his name associated with it. He was proven correct when Credit Anstalt went bankrupt and precipitated the depression in Europe in the 1930s.[21]

In recent times, however, the forecasts of "Austrian" economists have been mixed. They were largely correct in their predicting higher inflation, higher interest rates, the fall of the dollar, and the rise in the prices of gold and silver in the late 1960s and 1970s. But, in large measure, they failed to see the reduction in inflation and interest rates in the 1980s. As Hans Sennholz, professor of economics at Grove City College, admits, "The 1980s took us by surprise."

It is no wonder, as financier Bernard Baruch once remarked, that "I think economists as a rule . . . take for granted they know a lot of things. If they really knew so much, they would have all the money and we would have none."[22] Rothbard says practically the same thing: "If someone were really able to forecast the economic future, he wouldn't be wasting his time putting out market letters or econometric models. He'd be busy making several trillion dollars forecasting the stock and commodity markets."[23]

The Mind of the Speculator

Recent research, particularly by Eastern schools of thought, has shown that the world of investing is distinct from the academic world of economic analysis. The analytical and deductive mind, used by economists, is separate from the intuitive and emotional mind. Bennett W. Goodspeed makes this point in his intriguing book, *The Tao Jones Averages*:

> Looking at the brain and how it operates, it is interesting to see that we have two brains within our neocortex: a left and right hemisphere. Furthermore, each person is dominated by either one side or the other . . . our left hemisphere, which controls the right side of the body, is analytically oriented. It

21. Margit von Mises, *My Years with Ludwig von Mises* (Cedar Falls, Iowa: Center for Futures Education, [1976] 1984), 23–24.

22. James Brant, *Bernard M. Baruch* (New York: Simon Schuster, 1983), 324.

23. Quoted in Ramsey, *Economic Forecasting*,xii.

> reasons logically and sequentially and is responsible for our speech. It is adept at math, accounting, languages, science, and writing . . . . Our right-brain hemisphere, which controls the movements of the left side of the body, is unique. It operates non-sequentially, is intuitive, artistic, has feelings, is gestalt-oriented (sees the forest and not just the trees), and controls our visual perceptions.[24]

According to Goodspeed, left-brain oriented professions include most lawyers, editors, doctors, scientists, researchers and analysts, dancers, politicians, and entrepreneurs.[25] The point of Goodspeed's book is that a successful investor must use both sides of the brain effectively, relying on both in-depth research and analysis (left brain) and intuitive feelings (right brain).

Interestingly, Rothbard's method of reasoning is primarily *a priori*,[26] which fits the "left brain" analytical side, while successful investing usually requires a strong "right brain" artistic approach, according to Goodspeed. This may be one explanation of why Rothbard has shown little interest in giving investment advice or speculating in the markets.

Charles Hession, in his biography of John Maynard Keynes, argues that Keynes was both a creative economist and successful speculator because he was in essence "dual-minded," in a similar sense described by Goodspeed.

> In modern analyses of creativity there is a pronounced tendency to conceive it as a rhythmic process involving an interplay between opposite aspects of the mind . . . more recently, students of the lateral functioning of the brain have stressed that it is the polarity and integration of the two hemispheres, the complementary workings of the intellect and of intuition, which underlie creative achievement . . . .[27]

Hession goes further to suggest that Keynes' androgynous behavior

24. Bennett W. Goodspeed, *The Too Jones Averages: A Guide to Whole-brained Investing* (New York: Penguin Books, 1983), 22–23.
25. Ibid., 30.
26. Rothbard, "In Defense of Extreme Apriorism," *Southern Economic Journal*, 23, no. 3 (January 1957): 314–320.
27. Hession, *John Maynard Keynes*, 105–06.

was, in part, responsible for this creative ability, combining "the masculine truth of reason and the feminine truth of imagination."[28] Goodspeed's thesis also suggests that the left-brained analytical side is usually more developed in males and the right-brained intuitive side is usually more developed in females, and that men or women who adopt both sides of the brain might be more creative and entrepreneurial.[29]

Rothbard also recognizes the necessity of skill and intuition to be successful in business or finance. "Forecasting on the market is the function of the entrepreneur, and entrepreneurship in the final analysis is an art rather than a science, a matter of intuition, hunch, and deep insight into the slice of the market that the entrepreneur knows and is dealing with."[30]

The Personal Goals of the Economist

The study of finance and business is not the same as the study of economics. They are related fields, but being knowledgeable in economics does not make one an expert in finance. An academic economist may be totally engrossed in the theory of interest rates, inflation, or foreign trade, while showing little interest in the investment vehicles that profit from movements in interest rates, inflation, and foreign trade. Some economists, such as Keynes, find the markets intriguing; others, such as Rothbard, find them uninteresting.

An academic economist can certainly use the principles of economics to make investment decisions, but it is purely a voluntary decision that many economists eschew. In fact, many well-known economists, such as Milton Friedman, refuse to give investment advice when asked publicly. If there is one thing economists recognize, it's the fact that time is a scarce commodity and one cannot do everything in this lifetime. Therefore, one must allocate his time to achieve his most desired goals. These goals are not always materialistic.

As successful short-term traders know, keeping track of your speculative investments is a full-time job and can keep you from achieving many other non-pecuniary goals you may have. The troubles and sorrows

28. Ibid., 107.

29. Goodspeed, *The Too Jones Averages*, 117–18. This "dual-minded" theory does not justify, in my mind, a proclivity toward deviate sexual behavior as a prerequisite to creativity or financial success, as Hession seems to characterize Keynes.

30. Ramsey, *Economic Forecasting*, xi.

connected with substantial wealth can be counterproductive.

Being "rich" does not necessarily mean financial wealth. It can mean richness in wisdom, creative ideas, and charity toward mankind. Rothbard spends most of his time working on books and articles that will live far beyond his time. They are "classics" that will be read 100 years from now, far after the dust gathers on today's popular titles. As economist Leon Walras once commented, "If one wants to harvest quickly, one must plant carrots and salads; if one has the ambition to plant oaks, one must have the sense to tell oneself: My grandchildren will owe me this shade."

In conclusion, perhaps Murray Rothbard would agree most with his teacher, Ludwig von Mises, who told his new wife, Margit, "If you want a rich man, don't marry me. I am not interested in earning money. I am writing about money, but will never have much of my own."[31]

Hard-Money Response to Monetary Crises: Assessing Rothbard's Impact

Rothbard wrote a series of books and pamphlets, published in the early 1960s, that had a great impact on the hard-money movement. There were several major economic events that triggered the creation of the hard-money movement: the silver coin shortage in the United States in 1963–64, the dollar crisis in 1968–71, and the inflation crisis and commodity shortages of the 1970s.

Rothbard's popular works appeared a few years prior to this series of economic crises. The first book, *Man, Economy, and State*, published in 1962, was a treatise on economic principles and appealed primarily to a small group of dedicated followers who had some form of economic training.[32] In fact, most regard it as a graduate text in its degree of difficulty. Nevertheless, the book had a tremendous impact because it elucidated the principles of the free market, following in the footsteps of Rothbard's teacher, Ludwig von Mises, and his magnum opus, *Human Action*.

Moreover, *Man, Economy, and State* offered a full-scale critique of Keynesian economics, practically the only type of economic doctrine being taught in colleges in the 1960s. It was a breath of fresh air. When first exposed to Rothbard's magnum opus, the reaction of students of

31. Margit von Mises, *My Years*, 24.
32. Rothbard, *Man, Economy, and State* (Princeton: Van Nostrand, 1962; reprint, Los Angeles: Nash Publishing, 1970).

free-market economics seemed like Paul A. Samuelson's when he had read Keynes' *General Theory*: "Bliss was it in that dawn to be alive, but to be young was very heaven!"

As far as popularity was concerned, the next two works were far more significant for the intelligent layman. *America's Great Depression*, a revisionist history of the Great Depression in the 1930s, came out a year later, in 1963.[33] It explained in lucid terms the basics of a business cycle and why government monetary inflation was the cause of booms and busts, not the free market. It also offered a devastating critique of Keynesian and other business cycle theories.

Investment writer John Pugsley wrote, "Dr. Rothbard's *America's Great Depression* was both shocking and exciting in its revelation of the causes of the economic debacle in the thirties. I have always been impressed by careful scholarship and adherence to scientific principles, and Dr. Rothbard's book was a fine example of both."[34]

Rothbard's next work, a sixty-page pamphlet called *What Has Government Done to Our Money?*, published in 1964, probably had the greatest impact of any short work.[35] What *The Communist Manifesto* was to Marxists, Rothbard's *What Has Government Done* was to the hard-money movement. The booklet was highly influential, because, for the first time, it explained in simple, understandable terms what money is all about.

It took away the mystique of the dollar and foreign currencies. It explained the creation of money all the way from barter to the modern fiat money system. It showed the ill effects of governments meddling with money, why central banking was inflationary, and of the monetary breakdown of the West. Finally, he demonstrated that the only stable monetary system was a return to a pure gold standard. Financial writer Gary North recalls the influence Rothbard's works, especially *Man, Economy, and State*, had on him during the silver coin shortage in 1963–64. Rothbard's writings demonstrated how going off the gold standard allowed the government to be more and more inflationary. Meanwhile, the government had established a controlled price for silver at $1.29 per

33. Murray N. Rothbard, *America's Great Depression*, (Princeton: Van Nostrand, 1963; 2nd ed., Los Angeles: Nash Publishing, 1972; 3rd ed., New York: New York University Press, 1975; 4th ed., New York: Richardson and Snyder, 1983).

34. Pugsley, *Common Sense Economics*, v.

35. Murray N. Rothbard, *What Has Government Done to Our Money?* (Larkspur, Colo.: Pine Tree Press, 1964; 2nd ed., San Rafael, Calif.: Libertarian Publishing, 1982).

ounce. As inflation worsened, a shortage of silver coins was inevitable. This was interpreted by many free-market economists as an example of Gresham's law, which stated that "bad money drives out good money."

It was named after Sir Thomas Gresham, founder of the English Royal Exchange, who lived in the sixteenth century during the reign of Queen Elizabeth I. According to Gresham's law, if the government made two commodities equal in price, the overvalued ("bad") commodity would circulate, while the undervalued ("good") commodity would disappear. If two coins of equal nominal value were circulating, the one with the highest intrinsic value would be hoarded and the one with the lower intrinsic value would be spent. As John Pugsley states, "When you find you have a silver quarter and a copper plated quarter, you'll naturally follow Gresham's law by keeping the silver and spending the copper."[36]

North states, "In 1962, I read Rothbard's *Man, Economy, and State.* After reading his section on Gresham's law, I knew that silver dimes and quarters would gradually become scarce, and I started hoarding the coins. In the fall of 1963, the crisis hit, and silver coins disappeared from the big cities. The U.S. Mint had to introduce non-silver coins in 1964 to avert a nationwide shortage of small coins."[37]

After the silver coin shortage of 1963–64, the conservative publishing house, Arlington House, under Neil McCaffrey, began publishing a series of books on hard-money topics. One of the most popular books in 1966 was *Wooden Nickels*, by William F. Rickenbacher, who discussed the "decline and fall of silver coins" in America and how to profit from it. Rickenbacher said he had been influenced by Henry Hazlitt and Elgin Groseclose. He recommended buying silver coins and silver mining stocks.[38]

This book was followed by another in 1968, *Death of the Dollar*, in which Rickenbacher predicted the "inevitability" of more inflation, a devaluation of the dollar, and a rise in the dollar price of gold. In the final chapter, he recommended investing in collectibles, rare coins, real estate, gold and silver shares, and silver coins.[39]

By far the most popular financial book published by Arlington House

36. Pugsley, *Common Sense Economics*, 118.
37. Cf. Gary North, *How You Can Profit From the Coming Price Controls*, 2.
38. William F. Rickenbacher, *Wooden Nickels* (New York: Arlington House, 1966), 145–47, 154–55.
39. William F. Rickenbacher, *Death of the Dollar* (New York: Arlington House, 1968).

was Harry Browne's *How You Can Profit from the Coming Devaluation* in 1970. It reached the *New York Times* bestseller list and eventually sold nearly half a million copies (including paperback). Browne's book took a more direct investment approach than Rickenbacher's and also came at a more opportune time; the dollar was reaching a crisis stage in the foreign exchange markets in the early 1970s at the time when Browne's book was published. In his breakthrough work, Browne correctly predicted the devaluation of the U.S. dollar and the rise in the price of gold. "The greatest influence on my thinking at the time was Rothbard," Browne said. In the "acknowledgements" section of the book, Browne credits Rothbard: "In the field of money, the most important help has come from the writings of Murray Rothbard."

He cites several of Rothbard's works: *What Has Government Done to our Money?*, *America's Great Depression*, and the *Panic of 1819*. Using principles developed by Rothbard and other free-market economists, Browne concluded that the fixed exchange rate system and the fixed gold price ($35 per ounce) were in essence forms of price controls. Therefore, a run on gold and the dollar were almost inevitable, which in turn could only mean an "official devaluation," according to Browne. The devaluation occurred in 1971, soon after Browne's book came out.

Browne used Gresham's law as an investment tool:

> A good example of this took place in the United States during 1964 and 1965. The dollar was continuing to depreciate rapidly. American citizens couldn't legally own gold. But silver coins were available. At that time, the value of the silver in a silver coin was slightly less than the face value of the coin (a silver quarter had about 23 cents worth of silver in it).
>
> But the silver had value; the paper was intrinsically worthless. Consequently, the silver coins became scarce. Pretty soon, it became almost impossible to keep the cash register stocked with dimes, quarters, or half-dollars. It reached a point in which the government (after having tried to flood the market with 300 million ounces of new silver coins) gave up and switched to copper-nickel tokens.[40]

40. Harry Browne, *How You Can Profit from the Coming Devaluation*, 88–89.

Browne also noted, "Gresham's law can't tell us how soon a given reaction will occur. It's a mistake to take a general principle and try to predict specific short-term market activity from it."[41]

Based on Mises, Rothbard, and other Austrian economic thinkers, Browne applied these principles to the financial situation and concluded in 1970, "Because its only alternative is deflation, a devaluation is an overwhelming probability."[42] Browne says he was "lucky." In his *Devaluation* book, he declared, "I expect a devaluation to occur sometime between this coming Saturday and the end of 1971."[43]

As a result of the devaluation of the dollar, Browne expected a fall in stock prices ("with a good selection of stocks, a short seller might do surprisingly well at this time") and a rise in gold ("gold bullion is a prime beneficiary of devaluation"). He recommended buying North American and South African gold shares, silver ("silver bullion is one of the best all-around investments . . . . "), and Swiss francs ("the only currency to be recommended is the Swiss franc").[44]

Browne's *Devaluation* book was the first in a series of Arlington House books under the category, "Dollar Growth Library." Llewellyn H. Rockwell, Jr., was the senior editor in charge of the financial books. In 1971, Arlington House published *Panics and Crashes, and How You Can Make Money Out of Them*, by Harry D. Schultz. It also published two books by Donald J. Hoppe, entitled *How to Buy Gold Coins and How to Buy Gold Stocks and Avoid the Pitfalls*.[45]

Harry Browne followed with another financial book in 1974, entitled *You Can Profit from a Monetary Crisis*, which also became a bestseller.[46] Again, he acknowledged several books by Rothbard. In it, he argued that continued inflation in the 1970s would mean further rises in the prices of gold, silver, and Swiss francs. His expectations proved to be correct in the late 1970s. "All of these events were probable according to my understanding of economics, but no one could predict exactly when they would happen. The timing was very fortuitous."

Following the official devaluation of the dollar and the closing of

---

41. Ibid., 89.
42. Ibid., 124.
43. Ibid., 125.
44. Ibid., 148, 154–59, 162.
45. Harry D. Schultz, *Panics and Crashes and How You Can Make Money Out of Them* (New York: Arlington House, 1971); Donald). Hoppe, *How to Buy Gold Coins*; idem., *How to Buy Gold Stocks and Avoid the Pitfalls* (New York: Arlington House, 1972).
46. Browne, *You Can Profit from a Monetary Crisis*.

the gold window on Aug. 15, 1971, a whole industry was created. The mid-1970s witnessed a tremendous increase in hard-money books, newsletters, seminars, coin companies, survival retreats, food storage, and related businesses. In 1974, Robert D. Kephart, former publisher of *Human Events* and long-time follower of Austrian economics, began the first mass-audience investment letter, called the *Inflation Survival Letter*. Of course, many hard-money activities took place prior to these events, but the monetary crises, the OPEC oil embargo, and commodity shortages of the early 1970s gave great impetus to the movement.

Harry Schultz claimed to have sponsored the first hard-money investment seminar in 1967. James U. Blanchard, III, a free-market devotee and admirer of Rothbard, began his famous New Orleans investment conferences in 1974. There are several financial advisors who claim to be the "original gold bug," including Harry Schultz, James Dines, and Joe Granville, because they recommended buying gold shares in the late 1950s. However, Hans Sennholz and E. C. Harwood were two hard-money investment advisors who bought gold shares as early as 1950. Sennholz wrote several articles in *Human Events* in 1959 and 1960 predicting higher gold and silver prices. He also was one of the first hard-money investment counselors to invest in real estate.

Another well-known investment counselor and writer is Jerome F. Smith, who formed the ERC Publishing Co. in West Vancouver, British Columbia, in the early 1970s and helped investors open Swiss bank accounts. Smith has high regard for Rothbard and the "Austrian" school of economics: "Murray Rothbard has advanced economic science, in my view, more than any other living economist."[47] Smith's most famous book was *Silver Profits in the Seventies*, which argued that silver was greatly undervalued at the time because of inflationary pressure and annual figures indicating net consumption of silver throughout the 1970s. He predicted, "silver will double in price and then double again."[48]

Another writer influenced by Rothbard and the Austrian economists is Alexander P. Paris, who wrote *The Coming Credit Collapse* in 1974, analyzing the debt and banking crisis and the significance it would have on investments. Paris wrote, "My view of the business cycle and

47. *Jerome Smith's Investment Perspectives* (November 1984).
48. Jerome Smith, *Silver Profits in the Seventies* (West Vancouver, B.C.: ERC Publishing, 1972). Smith's book was updated in 1982; idem, *Silver Profits in the Eighties* (New York: Books in Focus, 1982). Smith calls his letter, "The Investment Advisory Newsletter Based on the Austrian School of Economics."

the cause of the recessions is a simple one and is based upon the role of money and credit in the economy. It is also strongly based on theories of the Austrian school of economics . . . ."[49]

John A. Pugsley also wrote a hard-money investment book in 1974, entitled *Common Sense Economics*, which sold more than 200,000 copies by mail order. He argued that the financial survivors of these turbulent years would be only "a more astute minority who will succeed because they have taken the time to understand the causes of the world's economic turmoil."[50]

Based on this economic analysis, Pugsley developed a "rational portfolio," which included an emphasis on gold and other inflation hedges: "I believe that the demand for gold from private holders will increase dramatically in the next few years as currency inflation accelerates."[51]

The Inflation-Deflation Debate

A recurring debate within the hard-money movement has been over the question of whether the economy would suffer a serious deflation or the continuation of inflation. The debate went on throughout the 1970s and continues even more fiercely in the 1980s. Murray Rothbard has been in the center of this battle for more than 10 years. The principal "deflationists" have been C. Vern Myers, John Exter, Don Hoppe, and James Dines. The "inflationists" have been led by Rothbard, Jerome Smith, James Blanchard, and Howard Ruff, among others.

The deflationists argued that business, consumer, and government debt were reaching such dangerous levels that a recession would lead to worldwide bankruptcies, a banking crisis, and a financial panic. The government would not be able to stop it. Official efforts would be futile, like "pushing on a string," because the demand for cash in a banking crisis would exceed the ability of the government to supply it. The deflationists have pointed to the sharp drop in commodity prices at various times to prove that deflation was "imminent."[52]

Rothbard wrote at least three articles for investment newsletters responding to the deflationists' arguments, covering the past 10 years.

---

49. Alexander P. Paris, *The Coming Credit Collapse*, 198.
50. Pugsley, *Common Sense Economics*,xii.
51. Ibid., 108–09.
52. The most popular deflationist book was C. Vern Myers, *The Coming Deflation* (New York: Arlington House, 1979).

The timing of the articles is helpful in examining Rothbard's views on the subject. His first article was written for *Inflation Survival Letter*, in 1975, at the bottom of the 1973–75 inflationary recession; the second for *World Market Perspectives* in 1979, at the height of double-digit inflation; and the third for *Jerome Smith's Investment Perspectives* in November 1984, during the "disinflationary" era.

In the first article, written in 1975, Rothbard makes a strong case for higher inflation ahead, despite the "inflationary depression" at hand. The Federal Reserve, Rothbard maintained, "can stop any deflationary process from taking hold and can ensure that inflation will continue." This is because the U.S. and the world are no longer on a gold standard, so that "restraints on Fed inflationary manipulation have been removed." He concluded, "[i]f, as seems likely, the current depression is substantially over by next year, this recovery will add further fuel to the fires of accelerated inflation."[53]

In 1979, writing for World Market *Perspective*, Rothbard acknowledged that the Federal Reserve can precipitate a major recession or depression. "The deflationists see correctly that our Keynesian policies of inflationary bank credit, propelled by the Federal Reserve System, have brought and will continue to bring about recessions . . . . " Rothbard refers back to the 1973–75 recession, noting that "inflation, though indeed stamped down to 6 or 7 percent per year, was yet not reversed."

Using Austrian economic analysis, Rothbard showed how the deflationists have been misled by declines in industrial commodity prices. He explained how it's perfectly natural for consumer prices to rise relative to commodity or wholesale prices during a recession. But Rothbard also raised the possibility that the "inflationist mentality" could be reversed.

> It is certainly theoretically possible that power in Washington will soon be assumed by sound-money men dedicated to stopping inflation in its tracks . . . the last few years have seen a notable economic education on the part of the public. Most people now believe that federal spending and deficits are in some important way a cause of chronic inflation, and are putting pressure on the politicians to reduce or slow down their spending and deficits. Even the money printing

53. "Inflation or Deflation?" *Inflation Survival Letter* (4 June 1975).

> process as a source of inflation is becoming known among the public . . . . Already the Carter administration has slowed down, though in no way stopped, the rate of inflating because of this public pressure.

Nevertheless, Rothbard dismissed the possibility of lower inflation: ". . . until hard-money trends among the public take hold and become more institutionalized in organized political pressure—inflation will probably continue to grow. Furthermore, it might even accelerate, because we have in the past few years gotten to the dangerous point where the public expects continued inflation . . . . "[54]

Finally, in late 1984, in the midst of a lower inflation environment, Rothbard responded to the question, "Is it really true that inflation is finished?" He stated, "I am notoriously leery about making forecasts in economics, but I am confident in repeating the same thing I have been saying, over and over, for several decades: Don't you believe it! Inflation is here to stay, a permanent feature of the economic landscape. No one can predict the precise percentage of price rise from year to year, but the direction—inflation—is here and will not be altered."

Rothbard noted that, if by deflation is meant a fall in *consumer* prices, it won't happen. He expressed great skepticism about President Ronald Reagan's "supply side" economics and the possibility of a return to some kind of gold standard. He noted that Congress, under the Monetary Control Act of 1980, gave the Federal Reserve increased power to "buy any asset whatever, even foreign currencies and shares of stock" to avoid a monetary crisis. Rothbard concluded, " . . . inflation is going to be permanent in the United States and throughout the world."[55]

Rothbard's Critique of the Kondratieff Cycle

Part of the deflationists' argument involved the use of what is called the "Kondratieff Cycle," frequently expounded by investment writers such as Donald J. Hoppe, Julian Snyder, Jim McKeever, and Bert Dohmen-Ramirez. Rothbard has been sharply critical of this cycle theory and of cycle theories in general.

---

54. "Inflation or Deflation-Which Way?" *World Market Perspective* (19 July 1979).

55. "What's Ahead? Resurging Inflation or Sudden Deflation?" *Jerome Smith's Investment Perspectives* (November 1984).

The Kondratieff cycle theory is named after the Russian economist Nikolai D. Kondratieff, who in the 1920s researched the proposal that Western business cycles go through a periodic "long wave," lasting approximately fifty to sixty years. The Great Depression of the 1930s represented a major cyclical point of reference for predicting the next depression. According to Kondratieff advocates, the next depression would be fifty to sixty years later; some proponents suggested the 1973–75 recession as a starting point, while others keep moving the date upward into the 1980s.[56]

Rothbard criticized the Kondratieff long-wave theory in both specific and general terms. In an article published in the *Inflation Survival Letter* in 1978, Rothbard demonstrates that the economic data does not fit the fifty- to sixty-year cycle. For example, the 1896–1940 trough-to-trough cycle lasted only 44 years. Moreover, Rothbard notes that Kondratieff observed the "long wave" only two-and-a-half times: "The idea of even hypothesizing, much less proclaiming, the existence of a cycle on the basis of only two-and-a-half observations must strike the unbiased observer as breathtaking in its presumption."

On a more general level, Rothbard criticizes the whole notion of cycle analysis:

> Correct business cycle theory is qualitative; it cannot predict the length or the intensity of any particular cycle. Specifically, the length of the boom period depends on how long the government authorities are willing to keep inflating the money supply at a rapid pace. It is manifestly absurd for economists or historians to claim that they can forecast precisely *when* the monetary authorities will stop or slow down their inflationary policies. This depends on complex qualitative political and psychological factors that manifestly cannot be squeezed into some predictable set of numbers.[57]

Still, despite Rothbard's and others' devastating critiques, the Kondratieff wave theory is still espoused by investment writers. Recently, for

56. For an in-depth critique of the Kondratieff cycle theory, see John A. Pugsley, "The Long Wave: Should We Praise or Bury Kondratieff?" *Common Sense Viewpoint* (November 1982).
57. "The Kondratieff Cycle Myth," *Inflation Survival Letter* (14 June 1978); see also, "The Kondratieff Cycle: Real or Fabricated?" *Investment Insights* (August and September 1984).

example, financial advisor Bert Dohmen-Ramirez suggested that the early 1980s was the "depression" that Kondratieff predicted. "I have often referred to the Kondratieff wave (K-wave), which is the long term, fifty-two- to fifty-six-year, economic wave. I believe we are presently at the end of that wave and that the K-wave crash (which many analysts are still expecting) occurred in 1980, when all the tangible assets collapsed."[58]

Rothbard's stinging criticism of wave or cycle theory could also apply to other recent cycle theories. For example, during the first half of the 1980s, some hard-money writers and analysts (especially Mary-Anne and Pamela Aden, chart analysts from Costa Rica) predicted that gold and silver would skyrocket by 1986, based on a so-called "six-year" cycle in gold and silver prices (gold and silver reached previous highs in 1974 and 1980). Forecasts of $2,000 to $4,000 per ounce for gold were made frequently. Although Rothbard did not comment publicly on the six-year gold cycle theory, he expressed grave skepticism about technical analysts who forecast higher prices based purely on "cycle" theory.

As Rothbard stated in 1979, "Computer models can only embody past quantitative linkages. But there is no guarantee that these same linkages and ratios will hold in the near or far future. Ratios and trends change. It is no great thing simply to extrapolate past trends into the next year: Anyone can do this with a ruler, and there is no need for high-speed computers. The real trick is to forecast sudden changes and reversals of trends; and econometricians have been spectacularly unsuccessful in doing so."[59] In 1982, when the six-year gold cycle became popular, Rothbard stated that "expectations are purely subjective, and cannot be captured by the mechanistic use of charts and regressions."[60]

Rothbard and the Financial Markets in the Eighties

Rothbard and the "inflationist" camp expected inflation to worsen in the 1980s. In 1979, Rothbard suggested that, barring the government adopting an anti-inflation policy, "the prognosis ahead can only be for more, and ever more, inflation."[61] Jerome Smith, Hans Sennholz, Howard Ruff, Jim Blanchard, Doug Casey, and other hard-money investment

58. Bert Dohmen-Ramirez, "The Long-Term Wave Phenomenon," *Wellington's Capital* (January 1986), 7.
59. Murray N. Rothbard, "Ten Most Dangerous Economic Fallacies of Our Time," *Personal Finance* (21 March 1979); see also my critique of the six-year gold cycle theory in *Personal Finance* (9 December 1981).
60. Rothbard, *America's Great Depression*, p. x.
61. "Inflation or Deflation—Which Way?" *World Market Perspective* (19 July 1979), 7.

writers expected double-digit inflation to worsen in the 1980s.

Jerome Smith, for instance, wrote in 1979, "the accelerating double-digit inflation rate of the 1970s (now around 15 percent) will lead to triple-digit inflation and destruction of the dollar (and all dollar-tied national currencies) in the 1980s."[62] Doug Casey, in his bestselling book, *Crisis Investing*, argued that an "inflationary depression" was inevitable, based on "Austrian" malinvestment theory of the business cycle. Casey suggested that "a hyperinflation seems almost inevitable."[63]

But higher inflation didn't materialize—in fact, the "Reagan Eighties" have so far been characterized by a reduction in inflation and a gradual decline in interest rates, following the severe 1981–82 recession. At that point, some hard-money investment advisors parted company with the "inflationists."

Harry Browne's views on the markets changed in the early 1980s, departing from Rothbard's inflationist viewpoint. In the book, *Inflation Proofing Your Investments*, Browne and co-author Terry Coxon developed one potential scenario in which the demand for money might rise substantially, offsetting the rise in the money supply and resulting in a "high interest, low inflation" environment.[64] But, according to Browne, Rothbard read the chapter in manuscript and thought such a possibility to be "remote." "He felt very strongly that deflation wasn't politically possible," Browne said. "I'm philosophically more in harmony with Ludwig von Mises, who was agnostic, skeptical, and non-political."

Despite the decline in interest rates and inflation in the 1980s, Rothbard has been staunchly critical of the monetary and fiscal policy of the Reagan administration and the Federal Reserve. In 1981, he commented, "there is no Reagan Revolution. There is no budget cut; there is no tax cut. The whole *brouhaha* is sound and fury, signifying nothing. Nothing is happening." Rothbard noted that Reagan's budget showed an increase in government spending, not a decrease.

Also, despite a reduction in the highest tax bracket from 70 percent to 50 percent, and a reduction in long-term capital gains rates to 20 percent, the tax bill for most Americans was going up, if one includes

62. Ibid., p. 1. See also Jerome F. Smith, *The Coming Currency Collapse—And what You Can Do About It* (New York: Book in Focus, 1980).

63. Douglas R. Casey, *Crisis Investing* (Los Angeles: Stratford Press/Harper and Row, 1980), 39–62, 278. See also Howard Ruff, *How to Prosper During the Coming Bad Years* (New York Times Books, 1979).

64. Harry Browne and Terry Coxon, *Inflation-Proofing Your Investments*, 45–83.

Social Security levies. As far as monetary policy is concerned, Rothbard criticized Federal Reserve Chairman Paul Volcker for achieving "neither stable nor slow monetary growth so far .... Federal Reserve actions, and the resulting money supply, have been unprecedentedly erratic and volatile." He added that " ... the Reagan program of gradually reducing the rate of money growth until a moderate level is achieved is not going to work. Gradualism won't work, now less than ever."

Nevertheless, Rothbard noted that a "disinflationary psychological impact" had already begun in the United States in 1981, with incredibly high deregulated interest rates and the dramatic drop in precious metals prices and other commodities. Rothbard was critical of his friends in the hard-money movement who were sympathetic with Reagan: "James Sinclair asserts that Reagan, Regan, and Volcker have been saying exactly the right things, which are exactly the *wrong* things for gold, and my old friend Dr. Mark Skousen persists in claiming significant future reductions in inflation and improvements in the economic climate." Rothbard summarized by stating:

> The bottom line is that the Reagan program is all talk and no action. In short order, the market will discover this, will realize that all we are getting is retread Nixon-Ford economics, and inflation will resume its accelerating course. The interesting question is: Will my friends in the hard-money movement wake up before, or later than, the market?[65]

Actually, a case can be made to explain the disinflationary phenomenon of the 1980s using "Austrian" principles of economics. F.A. Hayek and other Austrian economists have shown that fiat money inflation is inherently unstable, creating a boom-bust cycle. A monetary inflation inevitably leads to a recession, even if the central bank adopts a monetarist rule by expanding the money stock at a steady rate equal to average GNP growth. In fact, according to Hayek, the only short-term way to postpone a recession is to *accelerate* monetary growth (which, of course, can result only in a worse disaster in the long run, eventually

65. Rothbard, "The Reagan Budget Fraud," *World Market Perspective* (19 March 1981).

leading to what Mises called the "crack-up" boom).[66]

A corollary of this principle can be applied to the monetary policy of the eighties: if, after a "tight" money policy and severe recession, the government expands the money supply at a rate *equal* to the previous monetary inflation, general consumer prices will rise by an amount *less* than the previous rate (assuming that the recession is strong enough to break the inflationary psychology). Moreover, in order to reignite consumer price inflation to the previous high level, the Federal Reserve would have to reinflate at a more rapid rate. Why? Because the tight money policy and severe recession have left the capital goods industry in a precarious financial state, many of them close to bankruptcy.

In general, with a high debt exposure, the capital markets are in a more vulnerable position than at the beginning of the previous cycle. The level of "malinvestment" in the economy has grown as a result of the inflationary policy of the government. Thus, the "malinvested" capital markets require substantially greater resources to bring them out of their dangerous financial condition. Under this burden, the chances of reigniting an artificial boom, accompanied by sharply higher prices, are reduced.

Monetary policy in the first half of the 1980s appears to bear this out. The Federal Reserve under Carter expanded the money supply at double-digit rates, anywhere from 10 percent to 13 percent, depending on which definition of money you look at. The Federal Reserve under Reagan has expanded the money supply at similar rates. The result has been less consumer price inflation under Reagan than under Carter.

Admittedly, there are other significant factors at work that keep inflation down—e.g., the tight money in the early 1980s, the deregulation of the banking industry, the reduction of marginal tax rates, the collapse of OPEC, and the worldwide psychological impact of Reagan's conservative image. But the point is that, under Austrian analysis, the Federal Reserve under Reagan would have had to expand the money supply at significantly higher levels than it has been doing in order to reignite the fires of price inflation to equal the double-digit levels of the 1970s. And so far it has not done so.[67]

---

66. F.A. Hayek, *Monetary Theory and the Trade Cycle*, 111–32, 212–26. For more complete explanation of Hayek's monetary theory of the business cycle, see his *Prices and Production* (New York: Augustus M. Kelly, [1931] 1967).

67. Written extensively on this subject in my newsletter, *Forecasts & Strategies* (September 1985 and March 1985). In order for my thesis to occur, it is essential that the inflationary psychology be broken. If not, the result might be more price inflation, not less.

Despite the drop in interest rates and inflation in the 1980s, Rothbard takes a long-term view. In a 1985 interview, he said that "we will certainly see a reacceleration of inflation and interest rates . . . . I can't predict the exact time frame . . . but certainly over the next few years . . . . We've been in a permanent inflation for the last fifty years, and I don't see any sign that it's ending. The money supply has been going up about 10%, depending on which figures you look at. It's inevitable that prices will start reaccelerating again as the economy heats up. And when they do start to move, they will do so quickly. People have been lulled to sleep by the rhetoric of the Reagan administration."

He considered Volcker "less inflationary than Arthur Burns, but he's certainly no hero of the free market. The Reagan administration has been attacking Volcker for not being inflationary enough. In that sense, he's keeping monetary growth down. But based on any absolute criteria, the guy's an inflationist." When asked about the bull market in stocks, with the Dow at 1,300 at the time, he responded, "That's only 30 percent higher than it was in 1966. Consumer prices have tripled since then. I'd hardly call it a boom." He did, however, suggest that the stock market could go higher.[68]

The Prospects for Another Economic Crisis

Unlike an investment advisor, who has to be concerned about the short-term shifts in public psychology and trends in the financial markets, Rothbard is an academic economist who can take the long-term view. Despite good economic news in the mid-1980s—low inflation, falling interest rates, and a bull market in stocks—Rothbard points out that serious fundamental problems still exist. Consumer inflation is maybe 4 percent but—"Four percent was considered so terrible in 1971 that Nixon put on a wage and price freeze," notes Rothbard. The Federal Reserve still governs a totally fiat monetary system, which is both inflationary and economically destructive. As Rothbard states, "Since the Fed is no longer limited by gold restraints, it can now print dollars in unlimited amounts, unhampered by domestic statute or international obligations."[69]

---

68. *Predictions* (April 1985). By the summer of 1987, however, Rothbard had turned bearish on the stock market. In a private letter to a money manager, he suggested that a tight-money policy by the Federal Reserve could send stocks "plummeting" (Mark Skousen, *The Great Crash of 1987: Prelude to Financial Disaster?* [Potomac, Md.: Phillips Publishing, 1988], 7).

69. "Inflation of Deflation—Which Way?" *World Market Perspective* (19 July 1979), 2.

And the Federal government continues to run huge deficits and is always looking for ways to increase revenues. So the wise investor, while taking advantage of the temporary goods news in traditional investment vehicles, such as stocks and bonds, must be prepared for the bad economic news that Rothbard eventually foresees. Rothbard's viewpoint may not be a popular one today, but in the words of Josh Billings, "As scarce as truth is, the supply has always been in excess of the demand."

12 WHAT EVERY INVESTOR SHOULD KNOW ABOUT AUSTRIAN ECONOMICS AND THE HARD-MONEY MOVEMENT

"Genius without education is like silver in the mine."

—Benjamin Franklin

A specter is haunting Wall Street and the financial world—the specter of Austrian economics and the hard-money movement!

Since the late 1960s, the world has been rocked by monetary crises, double-digit inflation, severe economic slumps, and violent fluctuations in currencies, stocks, and precious metals. In short, we have been the victims of a volatile boom-bust cycle. The world economy has been at sea without rudder.

It is no accident that during this financial upheaval, we have witnessed a dramatic rise in unorthodox investment newsletters and conferences. In fact, the growth of the hard-money movement and Austrian economics is the most significant event to occur during this financial revolution. It is vital that you as an investor understand what this movement is all about and what it is trying to achieve—and how it can help you protect yourself from the terrible economic crises that we will be facing in the very near future.

If you have ever subscribed to a hard-money newsletter, you know that it is far different from anything you'll read in *Money* magazine. And if you have ever attended a "gold" conference, you know that you'll hear things you'll never hear at a seminar sponsored by Merrill Lynch.

Many well-known financial writers, advisors, and entrepreneurs are

---

Reprinted from "What Every Investor Needs to Know About the Hard-Money Movement" (Foundation for Economic Education, 1988).

said to belong to this hard-money movement, including Harry Browne, Gary North, Howard Ruff, Harry Schultz, Doug Casey, James U. Blanchard IE, Julian Snyder, Richard Band, Ron Paul, Adrian Day, and John Pugsley, among many others.

What is this movement all about? In the simplest terms, the hard-money camp is a group of investors and financial advisors who seek to circumvent the ill effects bad government may have on their wealth and business. They ardently believe in the principles of the free market, limited government, and a monetary policy linked directly to the gold standard. Thus, the hard-money movement has also been referred to as the "sound-money" or "honest-money" movement.

Members of the gold camp recognized early on that government was rapidly moving away from sound principles of finance since going off the gold standard in 1971. Rather than fight the government in the political arena, which often proved fruitless, the hard-money camp adopted a more positive approach. Gold-oriented investors sought ways to protect their assets and even to profit from the ravages of inflation, depression, and other government-induced monetary crises.

"Buy Gold, Buy Silver, Buy Swiss Francs!"

Specifically, hard-money investors seek to invest in real assets that circumvent the inflationary effects of a paper-money economy. These investments include precious metals (especially gold and silver), foreign currencies tied closely to multi-inflation policies (such as the Swiss franc), and other inflation hedges, such as real estate and collectibles, that may be a protection against the "bad times" caused by international monetary, banking, or economic crises. In the 1970s, the rally cry of the hard-money movement was, "Buy gold, buy silver, buy Swiss francs!" Today, there are many other investments that the hard-money follower might consider in an effort to protect his wealth.

Free-market followers are convinced that the instability and crises existing in the world economy today are caused not by free enterprise, as the government interventionists would have us believe, but by government intervention itself, and that there are numerous benefits, both personal and national, that can come from adherence to hard-money principles. Meanwhile, tremendous investment opportunities are created by these volatile government policies, opportunities from which intelligent investors can profit. Thus, the hard-money movement is indeed motivated primarily by the natural desire for financial gain.

Because of this sense of self-preservation, we are keenly interested in building our net worth, to protect ourselves in this age of economic uncertainty. But we are not just profit-seekers, out to make a killing in the marketplace at anyone's expense. We do look for speculative opportunities from time to time, but more often than not, we are *defensive* investors, primarily concerned with protecting what we already have from the triple threats of inflation, taxes, and government regulation. As Dick Russell says, "The person who wins is the one who loses the least."

Fundamental Investment Philosophy

We also adhere to an important investment philosophy that differs from many mainstream investors: We don't simply follow the charts as do technical analysts or cycle theorists, nor are we just trend followers. Such technical traders are little more than gamblers with a "system," betting on the likelihood that an established pattern will continue. They are hoping to beat the system, without trying to understand the system or hoping to improve it. Although we do look at historical data, charts of past prices are just one of many tools we use in our analyses of fundamental market factors.

Our financial point of view is grounded in the belief that market behavior is fundamentally more and more determined by artificial government policies of monetary inflation, excessive government spending, nationalization, wage-price controls, and foreign exchange restrictions. These forms of intervention can bring only economic harm to the majority of citizens. The hard-money movement came into being in response to thousands of free-minded individuals seeking to protect themselves from the unreasonable policies of the state.

There are ways to escape and even to profit from inflation, high interest rates, the boom-bust business cycle, and government-induced crises. There are ways to avoid high taxes and bureaucratic regulations, as well. (As Larry Abraham says, "There is not now, nor has there ever been, nor will there ever be, a tax law without legal loopholes.") The primary purpose of hard-money newsletters and seminars is to help people achieve these goals.

Of course, the world economy does not have to be government-run.

The world would be a much better place in which to live and work if it operated in a freely competitive and stable monetary environment, where businessmen and entrepreneurs could function without constantly worrying about uncertain government policies. We believe it is in the interest of all investors to reestablish a sound, non-inflationary monetary standard, encourage personal savings and capital formation, and eliminate government controls and regulations that hamper the free flow of goods and services throughout the world.

We believe that the free enterprise system—as characterized by thrift, hard work, creativity, good customer relations, and the profit motive—is the greatest source of wealth, and the key to increasing the standard of living for all people. But it can function efficiently only if we have a stable monetary system.

We applaud the recent collapse of socialist regimes and the new worldwide movement toward free markets, free trade, and free minds. We are encouraged by continuing efforts to privatize wasteful government enterprises, to reduce tax rates, red tape, and trade barriers, and to control fiscal and monetary policies. The triumph of capitalism has led to tremendous investment opportunities in developing and emerging markets around the globe—in Latin America, Europe, Asia, and Africa. We believe in investing in stock markets when the economic and political environment is favorable toward free-enterprise capitalism.

A Political Movement?

While we may be primarily interested in ways to profit and protect our money, we realize that if we don't fight the evils of government, the very foundation of our economic and political freedoms may collapse. As John A. Pugsley states, "Being a millionaire on a sinking ship is a bitter victory."

Consequently, the hard-money camp is also a political movement. But we are not a political party, and, in fact, many members of the hard-money movement think that we have passed the point of no return when it comes to effective political action through traditional channels. In a famous article written in the late 1960s, "The Death of Politics," Karl Hess argued that all major parties seek political power to control people's lives, and that the wave of the future is to take an "anti-political" or "non-political" approach.

It is hopeless to work toward making fundamental changes now, due to the thoroughly entrenched bureaucracy in the nation's capital. Politicians can be elected or rejected, but the bureaucrats are there for decades, until they retire. Consequently, many free-market followers have given up on traditional political action, because they have decided that the best we can hope for now is simply to *survive* as individuals and escape the inflation-welfare machine in Washington. If we can profit from inflationary policies in the meantime, so much the better.

Despite this somewhat hopeless outlook, we remain a political movement in the sense that we know that genuine prosperity and stability can be established in the Western world if we return to a stable monetary system under a government that maximizes economic and political freedom and minimizes interference with the marketplace. Therefore, many hard-money investors belong to a wide variety of organizations, spending their money, time, and energy to educate and influence others. You cannot change the government until you change the people!

In our own individual ways, we strongly oppose efforts by government leaders and representatives to expand the size of government, increase taxes, inflate the money supply, impose economic controls on us, or take away our basic rights to life, liberty, and property, and we will do everything possible to protect ourselves, our families, and our assets from these invasions. In the words of Thomas Jefferson, "What country can preserve its liberties, if its rulers are not warned from time to time that its people preserve the spirit of resistance?"

How to Win Friends and Influence People

How influential is the hard-money movement? Based on the number of hard-money newsletters and books being sold today, there are probably several million adherents to the sound-money philosophy (for a partial list of newsletters and books published by hard-money advocates, see the appendix). Many political groups have limited influence because they face great difficulties in raising funds to support their causes. The hard-money movement, on the other hand, has no such problem. Many investors have been extremely successful in making money, either in their businesses or in the markets, and are willing to give financial support to fight the evils of government. What creates power and influence in today's political world? Ideology *and* money. The hard-money movement has both!

A Short History of the Hard-Money Movement

The hard-money movement began in earnest in the 1960s, largely in response to the U.S. silver coin shortage in the early 1960s and the gold drain and dollar crisis of the late 1960s. Suddenly, hard-money newsletters, seminars, and related products proliferated in the 1970s. There is an ongoing good-natured debate over the question of "Who is the original gold bug?" with Harry Schultz, Jim Dines, Hans Sennholz, and Dick Russell, among others, as frontrunners for the title. (Personally, my vote goes to E.C. Harwood, a sound-money man from New England who recommended gold and silver stocks as an investment in the 1930s!)

It is significant, however, that there is really no single individual who is responsible for creating the underlying philosophy of sound money; as with the establishment of many new philosophies, it was the result of several intelligent and logical thinkers who were reaching similar conclusions at the same time.

Interest in the precious metals as an investment heightened during the 1960s, following the silver coin shortage in the United States and the dollar crisis overseas. William F. Rickenbacker wrote about these events in *Wooden Nickels* (Arlington House, 1966) and *Death of the Dollar* (Arlington House, 1968). In 1967, Harry Schultz held the first gold investment seminar. The heyday of the hard-money movement came during the inflationary seventies (during the energy crisis and the commodity shortages), with gold, silver, and "hard" currencies like the Swiss franc skyrocketing in value. During this time of shortages in basic commodities, the storing of food supplies and building a "survival" home became popular among hard-money followers.

The titles of certain nontraditional newsletters reflected this new era: *The Inflation Survival Letter*, published by Robert Kephart, and *The Ruff Times*, published by Howard Ruff. The first hard-money bestseller was Harry Browne's *How You Can Profit From the Coming Devaluation*, published by Arlington House in 1970. Other bestselling books included Browne's *You Can Profit From a Monetary Crisis* (Macmillan, 1974), Howard Ruff's *How to Prosper During the Coming Bad Years* (Times Books, 1979), and Doug Casey's *Crisis Investing* (Stratford Press, 1980). My own book, *The Complete Guide to Financial Privacy* (Alexandria House Books, 1978; Simon & Schuster, 1983) sold nearly half-a-million copies. Other bestselling hard-money books were written by Harry Schultz, James

Dines, Gary North, Jerome F. Smith, Donald J. Hoppe, Alexander Paris, John Pugsley, C. Vern Myers, and R.E. McMaster, among others.

The background of the hard-money advisors is worth noting: Very few of them came from the traditional Wall Street background with degrees in finance or positions in major brokerage firms. They were unorthodox from the very beginning, educated by experience and common sense, rather than by textbooks and sales techniques. Since then, the hard-money movement has continued to expand and mature as an investment *philosophy*, even though the hard-money hedges of the 1970s have not always been the high performers they once were.

Not by Bread Alone

The hard-money movement is not just a new way to "make more money." There's more to it than that. Recently, an exhibitor at an investment seminar approached me with a conspiratorial air and said, "Mr. Skousen, I'm here to make money, just like you." His attitude was that it's a dog-eat-dog world in the investment business, and that, in order to make money, he would take advantage of potential investors, perhaps gloss over important details or de-emphasize risks, just to make a sale. Well, I'm afraid this salesman had little understanding of me or of the attendees and subscribers who follow the hard-money movement. Sure, making profits is important.

Profit potential is the principal motivating factor behind all of our efforts to gain up-to-date knowledge and sound advice, so that we can improve as investors. But, as adherents to the free market, we also understand that any transaction is a cooperative effort and that, if a transaction includes a complete exchange of information as well, both the buyer and the seller gain. This short-sighted exhibitor seemed to have forgotten this simple economic principle in his zeal for easy profits.

I'm afraid that the zeal to gain at any price is reaching an all-consuming attitude in Western civilization these days. Donald J. Hoppe recently commented on this fact: "Now there is nothing wrong with making money or acquiring wealth, but when that alone becomes the central theme and dominant passion of a society, that society is corrupt and doomed. While we are so busy piling up the money and paper assets, what is our nation and civilization producing in the way of art, literature, philosophy, music, or drama?"

Even more important in today's economy than the profit motive is the protection instinct. Wise investors today are skeptical of high-risk speculations that appeal primarily to their sense of greed. Protecting what you already have from the ravages of a capricious government should be more important. Purchasing power lost to inflation, high taxation, invasion of financial privacy (through lawsuits and IRS audits), asset seizures, and stifling business regulations are just some of the threats posed by our government.

Moreover, government policies that change from year to year in the legislators' misguided attempts to "fix" things can lead to chaos in the marketplace and the financial destruction of the vast majority of hard-working citizens. Speculators may profit handsomely from the government's blunders, but the average worker can be devastated by high inflation, a credit crunch, or a depression. Government mismanagement inevitably makes new millionaires out of a small minority of speculators (including select government officials!), but the masses of people lose. And when the majority of countrymen are destroyed economically, they turn to extremists and revolutionaries who take away our precious freedoms.

In short, making money can be rewarding and of true value if it is used to preserve our quality of life. But it can also be sterile and useless if we do not use some of it to protect the foundations of our economic and political freedom.

The Philosophy of Hard Money

What do hard-money investors believe in? There are three major principles of the hard-money movement.

Foremost is a return to the gold standard. We believe that the best way to establish a stable monetary system is to back all national currencies by gold.

To understand why gold is so important, consider this question: "What kind of economy would most people like to live under?" I suggest the following five characteristics:

1. little or no inflation
2. low interest rates
3. high employment (low unemployment)

4. stable, predictable economic climate with no boom-bust business cycle
5. widespread economic freedom.

Wouldn't it be marvelous if we had such an economy today? Certainly, the inflationary fiat money standard of today has not achieved these goals. If anything, it has brought about just the opposite result: inflation, high interest rates, high unemployment, boom-bust cycles, and government controls. But a properly conceived gold standard could accomplish all five of these ideal goals. This view is, of course, a minority view; most conventional economists consider gold a "barbarous relic."

How would a gold standard solve our monetary problems? Historical experience demonstrates that prices are far more stable under a gold standard than under fiat money systems. In fact, in economies based on a gold standard, average prices of goods and services have usually declined slightly over time. After reviewing the monetary history of the United States before and after the repeal of the gold standard, Milton Friedman and Anna J. Schwartz state in their work, *A Monetary History of the United States, 1867–1960*, "The blind, undesigned, and quasi-automatic working of the gold standard turned out to produce a greater measure of predictability and regularity—perhaps because its discipline was impersonal and inescapable—than did deliberate and conscious control exercised within institutional arrangements intended to promote monetary stability" (10).

Gold Is the Ultimate Money

There are many reasons why gold has been considered the "ultimate money" over the years. It offers stability, divisibility, and convenience. In the words of economist W. Stanley Jevons, "Some of the metals seem to be marked out by nature as most fit of all substances for employment as money, at least when acting as a medium of exchange and a store of value." Gold provides a far more stable environment than a "fiat" paper money standard. Now, it's true that the price of gold has been highly volatile since the world went off the gold standard in 1971, but this is due to the instability of the state's monetary policy, not gold.

The total amount of gold on Earth is strictly limited, and new mine production actually increases the gold stock by marginal amounts. It is estimated that the world has produced only about 120,000 tons of gold in its entire history. Moreover, annual gold output has seldom increased the total stock of gold by more than 2–3 percent, except during the gold rush years. By contrast, paper money issued by the state has no official limits. In many countries, monetary inflation has exceeded 10 percent, 50 percent, or 1,000 percent, depending on the whims of the rulers. Once a country goes off the gold standard, investors should become highly suspicious of their government's policies to control spending and the money supply.

The main theoretical objection to gold as a monetary standard is that it would be too expensive to produce and store the gold. Milton Friedman estimates the cost to be 4–5 percent of the world's annual product. Yet the adoption of a fiat money standard has not reduced this expense at all; in fact, it may have increased it. Unstable monetary policy has resulted in a substantial increase in gold output and storage during the past two decades. Old mines have been reopened, new mining techniques have been developed, and geologists have been searching for new deposits.

Although all hard-money investment writers agree that a return to the gold standard is essential, they often differ as to what kind of gold standard should be adopted or how it should be reestablished. Some favor a return to a strict 100 percent gold standard, in which every banknote and checking account is fully backed by gold at a set price. Others favor a return to a "gold exchange standard," in which the nation's currency is fixed to a specified amount of gold bullion, and governments buy or sell gold at the official exchange rate to maintain an adequate store of gold. This was the system practiced in the U.S. prior to 1971. Still others favor "free banking" linked to gold. Whichever standard is adopted, the idea is to force government to sharply limit or even eliminate its inflationary powers to create paper money with no store of real value to back it up.

As the gold standard brings inflation under control, it also creates an atmosphere of general economic stability, with low interest rates, steady economic growth, and a free market. As economist Murray Rothbard states in *The Case for the 100% Gold Dollar*, a gold standard is "compatible with the fullest preservation of the rights of property . . . [and] . . . assures the end of inflation, and with it, the business cycle."

Are hard-money investors "gold bugs"? In the sense that they favor a return to a gold standard, the answer is "yes." But, if the term "gold bug" is intended to mean that hard-money investors cling irrationally to gold as an investment even when the price of gold is collapsing, the answer should be "no." No investor should be so enamored with gold that he allows himself to put the majority of his assets into precious metals and leave it there no matter what happens to the price. The Wall Street refrain, "Never marry a stock," has just as much significance for the gold bug as the stockholder. Unfortunately, too many gold enthusiasts have made this mistake.

Gold and Silver As "Survival" Hedges

At the same time, however, hard-money investors recognize that gold is a "survival" hedge against crises, inflation, war, and bad times. It is the ultimate insurance policy. In times of economic chaos, gold has always been recognized as a store of value, accepted in exchange for real goods and services, and thus is a way to protect oneself from the ravages of inflation, economic collapse, and government controls. Consequently, hard-money investment advisors usually recommend that 5–10 percent of one's assets should be invested in gold and silver in convenient form (coins, small bars, gold stocks, etc.).

Survival gold and silver should be a part of everyone's "permanent portfolio," never to be sold or exchanged, except when needed in an emergency. In this case, gold is not purchased as an investment but as insurance. Profit is not the motive, protection is. The French have long held this traditional attitude toward gold. They have learned by sad experience that it pays to hide a little gold under the mattress in case the government turns despotic. In the survival and monetary context, then, gold is not "just another commodity," as some traders and economists argue. It is the ultimate hedge.

Gold should also be treated as a speculation when the world is no longer anchored by a gold standard. In that case, it can be bought and sold like any other commodity. Hard-money investors must carefully distinguish between their "survival" gold holdings and their "speculative" gold holdings.

Followers of the Austrian School of Economics

In addition to the gold standard, the hard-money camp also has an ideological foundation in free-market Austrian economics. We have been heavily influenced by the writings of Austrian economists, especially Ludwig von Mises and Friedrich A. Hayek. Mises was a professor of economics at the University of Vienna. In the 1920s, he forecast the 1929–33 economic collapse. In 1929, he refused to take a major position with Credit Anstalt, the largest bank in Europe, because, he said, "Someday there is going to be a crash and I don't want my name associated with it!" (Two years later, the bank collapsed.) Mises left Europe during World War II and came to the United States. He wrote several influential works, including *Human Action* and *The Theory of Money and Credit*.

Hayek was one of Mises's colleagues and, as director of the Austrian Institute of Business Cycle Research, also predicted the stock market crash in 1929. He taught economics at the London School of Economics in the 1930s and won the Nobel Prize in Economics in 1974 for his work in business cycle theory. Following the tradition of these Austrians have been economists such as Murray N. Rothbard, Henry Hazlitt, Hans Sennholz, Jacques Rueff, and Wilhelm Ropke. Hazlitt's popular little book, *Economics in One Lesson*, is written from a classic Austrian perspective. The late Professor Rothbard, more than any other economist, has popularized Austrian economics among investors through such works as *What Has the Government Done to Our Money?* and *America's Great Depression*.

Austrian economics need not be purely academic in nature. It can be of supreme practical value in helping you foresee what's ahead for the economy and for your personal investments. As Adrian Day states, "Austrian economics, far from being ivory tower theory, is of immense practical value. An understanding of basic economic principles can certainly help you become a better investor."

What do we mean by Austrian economics? Basically, it's the scientific theory of free-market economics. Its essential conclusions are:

(1) *One of the keys to economic growth and prosperity is a high rate of personal savings and capital formation*. This Austrian approach is in complete opposition to today's often accepted Keynesian analysis, which emphasizes increased consumption and government spending as the key to prosperity. However, Austrian economists rightly note that the countries with the highest level of economic growth in the post-war period (Europe and Asia) have also had the highest rates of savings and capital formation. Thus, government policy should promote savings and capital growth, rather than consumption.

(2) *Free markets provide a higher standard of living for all.* Nations that have encouraged the development of new businesses, new technology, and free trade have seen a rapid increase in living standards in their countries. Meanwhile, countries that have restricted imports, severely limited foreign workers and foreign capital, imposed wage-price controls, and restricted the free flow of goods and services have seen a sharp decline in real income. Austrian economists have long predicted these results: Government intervention restricts national output, while government deregulation and privatization expand national production.

With this in mind, investors should search for the most profitable opportunities in countries which provide political and economic stability and a free-enterprise attitude. As mutual fund advisor John Templeton states, "Avoid investing in those countries with a high level of socialism or government regulation of business. Business growth depends on a strong free-enterprise system .... Governments should stop interfering with what people want to do."

(3) *High taxes and government regulations stifle economic activity.* Austrian economists and hard-money investors favor a reduction in tax rates to encourage business activity and reduce the underground economy. When tax rates are too high, businessmen and investors waste millions of dollars in high-risk tax shelters and illegal or fraudulent schemes. Nations that minimize taxes, especially on savings and capital gains, usually provide the best environment for business. If a country faces a high degree of tax evasion and underground activity, the answer is not to increase forced compliance, but to reduce tax rates to acceptable levels.

In today's world of burdensome state regulations, the watchwords are "compliance" and "full disclosure" to capricious rules imposed by government agencies. But the hard-money movement resists blind obedience to unnecessary government bureaucracy. Their rallying cry is "resistance" and "minimal compliance."

(4) *Government inflationary policy is responsible for the boom-bust business cycle.* Mises, Hayek, and other Austrian economists have convincingly shown that it is government intervention, not the free market, which is responsible for the business cycle. Monetary inflation, unbacked by gold, distorts interest rates and savings patterns, causing a boom in the capital-goods markets that cannot last and eventually ending in an economic collapse. The conventional Keynesian economists blame the depression on the lack of investment and consumer spending, which they hope

to alleviate in future generations by forcing increased consumption, through direct government spending. Monetarist economists think the best alternative is to stimulate the economy by expanding the money supply again.

Free-market Austrians reject this "something for nothing" approach, however. They believe that the best solution is to stop inflating, which caused the boom-bust cycle in the first place; endure the transition period which should not last long *if* (an important if) the government lets prices and wages to fall to market levels; and allow the markets to adjust to a new and more realistic schedule of production based on real supply and demand. They also believe that the best way for "developing" countries to achieve a high growth rate and general economic prosperity is for their governments to get out of the way—by reducing taxes, stopping the printing presses, encouraging foreign capital (which includes permitting foreign companies to own property and hire foreign as well as local workers), privatizing government enterprises, and eliminating foreign exchange controls.

But the hard-money movement harbors no delusion. Most governments, believing it is their duty to solve all problems, will continue to intervene and engage in an inflationary cycle. As Harry Browne warns, "Monetary crises are here to stay—the latest is not the last."

How to Profit From the Business Cycle

While hard-money investors have an idealistic philosophy which could solve the world's economic ills, they are realistic enough to recognize what will happen if government policies continue in their current direction, and they have learned how to profit from predictable market reactions. We are well aware of the investment implications of this government-induced business cycle. Under today's non-gold fiat money standard, the business-investment cycle falls into four basic categories:

(1) The inflationary boom. As the central bank expands the money supply, capital-intensive industries are stimulated with new money and easy credit. In the early stages, the income and profits of these businesses tend to rise, and because companies listed on the stock exchange are highly capital-intensive, the stock market goes through an expansionary phase or bull market. However, at the later stages of the inflationary boom, consumer prices start catching up, and the stock market may lose

some of its luster. At that point, inflation hedges such as gold, silver, and real estate tend to move up sharply.

(2) The credit crisis. Once consumer prices start rising sharply, interest rates generally move up as well. In addition, the central bank, concerned about price inflation, may apply the brakes and cause a credit crunch. Many businesses may find their costs rising faster than their revenues, squeezing their profits. Interest rates may rise rapidly as corporations scramble for funds. The best investment during the credit crunch: short-term money market instruments in safe financial institutions.

(3) Recession. Production of capital goods falls more sharply than consumer goods. Gross national product declines, and stocks continue to fall. Interest rates start dropping as demand for credit declines, especially if the central bank decides to loosen the money supply. Prices for commodities and capital goods tend to fall more sharply than consumer goods. The best investment during a recession: top-quality money-market instruments and high-quality bonds.

(4) Economic recovery. The recession in capital goods ends as the economy bottoms out. Prices for commodities and capital goods stop declining. How long the recovery lasts depends on government monetary and fiscal policy. The best investment for this stage of recovery: stocks and bonds.

How to Trade the Markets

Hard-money investors have learned to adjust to the conditions in the marketplace. It may seem unnatural for "gold bugs" to invest in traditional stocks and bonds, but there is a time and place for everything. Gold is an essential feature in any hard-money portfolio, but in times of temporary stability, low inflation, and deregulation, the stock market may play a bigger role than gold and other "inflation hedges."

One thing is clear, however. It is impossible for a country's economic condition to remain stable under a fiat money standard where the government continues artificially to inflate the money stock. Another recession is inevitable. As Howard Ruff states, "The course that our government leaders have plotted can only end in fiscal chaos." This is true even if a country adopts a monetarist rule of increasing the money supply at a constant rate. Only a pure commodity-money standard can eliminate the distortions inflation creates.

Conventional investors who have no basic understanding of Austrian economics may be lulled to sleep by temporary good economic news. In the eye of the hurricane, everything appears to be calm. But hard-money investors realize that good economic news is temporary only if the government has not put its house in order and adopted truly sound policies rather than makeshift solutions. With today's huge personal, business, and government debt structure, a banking crisis looming, and political instability popping up around the world, the wise investor will keep his powder dry.

Many investors seek to maximize their profits by switching among stocks, bonds, gold, and money funds, depending on which phase the business cycle is in. Moving in and out of markets is, however, not so simple. As the old Wall Street saying goes, "No one rings a bell when the bull market is over." Investors who study the Austrian theory of the business cycle do not necessarily call every turn in the market. No one pretends to have a crystal ball. Many hard-money investors, for instance, invested in gold and silver when they were cheap in the early 1970s, but failed to get out in 1980, when silver reached $45 per ounce and gold $850.

Nevertheless, some financial writers did get out in time because they understood the basic principles of economics and investor psychology. In addition, many hard-money advisors recognized early that the Reagan 1982–87 bull market was largely induced by monetary inflation and, like any speculative bubble, had to burst at some point.

The same can be said of the bubble in Japanese stocks and real estate, which ended in the early 1990s. Austrian economists and financial writers will be the first to admit that no one has all the answers. In fact, one of the tenets of Austrian economics is that people are not machines. They respond differently to a new set of circumstances. Nevertheless, you as an investor will definitely be ahead of the pack if you study and apply the principles of free-market economics as taught by Mises, Hayek, and Rothbard.

Inflation-Deflation Debate

In conjunction with the business cycle, there is a growing debate among hard-money advocates: Will we have more inflation (even run-away inflation), or will we suffer a catastrophic deflation and depression? This "inflation-deflation" debate rages on in the pages of investment newsletters and at financial seminars. The deflationists, led in the past by such hard-money followers as Donald J. Hoppe, C. Vern Myers, John Exter, and James Dines, have argued that business, consumer, and government debt have reached such dangerous levels that another recession could lead to worldwide bankruptcies, a banking crisis, and a financial panic. The deflationists see this depression as the market solution to an artificial boom. According to these hard-money supporters, the deflationary bust is nothing more than market forces finally overcoming the forces of government. The government would try to inflate, but it would be "too little too late." Official efforts would be fruitless because the demand for cash would far exceed the ability of the government to supply it. The deflationists point to the frequent sharp drops in stocks, commodities, and other investments from time to time as evidence of their thesis that deflation is "imminent."

The inflationists, led in the past by Howard Ruff, Jerome Smith, Jim Blanchard, and Murray Rothbard, argue that deflation is indeed the market solution to government mismanagement of the world's money supply. But for a variety of reasons, the government has far more power than the deflationists realize to keep the deflation from happening. Officials have a variety of effective tools to keep the debt pyramid from collapsing, including control over the money supply, bank reserve requirements, nationalization, declaring bank holidays, etc. Moreover, governments have been willing to impose recessions from time to time without precipitating an economic crisis, and this has been a healthy trend. Recessions force businesses and banks to adopt sound accounting practices and avoid wasteful, inefficient projects.

Who's right? In a sense, both are right. Deflation and inflation are two sides of the same coin, the fiat money standard. It's difficult to predict what will happen in the end. It all depends on whether deflationary market forces eventually overwhelm the government's inflation forces. The battle may rage on for years before the final outcome is clear. At least both camps agree on one thing: when a financial panic strikes, whether in the form of deflation or inflation, gold bullion will be an excellent hedge against uncertainty.

Personal Survival Tactics in a Worldwide Breakdown

Austrian economics teaches that the government's reckless policies are capable of creating massive chaos. In the past, we have witnessed the tragic effects of runaway inflation, totalitarianism, and world war. Hard-money followers have no illusions; it could happen again. The government could lose control of events, resulting in a temporary breakdown of the civilized world. Whether the country is struck by a banking crisis, runaway inflation, famine, or nuclear war, we know that our government leaders may not have the answer. In fact, they will undoubtedly be part of the problem. We will be left to our own wits to survive.

Thus, hard-core survivalists have favored the long-term storage of food supplies, fuel, basic tools, gold and silver coins, and other necessities in the event of a complete breakdown. In troubled times, people would be wise to reduce their personal and business debt as much as possible and get their house in order. They should be encouraged to use part of their wealth to develop self-sufficiency. They should learn practical skills and useful avocations that would be essential during a national emergency. It's what John Pugsley aptly called "the Alpha Strategy." While such a breakdown has not yet occurred, it's better to be too early than too late.

The Case for Financial Privacy

Finally, we must protect our wealth from the privacy invaders. We live in an "age of envy," as Gary North calls it. We must keep our private wealth from being taxed, confiscated, sued, or stolen. Moreover, when a depression, financial panic, war, famine, or other bad economic news strikes, the "surplus" economy may suddenly become a "shortage" economy. There is no telling what methods the government may engage in to "protect the public" from "speculators" and "hoarders" who are involved in the "underground." In the past and even today, many governments have confiscated gold, imposed foreign exchange controls, prohibited foreign bank accounts, etc.

Thus, many hard-money investors believe that it is essential to maintain a "low profile" with an all-powerful state. "Privacy from government may perhaps be the most important thing in life right now," says Harry Schultz. Government agents and their sympathizers are increasingly engaged in monitoring citizens' political activities and financial affairs through the use of computers, tax returns, and exchanges of information with foreign governments. To avoid the privacy invaders, many investors seek to:

1. Buy gold and silver coins privately in person using cash, so as to avoid being placed on official lists of gold investors.
2. Invest outside their country through foreign bank accounts, in countries such as Switzerland and other stable money havens. (As Doug Casey has said, "Get your money out of the country before the country gets the money out of you!")
3. Maintain a low profile in financial affairs and personal way of living.

The Future of Hard Money

The hard-money movement is here to stay. While we have had a strong influence around the world on individual investors as well as government policy, there is still a great deal more to do. We in the hard-money camp were the first to realize the tremendous profitable opportunities available in markets the government tried to manipulate. Governments everywhere continue to intervene and inadvertently create speculative opportunities. We will continue to capitalize on government's interventionist policies and even profit when it decides to stop intervening.

Yet we in the hard-money camp are not as callous and self-serving as to hope that economic conditions worsen in order that we may make higher profits. I think I speak for most hard-money investors in saying that it would be fine if the price of gold stayed low forever, because that would mean the economy is under control. There are plenty of investment opportunities in the traditional stock and bond markets under stable economic conditions. We don't need high inflation and financial chaos to make money. As the Wall Street maxim states, "There's more than one way to climb to the top of the mountain."

But we are not Pollyannas either. We recognize that our economic problems are not behind us; we are facing an impending monetary crisis, another potential recession, more inflation, and more politics of envy. Volatility in the stock, bond, and currency markets prove that government continues to be a source of instability in the world economy. Whatever the outcome of these crises, we are prepared to protect ourselves and do what is necessary to preserve our wealth and our freedom. Lord Acton said it best, "At all times sincere friends of freedom have been rare, and its triumphs have been due to minorities."

Recommended Hard-Money Investment Newsletters

The best way to keep up to date on the hard-money philosophy and financial advice is to subscribe to several investment newsletters. Most of the hard-money writers have written financial books that explain their basic philosophy.

Note: Many of these newsletters and services are no longer in print or are being written by other editors/publishers. Some of the writers have passed away.

Larry Abraham, *Insider Report*, PO Box 84903, Phoenix, Arizona 84903

Richard E. Band, *Profitable Investing*, 7811 Montrose Rd., Potomac, Maryland 20854

James U. Blanchard El, *Gold Newsletter*, 2400 Jefferson Hwy., Jefferson, Louisiana 70121

R.W. Bradford, *Analysis & Outlook*, PO Box 1167, Port Townsend, Washington 98368

Joe Bradley, *Investor's Hotline*, 10616 Beaver Dam Rd., Hunt Valley, Maryland 21030

Harry Browne, *Harry Browne's Special Reports*, PO Box 5586, Austin, Texas 78763

Douglas R. Casey, *Crisis Investing*, 824 E. Baltimore Ave., Baltimore, Maryland 21202

Jim Davidson, *Strategic Investment*, 824 E. Baltimore Ave., Baltimore, Maryland 21202

Adrian Day, *Investment Analyst*, 824 E. Baltimore Ave., Baltimore, Maryland 21202

James Dines, *The Dines Letter*, PO Box 693, Belvedere, California 94920

Bert Dohmen, *The Wellington Letter*, 6700 Kalanianaole Hwy., Suite 218, Honolulu, Hawaii 96825

Kenneth J. Gerbino, *Investment Letter*, 9595 Wilshire Blvd., Suite 200,

Beverly Hills, California 90212

Don McAlvany, *The McAlvany Intelligence Advisor*, PO Box 5150, Durango, Colorado 81301

Rich Maybury, *U. S. Early Warning Report*, PO Box 1281, Orangevale, California 95662

Ian McAvity, *Deliberations*, PO Box 40097, Tucson, Arizona 85717

R.E. McMaster, *The Reaper*, PO Box 39026, Phoenix, Arizona 85069

John Myers, *Myers' Finance & Energy*, PO Box 18586, Spokane, Washington 99208

Gary North, *Remnant Review*, PO Box 8204, Ft. Worth, Texas 76124

Ron Paul, *Survival Report*, PO Box 602, Lake Jackson, Texas 77566

John Pugsley, *John Pugsley's Journal*, 23-00 Route 208, Fair Lawn, New Jersey 07410

Howard Ruff, *The Ruff Times*, PO Box 25, Pleasanton, California 94566

Richard Russell, *Dow Theory Letters*, PO Box 1759, La Jolla, California 92038

Harry Schultz, *International Harry Schultz Letter*, Box 622, CH-1001 Lausanne, Switzerland

Mark Skousen, *Forecasts & Strategies*, 7811 Montrose Rd., Potomac, Maryland 20854

Sound Money Investors, 531 Versailes Dr., Suite 110, Maitland, Florida 32751

James Turk, *Free Market Gold and Money Report*, PO Box 4634, Greenwich, Connecticut 06836

Martin Weiss, Weiss Research, PO Box 2923, West Palm Beach, Florida 33402

Books and Other Hard-Money Sources

I recommend the following books for information about the hard-money movement and Austrian economics:

Hans F. Sennholz, *Money and Freedom* (Cedar Falls, Iowa: Center for Futures Education, 1985).

Henry Hazlitt, ed., *The Inflation Crisis and How to Resolve It* (Irvington-on-Hudson, N.Y.: The Foundation for Economic Education, 1995).

Inflation Is Theft (Irvington-on-Hudson, N.Y.: The Foundation for Economic Education, 1995).

The Lustre of Gold (Irvington-on-Hudson, N.Y.: The Foundation for Economic Education, 1995).

The following organizations offer free catalogs with numerous books concerning hard-money, Austrian economics, and many other subjects:

The Foundation for Economic Education, 30 South Broadway, Irvington-on-Hudson, NY 10533; telephone (914) 591-7230; fax (914) 591-8910.

Laissez Faire Books, 808 St. Paul Street, Baltimore, MD 21202. www.lfb.org

13 THE ECONOMIST AS INVESTMENT ADVISOR

"Economics cannot teach you how to get rich."

—Roy J. Ruffin and Paul R. Gregory, *Principles of Economics* (1988)

Economists frequently underestimate the power their theories can have in everyday use. Ruffin and Gregory warn students that economics does not supply magic formulas that tell them Mow to choose a winning stock, or which way interest rates or the dollar are headed; economics is unable to predict the IBM of tomorrow.

The top ten textbooks are remarkably silent regarding the investment markets, despite the critical role investments play in the economy. (Only one text, Baumol and Blinder's, has a chapter devoted to stocks and bonds.) Many academicians do not believe that the financial markets are very important; they may actually be disruptive. Economists draw a sharp distinction between the money economy, represented by the financial markets, and the real economy, the actual production of goods and services.

What's important, they believe, are capital goods, not capital. Stock market fluctuations have very little to do with the real economy, they reason. Thus, Hyman Minsky has rightly criticized the neoclassical model as "the economics of capitalism without capitalists, capital assets, and financial markets."[1] The purpose of this chapter is to dispel this orthodox notion and to demonstrate why the investment markets are far more important than economists realize.

Published as chapter 19 of *Economics on Trial: Lies, Myths and Realities*, by Mark Skousen (Homewood, IL: Business One Irwin, 1991).

1. Hyman Minsky, *Stabilizing an Unstable Economy* (New Haven: Yale University Press, 1982), 120.

It is unfortunate that textbooks do not spend more time on the investment markets. The world of high finance provides an excellent laboratory in which to test economic theories. Prices of stocks, bonds, gold, and currencies vary every day in response to changing supply and demand; new information; economic crises; and the attitudes of millions of businesspeople, investors, and speculators. The opportunity is always present to make considerable profits and suffer losses. Economic analysis is also very useful in choosing which investment theories make sense and which don't—fundamental, technical, cyclical, contrarian, etc.

When I became the editor of a financial publication in the early 1970s, I felt woefully inadequate in my knowledge of the financial world. Economics is a cousin to finance, but I found that the academic world makes it a distant cousin. Even though I had majored in economics in college and received a master's degree and a doctorate in economics and banking, I knew very little about price-earnings ratios, margin buying, selling short, futures, and options. My academic teachers never spent much time explaining the basics of high finance, probably because they did not know much about high finance themselves. I had to learn everything on my own. I took intensive courses and workshops, read books and magazines, studied manuals, and passed commodity and stock market examinations.

Economists and Financial Advice

THE ARMCHAIR ECONOMIST

There are two problems with economists when it comes to financial advice. First, economists are all too often uninterested in applying economics to specific investment decisions, and therefore they downplay the value of such application. They are seekers of knowledge, not mundane materialists. Ludwig von Mises once told his fiancée, "If you want a rich man, don't marry me. I am not interested in earning money. I am *writing* about money, but will never have much of my own."[2] Jenny Marx once complained about her husband, "I wish Karl would accumulate capital instead of just writing about it."[3] Financial economist Burton G. Malkiel summarizes the academic disdain for monetary

2. Margit von Mises, *My Years with Ludwig von Mises*, 2nd ed. (Cedar Falls, Iowa: Center for Futures Education, 1984), 24.

3. Quoted in Paul Johnson, *Intellectuals* (New York: Harper & Row, 1989), 74.

success: "A professor may inherit lots of money, he may marry lots of money, and he may spend lots of money, but he is never, never supposed to earn lots of money; it's unacademic."[4]

Generally, the economists who have made a lot of money have done so through book royalties and speeches, not through shrewd investing in the futures markets. Friedman, Samuelson, and other wealthy economists are adamant about not rendering specific short-term investment advice.

CAN TRADERS BEAT THE MARKET?

Second, many economists do not believe that you can beat the market. That is, they believe that investors cannot consistently make big money in stocks, commodities, or any other financial market. I heard this peculiar view when I was an undergraduate, and it is still very much in vogue among academic theorists. It's called the "efficient-market theory," and it remains the dominant theory in finance schools.

Samuelson and Baumol and Blinder discuss it favorably, and proponents of rational expectations often support it. It is the notion that markets are extremely efficient in the sense that in them all new information is quickly discounted. Therefore, no one can capture consistent profits by trading stocks, commodities, or options. As Samuelson summarizes, "You can't outguess the market." I call the efficient-market theory the perfect competition model of the financial world.

Efficient-market theory proponents point to numerous studies indicating that most professional money managers, stockbrokers, and investment advisors are unable to beat the averages (as measured by the Dow Jones Industrial Average or the S&P 500) or to perform better than a randomly selected portfolio of stocks. Nor can they accurately predict earnings by major corporations over a one-year or five-year period.

The Random Walk Method of Investing

The best alternative, says the armchair theorist, is to select stocks on a random basis. This is called the "random walk method" of investing. The most popular book on this subject is *A Random Walk Down Wall Street* (now in its fourth edition), by Burton G. Malkiel, dean of

4. Burton G. Malkiel, *A Random Walk Down Wall Street*, 4th ed. (New York: W.W. Norton, 1985), 17.

management at Yale University. Malkiel defines random walk as follows:

> A random walk . . . means that short-run changes in stock prices cannot be predicted. Investment advisory services, earnings predictions, and complicated chart patterns are useless . . . . Taken to its logical extreme, it means that a blindfolded monkey throwing darts at a newspaper's financial pages could select a portfolio that would do just as well as one carefully selected by the experts.[5]

While Wall Street analysts often dismiss the random walk method as academic nonsense, mainstream economists are enamored by it. Paul Samuelson likes Malkiel's book so much that he says he has given each of his children a copy. On the cover of Malkiel's first edition, Samuelson is quoted as saying, "There is no sure way to investment affluence, but Malkiel has outlined some of the booby traps and improved the odds in the reader's favor."

Baumol and Blinder also subscribe to the random walk idea, believing that forecasting individual stock prices is virtually impossible: "There is a mass of statistical evidence that the behavior of stock prices is in fact unpredictable."

The random walk method does not mean people should not invest in the stock market. Rather, proponents recommend that investors adopt a "buy-and-hold" strategy because stocks as a whole have an upward trend. Studies indicate that over the past sixty years, the U.S. stock market in general (as measured by the S&P 500 or its equivalent) rose at an average compounded rate of 10 percent.[6] Proponents of the random walk method usually oppose any form of trading the market because one cannot consistently predict the direction of the market in the short term, and because commissions and taxes will reduce the overall return. It is understandable that major brokerage firms do not usually subscribe to this approach; it would significantly reduce their role in the marketplace.

What's Wrong With the Efficient-Market Theory

In reality, there are several major objections to the efficient-market

5. Ibid, 16.

6. Charles P. Jones, *Investments: Analysis and Management* (New York: John Wiley & Sons, 1987), 242.

theory and the random walk method to investing. First, a minority of investment counselors and money managers have had superior market performance over the long run. Famous examples include the mutual fund magnate John Templeton; the investment advisor and founder of the Value Line Investment Survey, Arnold Bernhard; and the fundamental analyst Warren Buffett, to name a few.

According to *Forbes'* annual survey of mutual funds, a number of money managers have outperformed the market over a long period of time and are regularly featured in the magazine's honor roll. Peter Lynch, former manager for the Magellan Fund, is an example. Recent studies indicate that the stock selections by the Value Line Investment Survey have consistently outperformed the market averages, and that its earnings forecasts have been more accurate than sophisticated methods based on past performance. One of the efficient-market theory's proponents, Fischer Black, a former professor at MIT who is currently with Goldman Sachs, concludes, "Value Line rankings . . . are certainly one of the exceptions to my rule that active portfolio management is generally worthless."[7]

In response, critics contend that it is always possible, even in random betting, that a small minority of investment experts will outperform the market. A person flipping coins could possibly get heads ten times in a row, for example. But consistent market performers do not engage in randomly flipping coins or blindly choosing stocks, and their record has been consistent for thirty years or more. Moreover, making superior returns year after year typically involves making hundreds of investment decisions each year.

Second, certain groups of investors tend to beat the market—for example, corporate insiders and specialists on the New York Stock Exchange. Richard Band, editor of *Personal Finance* and a certified financial analyst, studied the stock trading habits of officers and directors of publicly traded companies and concluded that "the insiders certainly do much better than the public at trading shares of their own companies."[8] Insiders apparently take advantage of knowledge not generally available to other investors.

---

7. Fischer Black, "Yes, Virginia, There Is Hope: Tests of the Value Line Ranking System," paper presented at the Center for Research in Security Prices (Chicago: University of Chicago, Graduate School of Business, 1971). See also Lawrence Brown and Michael Rozeff, *Journal of Finance*, March 1978. These articles are summarized in Arnold Bernhard, *How to Use the Value Line Investment Survey* (New York: Value Line, 1988). Since these studies, Value Line has, except for a few years, outperformed the S&P 500.
8. Richard E. Band, *Contrary Investing* (New York: McGraw-Hill, 1985), 66.

Third, certain methods of investing consistently outperform the averages. Efficient-market theory proponents argue that professional traders will eliminate such anomalies over time, but this has not happened. One example is the January effect, the fact that stocks rise in January more consistently than any other month. (Why haven't investors recognized this well-advertised situation and started buying in December?)

Another example is the method of buying stocks based on low price-earnings (P/E) ratios. Financial analyst David Dreman has used this approach to make consistently higher profits. He recommends buying a diversified portfolio of low price-earnings stocks and holding them for varying periods, in some cases up to nine years. Comparing his method to other investment techniques, he discovered, "Low P/E stocks not only gave you better performance but they were also marginally safer."[9]

Fourth, although the efficient-market theory states that markets have incorporated nearly perfect knowledge, it is hard to imagine that the markets reflect current knowledge of corporate, earnings and other financial data on the eve of a financial crisis or stock market crash. The October 1987 stock market debacle shook the foundations of the efficient-market theory because it became clear that, prior to the crash, the market did not contain all the vital information. The public is clearly wrong when trends suddenly and dramatically change.

The Key to Understanding Market Action

In my studies of investment analysis, I have found that economists and followers of the markets fall into three basic categories. Each group fits somewhere along a continuum of market philosophy. The following spectrum illustrates the different types of investment philosophy.

Perfect knowledge of future	⟵	Imperfect knowledge of future	⟶	No knowledge of future

Those investors who fall into the "perfect knowledge of future" category are often technical traders who believe that the markets are totally rational, predictable, and mechanically precise. They feel that recent trends, volume, momentum, and other investment data reveal the future of asset

9. David Dreman, *The New Contrarian Investment Strategy* (New York: Random House, 1982), 149.

prices, especially in the short run. They may also rely on previous cycles or wave analysis to determine the future direction of prices. Some may even go so far as to predict exact dates for financial or economic events (such as the next depression) and specific targets for prices of investments. They strongly believe that there is a direct correlation between past events and future events.

This category also includes econometricians who believe that there is a strong direct correlation between markets and movements in interest rates, the money supply, elasticities, and other stringent relationships. This would include strict monetarists, who accept the crude quantity theory of money, i.e., that if the government doubles the money supply, prices will exactly double in the long run—although monetarists usually argue that economic activity is unpredictable in the short run.

Interestingly, I have found that the academic background of many technical traders is in the physical sciences. Such traders often majored in engineering, physics, mathematics, or other pure sciences. Consequently, they search for mechanistic formulas in the stock market and the economy.

At the other extreme, there are those investors who believe that the markets are totally irrational and unpredictable in both the long run and short run. They fit into the "no knowledge of future" category. They believe that the market knows and instantly discounts everything, but the individual analyst knows nothing. Where will the market go next week, next month, or next year? "I don't know" is their most common response. "No one can predict the future" is another familiar phrase. The random walk and efficient-market theory followers are usually in this group.

The no-knowledge group includes some market traders who depend on moving averages to decide whether to invest in stocks or mutual funds, or to be on the sidelines. They believe they can beat the market by following the trends, switching into the market when the trend is upward, and switching out of the market when the trend is downward. To determine a stock's moving average, analysts add up the stock's price for a certain number of weeks, divide by that number to find the average price, and then compare it to the current price. If the current price rises above its moving average, you buy; if it falls below its moving average, you sell. Switchers argue over which moving average is best (17 weeks, 39 weeks, 200 days, etc.), but they claim they can beat the averages even though they suffer occasional whipsaws (losses caused by short-term switches when the market is nearly trendless).

Keynesian economists often fit into the no-knowledge group. John Maynard Keynes, who was an avid speculator, believed that our knowledge of the future was virtually unpredictable. He likened the stock market to a casino or game of chance. In *The General Theory*, he opined, "For it is, so to speak, a game of Snap, of Old Maid, of Musical Chairs—a pastime in which he is victor who says Snap neither too soon nor too late, who passes the Old Maid to his neighbour before the game is over, who secures a chair for himself when the music stops."[10] A year later he wrote, "The fact that our knowledge of the future is fluctuating, vague and uncertain, renders wealth a peculiarly unsuitable subject for the methods of the classical economic theory." Regarding the future of events, he wrote, "there is no scientific basis on which to form any calculable probability whatever. We simply do not know."[11]

The Middle Ground: Knowledge is Imperfect

I believe the truth lies somewhere in the middle ground between the two extremes of perfect knowledge and no knowledge. Our knowledge of the markets and the future is not perfect, but neither is it totally imperfect. Economic events and investment prices are not always predictable, but sometimes they are quite predictable. Markets are not totally efficient, but neither are they completely inefficient. This middle-ground position is similar to Hayek's view of money in the economy—not as a "tight joint" nor as a "broken joint" but as a "loose joint."

In making investment decisions, we must always remember that economic activity and the financial markets in particular are based on the social science of human action. People are not like machines; we have free will. We learn from our mistakes and can alter our outlook. The social sciences are quite distinct from the physical sciences. Sir Isaac

---

10. John Maynard Keynes, *The General Theory of Employment, Interest and Money* (London: Macmillan, 1936), 155–56, 159.

11. John Maynard Keynes, "The General Theory of Employment," *Quarterly Journal of Economics* (February 1937), and *The Collected Writings of John Maynard Keynes*, vol. XIV, 114. Contrary to current belief Keynes was not a completely successful investor. He did have an uncanny ability to buy stocks near their bottom and hold for the long run. Consequently, his net assets increased dramatically from £16,000 to over £400,000 by time he died in 1946. (Does this mean, "In the long run, we are all wealthy"?) On the other hand, he was unable to predict the 1929 crash or 1937 recession and was completely helpless in getting out at the top. As a result, he lost three-fourths of his wealth in 1929 and two-thirds in 1937! See Donald E. Moggridge, "Keynes as an Investor," in *The Collected Writings of John Maynard Keynes* (London: Macmillan, 1983), vol. 12.

Newton once said, "I can calculate the motions of heavenly bodies, but not the madness of crowds."

There is some truth in the old refrain "history repeats itself." Past trends do repeat themselves *sometimes*. That is the partial truth underlying technical chart analysis, which sometimes reflects the repeatable psychology of investors. Financial history is replete with stories of speculative manias and man-made crises. Markets tend to go through cycles of optimism and pessimism, euphoria and depression, speculative bubbles and fantastic bargains. Psychologically, the public vacillates between greed and fear. Smart investors who act quickly, before the crowd acts, should be able to profit from overvalued and undervalued situations.

But investors must never forget that people are not totally predictable. History does repeat itself, but never in the same fashion and never according to the old timetable. Chartists usually discover this fact after a few years of experience in the markets—the cycles or waves shorten or lengthen unexpectedly. Chartists often remark that there is nothing wrong with the charts, only the chartist. Speculative bubbles and fantastic bargains will continue, but they will not always follow the same time pattern, nor in the same investment arena. People's visions of the future change and so do investment fads. One year the hot investment may be diamonds, another year high technology stocks, and the next year Parisian real estate.

The Speculator as Entrepreneur

The speculator/entrepreneur plays a key role in forecasting changes in the economy and the financial markets. The efficient-market theory, like the model of perfect competition, basically denies the analytical ability of the speculator/entrepreneur by concluding that the individual investor cannot outwit the market. According to a strict interpretation of the efficient-market theory, profit-seeking activity by traders is virtually irrational because investors are penalized by taxes when they sell and transaction costs when they trade.

But the truth is that markets are not always efficient and all-knowing, nor do they all offer the same reward. Uncertainty exists in all investment markets, although some markets are less uncertain or less efficient than others. The stock market is certainly more efficient than the rare coin, diamond, or real estate markets. Some markets can be severely overvalued or undervalued for weeks, months, or years. Accurate information is often costly and sometimes unavailable. Insiders may know something that the average investor does not.

As such, it pays to be a specialist—to be more alert and more knowledgeable than other investors or the public in general. The public is sometimes wrong about its decision to buy or sell stocks; markets are not perfectly coordinated. Hence, there is a wide scope of potentially profitable opportunities for speculators willing to do their own research and take a risk. All actions involve the potential for both profit and loss.

The speculator plays a vital role in moving the uncoordinated and imperfect market toward equilibrium, just as the speculator/entrepreneur is vital in providing goods and services that customers desire. Contrary to the provincial views of Marxists and some Keynesians, the speculator does play a beneficial role in society. Baumol and Blinder make this point explicitly, noting that speculators make it possible for producers and consumers to hedge and thus help smooth out price fluctuations. Speculating in stocks and commodities is not a zero-sum game, nor is it simply a gamble.

Successful speculators are rewarded through profits, whereas unsuccessful speculators lose money. Competition is keen in the financial markets, making it more challenging (but not impossible) for speculators to make superior returns. They must always be alert to changes in market conditions or new investment opportunities. Investors who seek to repeat profitable adventures of the past may be disappointed. Moreover, when speculators look at an overvalued situation, they must decide whether the market is temporarily undervalued or permanently undervalued.

Yet the end result is the same as that in the production process. Through trial and error, the market is a weeding-out process, rewarding those who have the capacity to make good judgments about people and their needs while discouraging those who make bad judgments.

Economics as a Subjective Science

Economics is, of necessity, a qualitative science. Even though the financial pages give the impression that investing is a numbers game based on averages, yields, cash flows, and ratios, it should be realized that the market is a human arena and therefore subjective. Events in the economy and in the financial markets are often based on the emotions and attitudes of people, not the physical nature of things, and therefore cannot be precisely measured.

Economists cannot predict the exact timing of an event or the magnitude of price and quantity changes. They may be able to predict the direction of interest rates, the exchange rate of the dollar, or the value of the stock market, but they cannot say definitively when something is going to change or by how much. If a worldwide famine hits, economists and commodity traders can predict that the price of wheat is going to skyrocket, but they cannot be sure how high the price will go.

Investors should be wary of any financial advisor who predicts that the stock market is going to go to 1,000 by July 4th. Yet it is amazing how often this kind of "voodoo investing" is attempted. Many economists have tried in vain to adapt the scientific method to analyze economic events and financial markets. Like the classical economists who sought an objective, intrinsic theory of value, such economists are bound to be disappointed.

The Theory of Contrary Investing

Timing is critical in the fast-moving marketplace. Not everyone can get out at the top or buy at the bottom. Why? Because prices of all assets are determined by marginal buyers and sellers. For every buyer there is a seller. Hence, if everyone tried to get out at the top in expectation of a crash, prices would collapse immediately and no one could get out in time. Or if everyone tried to buy at the bottom, prices would rise so rapidly that no one would get a bargain. This is the core of truth in the theory of contrary investing.

Therefore, because of the very nature of markets, only a small minority of speculators can sell at the top or buy at the bottom in any particular case. A contrarian must be a loner. He practices an art, not a science. Although there are technical benchmarks to help determine the top or bottom of a market, there is no scientific formula to prove either to be the case. Risk and uncertainty always exist, although they can be minimized through research and superior thinking. It is a self-contradiction to suggest that everyone should be a contrarian; the crowd cannot go against the crowd.

However, this fact does not mean that most people must lose in the financial market. I have found that the vast majority of investors are conservative by nature and seek to buy and hold individual stocks and bonds for the long run. If the economy is sound and continues to grow over the long run, the stock market will rise. Prices of stocks may not be predictable on a short-term basis, but over the long run, prices will tend to rise as earnings expand in a growing economy. In the long run, earnings determine the value of securities. This is the nugget of truth in fundamental analysis, and it is the reason securities analysts like Benjamin Graham were successful investors—they took the long view.

In addition, although only a minority of people may make a killing in a market by buying low and selling high, it is possible that a much larger number of individuals, perhaps even a majority, could make extremely high profits in other markets that come along. There are literally hundreds of undervalued or overvalued opportunities that occur every year around the world. Large numbers of investors can go bargain hunting as long as they look in many places and at more than one industry, investment market, or foreign country. As the old Wall Street adage goes, there's more than one way to climb a mountain. Moreover, individuals may be so successful with only a few trades that they could place their profits in bonds or money-market funds and live off the proceeds. If they are successful enough at first, they need not continue trading and risk losing what they have already gained.

How Useful is Economics?

Clearly, economics can be valuable in the world of business and high finance. Businesspeople and investors who apply the principles of economics correctly can achieve financial success. Economics cannot provide all the answers, but it can lay the foundation for prosperity.

As an investment newsletter writer and financial analyst, I have found my background in economics to be extremely beneficial. For example, knowledge of central bank policies regarding interest rates, open market operations, and the money supply is valuable in making investment recommendations. Market behavior is being more and more influenced by negative government policies—monetary inflation, excessive government spending, nationalization, wage-price controls, foreign exchange restrictions, and war.

On the positive side, such government actions as deregulation, privatization, and anti-inflation policies also influence market behavior.

Understanding the basics of the business cycle can be extremely useful for a businessperson or an investor, and so can the economist's view of the structure of production. An economist who understands subjective value can also help distinguish between good and bad financial theories.

How Government Policy Affects Investment Decisions

Businesspeople and entrepreneurs recognize that government policy, good or bad, has a dramatic impact on the economy and on financial markets. John Templeton, whose mutual funds are invested around the world, learned early in his career that the most profitable opportunities are found in countries that provide political and economic stability and a free-enterprise attitude: "Avoid investing in those countries with a high level of socialism or government regulation of business. Business growth depends on a strong free-enterprise system . . . . Governments should stop interfering with what people want to do."[12] (Templeton, by the way, earned a degree in economics at Yale University before Keynesianism took over.)

Over the years, Templeton has invested in such countries as Japan, West Germany, and the United States, all of which have encouraged free enterprise. He was one of the first to invest in Japan after World War II. Japan and the four tigers have been stellar performers both economically and financially because they offer low tax rates on investment, a small but stable government, and a strong belief in hard work and savings. Meanwhile, Templeton has avoided highly socialized countries such as Israel, Sweden, and Mexico.

The intelligent investor should also be on the lookout for changes in government policies that might affect the stock market and exchange rates. A generous tax exemption for stock purchases sharply boosted the French market. Privatization and elimination of the foreign exchange controls lifted Britain out of its malaise. High real interest rates in Australia brought about a recovery in the Australian dollar. On the other hand, the political victory of the socialists in France caused the French stock market and the franc to decline initially. Runaway inflation in Brazil created havoc in the financial markets and in the value of the cruzado. A general strike in the Chilean copper mines caused a sharp increase in copper prices.

The business cycle is largely a government-induced phenomenon.

12. Quoted in William Proctor, *The Templeton Prizes* (Garden City, N.Y.: Doubleday, 1983), 71.

An unanticipated monetary inflation by central banks may cause a temporary investment boom that business people and speculators can profit from. But as the Austrian economists have taught us, to depreciate the nation's currency is to destabilize the economy. Runaway inflation can be disastrous, causing rising prices and falling real output. A boom must eventually end in a bust if it creates an imbalance between capital-goods industries and consumer-goods industries. Falling interest rates become rising interest rates, cutting the boom short.

Over the years, the fiat money standard has created a series of boom-bust cycles and economic crises and will continue to do so. The battle lines are drawn between the government forces of inflation and the free-market forces of deflation. The nimble speculator will attempt to profit from these countervailing forces, whereas the conservative investor often becomes the victim. Businesspeople and investors all hope to protect themselves from an economic and financial downturn, but it is impossible for everyone to do so; there are bound to be casualties. The problem is often one of timing and liquidity. Some businesses cannot sell out quickly enough when the boom ends.

The worldwide increase in the demand for gold and silver coins responds directly to the fickle, unstable government policies that create inflation, recession, and crises. Gold and silver are bought by conservative investors as an insurance hedge against such troubled times.

The Principles of Financial Success

Economics explains why some businesses succeed and others fail. What are the principles of success? They are best summed up by Rosenberg and Birdzell, the authors of *How the West Grew Rich*. Rosenberg and Birdzell list four basic concepts:

1. The ability to accumulate large amounts of capital.
2. The need for innovation, discovery, and entrepreneurship.
3. A stable political government.
4. The encouragement of open markets and competition.

Individuals will be financially successful—and a nation as a whole will increase its standard of living—if they save and invest wisely in the competitive business world, either directly through their own entrepreneurship or indirectly through investing and speculating in the financial markets. In any case, a stable government and a competitive, open environment are absolutely essential in order for individuals and businesses to flourish.

Unfortunately, economics textbooks are often schizophrenic when it comes to the value of saving and investing. In their sections on economic growth, writers readily admit the need to postpone current consumption in order to achieve greater consumption in the future, but in the macroeconomic section they are overly influenced by the Keynesian anti-savings mentality, arguing that new savings can hurt the economy. In an economic downturn, savings are supposed to be bad whereas consumption and consumer debt are supposed to be good. Such an attitude, if taken to an extreme, could lead to individual and national bankruptcy.

John Templeton has the right approach. He is opposed to the consumerist, big-spending attitude that is at the root of Keynesian thinking. Templeton is a strong advocate of thrift, especially during hard times. During the Great Depression, he ignored the advice of economists John Maynard Keynes and Frank Taussig, who irresponsibly encouraged people to go out on a spending spree to stimulate the economy. Instead, he pledged to set aside 50 percent of his income for his personal investment portfolio.

> And after the crash of 1929 and the advent of the Great Depression, the importance of thrift became even more apparent. There was ample evidence on the streets of the 1930s to reinforce the notion that saving as much of your money as possible and investing it wisely are essential to security and success. Quite simply, those who practiced thrift received great rewards, and those who didn't suffered much more from financial setbacks and economic uncertainties.[13]

Templeton knew that money spent is money lost. Money should be set aside so that it can be put to work to make more money. This is a basic principle of financial responsibility that should be taught in today's classrooms.

13. Ibid, 50.

Summary

Investors as entrepreneurs can make money and can even beat the market if they are nimble enough. They represent only a select class of individuals, however. It is not irrational to seek a better return, but neither is it easy. Just because only a few actors become celebrities does not mean that a struggling actor should quit trying. The principles outlined in this chapter should help you become wealthy if that is what you seek.

Recommended Reading

Browne, Harry. *Why the Best-Laid Investment Plans Usually Go Wrong*. New York: William Morrow, 1987. A critical analysis of financial theories. Browne makes the case for a permanent portfolio consisting of stocks, bonds, gold, and cash.

Clason, George. *The Richest Man in Babylon*. New York: E.P. Dutton, 1955. The most important financial book ever written.

Dreman, David. *The New Contrarian Investment Strategy*. New York: Random House, 1982. A stimulating review of the major investment theories and why his form of contrarian advice works.

Malkiel, Burton G. *A Random Walk Down Wall Street*, 4th ed. New York: W.W. Norton, 1985. Fortunately, Malkiel's book is not just ivory tower thinking—he is a veteran of Wall Street and has been a successful investor over the long term. Even though I reject many aspects of the random walk thesis, I highly recommend Malkiel's book. He himself admits, "I have never claimed I was a 100 percent random walker. I am a random walker with a crutch." (*Forbes*, June 26, 1989.)

14 KEYNES AS A SPECULATOR

"A speculator is one who runs risks of which he is aware and an investor is one who runs risks of which he is unaware."

—J. M. Keynes, 1938

It is a widely accepted belief that John Maynard Keynes was not only a great theoretical economist but also an ingenious practical economist, whose rare abilities also extended to the financial markets. Relying on an extensive study by Donald Moggridge, editor of Keynes' collected works, *Forbes* magazine writer Lawrence Minard called Keynes the "original contrarian," concluding that he "was a highly successful investor and speculator" (Minard 1983, 42).

Indeed, as an extremely active investor in commodities, foreign currencies, and stocks, Keynes' net worth climbed from £16,315 in 1920 to £411,000 in 1946, the year he died *(see Figure 10.1)*.That's an annual compounded rate of 13 percent, far better than most professional money managers produced in an era when there was little or no inflation and, in fact, much deflation. His performance as a money manager for various insurance companies and for King's College, Cambridge, showed similar results.

My own review of Keynes' financial history confirms his overall worldly and wise ability to make money both for himself and as a professional money manager. However, the wizard of Cambridge was not a uniformly successful investor; he made his share of monumental blunders.

Published in *Dissent on Keynes: A Critical Appraisal of Keynesian Economics*, ed. by Mark Skousen (New York: Praeger Publishing, 1992).

With an uncanny ability to select stocks at cheap prices, he was nevertheless absolutely incapable of getting out at the top. Moreover, his economic theories failed him miserably at anticipating the major crises of the 1930s. My thesis is that his "general theory" of economic activity was highly influenced by his own inability to predict crashes and major short-term trends in the financial world.

Keynes's Investment Performance, 1905–1945

Figure 10.1

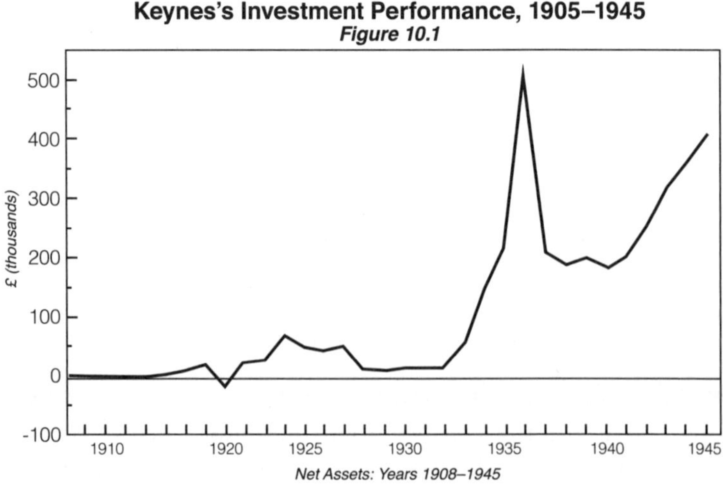

Keynes and Insider Trading

Roy Harrod, Keynes' official biographer, claimed that Keynes had virtually no capital and did not begin speculating until September 1919 (Harrod 1957). In fact, Keynes had become rather well-to-do by this time, much of his wealth the result of timely investments in the stock market. Keynes began investing on the London stock exchange when he purchased four shares of Marine Insurance Company in 1905. He speculated briefly in U.S. Steel and Canadian Pacific right before the First World War. His net position in securities increased dramatically from £197 in 1908 to £4,617 in 1914, at the beginning of the war, and had reached £14,453 by 1919.

Harrod failed to report these securities transactions because of accusations that Keynes had profited from inside information while working for the Treasury (1915–1919). A review of Keynes' financial position before 1920 indicates that his dealings were almost exclusively limited to purchases of securities. However, there is no explanation of how Keynes more than tripled his net worth during the war. Thus, the debate over Keynes' insider-trading activities during World War I continues (Skidelsky 1983, 286–88).

The Roaring Twenties

It appears that Keynes did not become a serious trader in the markets until he left His Majesty's Treasury in 1919 and plunged into the foreign-exchange markets. If Keynes used inside information at this time, it was hardly to his advantage. By 1920, less than a year after he had started trading, his leveraged position was completely wiped out when the European currencies recovered. After this unexpected turn of events, he borrowed £5,000, secured an advance from Macmillan for *Economic Consequences of the Peace*, and jumped back into the foreign-exchange markets, where he was able to recoup his losses, turning an £8,587 deficit into a £21,588 net profit.

Another rumor circulated about Keynes, that he conducted his financial affairs from his bedroom, was apparently true. Biographer Charles Hession writes, "Some of this financial decision-making was carried out while he was still in bed in the morning; reports would come to him by phone from his brokers, and he would read the newspapers and make his decisions" (Hession 1984, 175).

Throughout the 1920s, the British economist was a heavy trader in currencies and commodities. However, by the mid-1920s, noticing the burgeoning stock market boom in America and Europe, he became keenly interested in buying securities for himself and for several institutions he represented. He was chairman of the National Mutual Life Insurance Company and Bursar of King's College, Cambridge. His personal account included a heavy commitment to several British automobile stocks, such as British Leland and Austin Motor Company.

Keynes Miscalculates the Crash

According to Felix Somary, a Swiss banker as well as an Austrian economist, Keynes came to Germany during the mid-1920s eager to ask Somary for some stock recommendations. But Somary refused, warning Keynes of a speculative bubble developing on Wall Street and predicting an impending crash. Keynes responded, "There will be no more crashes in our lifetime" (Somary [1960] 1986, 146–47).

Keynes believed the conventional wisdom that the central banks, particularly the Federal Reserve Board, could properly manage the monetary system and prevent any crash or deflation. Why he would think so, in the face of Britain's disastrous policy of returning to the gold standard at an overvalued sterling exchange rate in 1925, is difficult to explain. Keynes correctly predicted the British depression, caused by the overvaluation of the pound, but he had no such luck in prognosticating the economy across the Atlantic. He hailed the management of the dollar by the Federal Reserve Board from 1923 to 1928 as a "triumph" of central bank management and remained unconcerned about the huge rise in stock prices on Wall Street.

In late 1928, Oswald T. Falk, one of the members of the board of National Mutual Life Insurance Company, became alarmed at the "dangerous inflation" in the United States, suggesting that the company liquidate most of its American holdings. But Keynes wrote two papers disagreeing with Falk. In the second paper, dated Sept. 1, 1928, "Is There Inflation in the United States?" he reviewed the data on the cost of living and business credit and concluded that there was "nothing which can be called inflation yet in sight."

Referring to real estate and stock values in the United States, Keynes added: "I conclude that it would be premature today to assert the existence of overinvestment .... I should be inclined, therefore, to predict that stocks would not slump severely (i.e., below the recent low level) unless the market was discounting a business depression." Such would not be probable since, he asserted, the Federal Reserve Board would "do all in its power to avoid a business depression" (Keynes [1928] 1973e, 52–59; Hession 1984, 238–39). By the time he had completed his *Treatise on Money* in 1930, however, the Cambridge economist had admitted having been misled by stable price indices in the 1920s, and that a "profit inflation" had developed in 1928 (Keynes 1930a, 190–98).

How did Keynes fare personally during the 1929 crash? According to Moggridge, he lost three-quarters of his net worth between 1928 and 1930, primarily due to commodity losses. He was long rubber, corn, cotton, and tin when the markets suddenly turned against his position in 1928. He also lost heavily on his British automobile stocks during the stock market crash in 1929. He tenaciously refused to sell on the way down. In short, he was almost wiped out during the crash

(Moggridge 1983,15–17).

However, Keynes was a stubborn investor, and he held onto his stocks and added substantially to his portfolio starting in 1932. Although he failed miserably at getting out at the top, he had a canny ability to acquire stocks at the bottom of the market. In 1944, he wrote a fellow money manager, "My central principle of investment is to go contrary to general opinion, on the ground that, if everyone is agreed about its merits, the investment is inevitably too dear and therefore unattractive" (Keynes [1944] 1983, 111).

In the early 1930s, he played the commodity markets (where his success record was checkered) less and the stock markets more. During the panic period of the Great Depression, he took a contrarian position by acquiring the preferred shares of the big utility holding companies in the United States. "They are now hopelessly out of favor with American investors and heavily depressed below their real value" (ibid., 61). He bought National Power and Light Preferred, which, he noted, yielded 15 percent, was awash in cash, and whose earnings were rising again.

Keynes as the Original Gold Bug?

For years, hard-money investors have debated the question, "Who is the original gold bug?" Unconventional Wall Street analysts who recommended gold and gold stocks early have included Jim Dines, Harry Schultz, Dick Russell, Joe Granville, William Baxter, and E. C. Harwood. But, amazingly, Keynes—one of the most vociferous opponents of gold as a monetary standard, calling it a "barbarous relic"—was one of the first to buy gold stocks in the early 1930s. His opposition to the gold standard did not prevent him from taking advantage of an undervalued opportunity when South Africa went off the gold standard in December 1932 and before the United States raised the price of gold to $35 per ounce.

He bought South African gold mining shares in January 1933, for the first time for both his personal account and an insurance company he represented. This gamble startled some of his associates, but he justified his speculation, saying, "I regard recent developments as not really primarily within the mining sphere itself, but an adjustment to a new exchange situation . . . and not a speculation about the contents of a prospective hole in the ground" (ibid., 54).

Keynes wrote an article on the subject for the *Daily Mail* (Feb. 7, 1933), concluding, "*Auri sacra fames!* Gold has its special glamour, its age-long appeal to the grasping palm, to those who would be safe and greedy at the same time. This may be an evil way in which to run our economic life. But seen realistically, it is by such tokens in the world as it is, that prosperity waxes and wanes" (Keynes [1933] 1982, 229). In Keynes' case, his prosperity waxed considerably, as the South African mining shares soared during the 1930s.

Keynes' Boom and Bust in the Thirties

Keynes was also optimistic about Franklin D. Roosevelt's New Deal, which he felt would be favorable toward the stock market. In fact, he was so convinced of the American recovery that he leveraged his position to the hilt. In 1929, his margin debt was £14,000; by 1936, it was £300,000! Frequently, more than half of his securities were in borrowed money. Yet his stock selections were so successful that his net worth rose to £500,000 in 1936.

However, as in 1929, Keynes was totally unprepared for the 1937 recession. Encumbered by his highly margined position, by 1938 he had lost nearly two-thirds of his net worth, which fell to £180,000. After the 1937 debacle, his portfolio recovered along with the general market as war engulfed the world, reaching £400,000 at the end of the war, but Keynes never regained his 1936 high-water mark.

A Summary of Keynes' Finances

In summary, Keynes was a superior, albeit erratic, investor. In terms of his personal investment portfolio, he became fabulously wealthy, but he suffered through three devastating financial crises (1920, 1928–29, and 1937–38) on his road to success, as Figure 10.1 demonstrates.

His performance as a money manager for various insurance companies and for King's College showed a similar pattern. According to a study by J. H. Chau and R. S. Woodward, Keynes was an outstanding portfolio manager of the Chest Fund at King's College, Cambridge. Between 1927 and 1945, he beat the UK market by a large margin, with an annual mean return of 13 percent, compared to 0 percent for the UK market as a whole *(see Table 10.1)*. But the return-on-investment strategy was much more volatile than that of the general market; he lost more during bear markets (down by 48 percent in 1938) but regained more during bull markets (up by 50 percent in 1936 and 1943). Overall, he outperformed the markets. Chau and Woodward conclude, "Keynes' performance was superior to that of the market on the basis of both total variance and systematic risk" (1983, 234).

Keynes's "Chest Fund" Performance at King's College, 1927–1945
Table 10.1

Year	Chest Fund Index	Chest Fund Return	U.K. Market Return	Treasury Bill Rate
1927	100.0			
1928	96.6	-3.4%	7.9%	4.2 %
1929	97.4	0.8	6.6	5.3
1930	65.8	-32.4	-20.3	2.5
1931	49.6	-24.6	-25.0	3.6
1932	71.8	44.8	-5.8	1.5
1933	97.0	35.1	21.5	0.6
1934	129.1	33.1	-0.7	0.7
1935	186.3	44.3	5.3	0.5
1936	290.6	56.0	10.2	0.6
1937	315.4	8.5	-0.5	0.6
1938	188.9	-40.1	-16.1	0.6
1939	213.2	12.9	-7.2	1.3
1940	179.9	-15.6	-12.9	1.0
1941	240.2	33.5	12.5	1.0
1942	238.0	-0.9	0.8	1.0
1943	366.2	53.9	16.5	1.0
1944	419.2	14.5	5.4	1.0
1945	480.3	14.6	0.8	1.0

Source: Jess H. Chau and Richard S. Woodward. 1983. "J. M. Keynes's Investment Performance: A Note." Journal of Finance 38:1 (March), pg 233.

On the negative side, Keynes had a serious weakness. He suffered significant, demoralizing setbacks by holding stocks and bonds long term, no matter what the short-term predicament. A one-armed contrarian who bought at the bottom but could never get out at the top, he apparently had no reliable macroeconomic model with which to avoid the mind-boggling bear markets of 1929–32 and 1937–38. He tried to develop a "credit cycling" model for selecting investments, but failed miserably (Keynes 1983, 100). He did not believe in market timing (ibid.). Keynes joined the other established economists, such as Irving

Fisher, Ralph Hawtrey, and Wesley C. Mitchell, in their "new era" optimism about America in the 1920s and shared their notion that no depression was possible as long as commodity prices were stable and the central banks were in control (Skousen 1992).

Keynes' inability to predict short-term movements in the financial markets influenced his "general theory" of the capitalist system. The market economy was inherently unstable, he reasoned, because investment was unpredictable and ephemeral. Government, he argued, needs to step in to keep the capital markets and the economy from going off their tracks. In particular, investment should be "socialized" (a national investment program) in an effort to make future expectations predictable and investment stable (Keynes 1936, 378).

The Stock Market as a Casino

According to Keynes' experience, short-term market fluctuations were totally unpredictable. In *The General Theory*, he likened the stock market to a casino or a game of chance. "For it is, so to speak, a game of Snap, of Old Maid, of Musical Chairs—a pastime in which he is victor who says *Snap* neither too soon nor too late, who passes the Old Maid to his neighbor before the game is over, who secures a chair for himself when the music stops" (ibid., 155–56). Regarding the future of economic or financial events, he later wrote, "there is no scientific basis on which to form any calculable probability whatever. We simply do not know" (Keynes 1973, 114).

It may seem paradoxical that Keynes, an avid speculator himself, contended that the speculator and the short-term trader are socially destabilizing and exhibit antisocial behavior. "Wall Street . . . cannot be claimed as one of the outstanding triumphs of *laissez-faire* capitalism," he wrote (Keynes 1936, 159). He recommended eliminating much of the short-term speculation in the financial markets because of its destabilizing influence on long-term expectations and business prospects. If Wall Street were indeed a casino, then that casino should not be available to the general public. "It is usually agreed that casinos should, in the public interest, be inaccessible and expensive. And perhaps the same is true of stock exchanges" (ibid.).

To mitigate speculative fever on Wall Street, Keynes recommended the introduction of a "substantial government transfer tax" on all stock transactions (ibid., 160). Paradoxically, Keynes' recommendation would destroy the vitality of the market. Clearly, he failed to recognize the benefits that short-term trading provides for long-term investors, particularly the much needed liquidity that allows long-term investors to get into and out of the market without being hurt. Short-term trading also plays a critical role in raising venture capital; a stock certificate is, after all, not a lottery ticket but part-ownership in a business.

Essentially, however, Keynes' model of the capitalist financial system was, to a large extent, an expression of his personal experience in the marketplace. Overall, he made a lot more money by being a long-term investor in stocks than a short-term speculator in commodities and foreign currencies.

Keynes also attacked people's desire to hold cash, which he termed "liquidity preference." He stated, "Of the maxims of orthodox finance none, surely, is more anti-social than the fetish of liquidity, the doctrine that it is a positive virtue on the part of investment institutions to concentrate resources upon the holding of 'liquid' securities" (ibid., 155). Of course, it makes sense to hold liquid cash in times of danger and crisis, such as during the 1929 crash. Keynes was undoubtedly expressing his bitterness toward those rash speculators and frightened conservative investors who dumped stocks in favor of liquidity during such crises. Such "waves of irrational psychology" could do much damage to long-term expectations.

Post-Keynesians and the Financial-Instability Hypothesis

The principal heir to Keynes' investment theory is Hyman P. Minsky, professor of economics at Washington University in St. Louis. He contends that conventional "neoclassical" economics, including most Keynesianism, ignores Keynes' principal thesis: "The essential aspect of Keynes' *General Theory* is a deep analysis of how financial forces—which we can characterize as Wall Street—interact with production and consumption to determine output, employment, and prices" (Minsky 1986, 100).

According to Minsky's thesis, which he terms the "financial-instability hypothesis," the financial structure of capital assets determines the degree of instability in boom-bust capitalism. Perverse banking practices, speculative fever, excessive corporate debt, and deep uncertainty about the future create inherently unstable conditions and a fragile economic system. Moreover, "instability is an inherent and inescapable flaw of capitalism" (ibid., 120), and this instability "is not due to external shocks or to the incompetence or ignorance of policy makers" (ibid., 10). Like Keynes, Minsky does not reject capitalism, but argues that its unstable nature can be contained through deficit spending and reinflation by a central bank. According to post-Keynesians, big-government capitalism is more stable than laissez-faire capitalism.

Minsky is quite correct in pointing out that neoclassical economics largely ignores the influence of the financial markets on the economy: "The neoclassical synthesis became the economics of capitalism without capitalists, capital assets, and financial markets" (ibid., 120). Indeed, orthodox Keynesians are not the only ones to ignore the stock market and its role in economic progress and expectations. The monetarists and new classicists also minimize the role that financial markets play in the economy. The Austrian economists, on the other hand, have always paid particular attention to the financial markets as an integral part of the economic process and the business cycle. As Murray Rothbard states, "Stocks . . . are units of title to masses of capital goods" and therefore respond, sometimes violently, to changing business conditions (Rothbard 1983a, 74–75).

Minsky mistakenly blames the market itself for its instability, when in reality investment volatility is caused by exogenous variables, that is, by monetary and fiscal policies. State intervention in the macroeconomic sphere is the principal source of uncertainty, false expectations, and the boom-bust investment cycle. Speculation is normally beneficial in the marketplace; it is distorted only policies regarding taxes, expenditures, regulations, monetary inflation, and manipulations of interest rates that can make speculative financing and what Minsky terms "Ponzi financing" destabilizing.

Certainly, big-government capitalism can be stabilizing, especially if, in the words of Minsky, "the policy emphasis should shift from the encouragement of growth through investment to the achievement of full employment through consumption production" (Minsky 1982, 113). But a more accurate description of big-government capitalism would be lethargy, characterized by inflation, low growth, bureaucracy, and capital consumption. The Keynesian prescription of inflation, consumption, and big government is precisely the one most Western nations have adopted since the end of World War II. In contrast, the Far East nations of Japan, Taiwan, Hong Kong, and Korea, among others, have adopted a distinctly non-Keynesian approach by stimulating investment and "excessively" high savings rates. The results are telling: The growth rates of the Far East have outstripped the West by a wide margin for the past thirty years.

Keynes' Principles of Investment

As Keynes matured, he discovered that the most successful investors are those who invest in sound companies at reasonable or bargain prices and hold for the long term. They ignore short-term bear markets or use them for opportunities to buy. In 1938, Keynes listed three principles for successful investing: (1) A careful selection of a few investments that are "cheap" relative to "intrinsic" value; (2) a steadfast holding of these investments through "thick and thin"; (3) a "balanced" investment portfolio with a variety of risks, including gold shares (Keynes [1938] 1983, 107). Later, in 1940, he wrote, "I am still convinced that one is doing a fundamentally sound thing, that is to say, backing intrinsic values, enormously in excess of the market price, which at some utterly unpredictable date will in due course bring the ship home" (Keynes [1940] 1983, 77; see also 38).

Keynes is famous for his remark, "In the long run, we are all dead." But perhaps it would be more accurate to say, in Keynes' case, "In the short run, Keynes was sometimes dead; in the long run, he became incredibly rich."

Bibliography

Chau, Jess H. and Richard S. Woodward. 1983. "J.M. Keynes' Investment Performance: A Note." *Journal of Finance* 38(1): 232–35.

Harrod, Roy. 1957. "Review of Clive Bell's Old Friends." *Economic Journal*: 693–99.

Hession, Charles H. 1984. *John Maynard Keynes*. New York: Macmillan.

Keynes, John Maynard [1928] 1973e: *The General Theory and After. Part I. The Collected Writings of John Maynard Keynes*. Vol. VIII. London: Macmillan.

Keynes, John Maynard. 1930a. *A Treatise on Money*. 2 vols. London: Macmillan.

Keynes, John Maynard. 1936. *The General Theory of Employment, Interest, and Money*. London: Macmillan.

Keynes, John Maynard. [1933] 1982. *Social, Political, and Literary Writings. Collected Writings*. Vol. XXVII. London: Macmillan.

Keynes, John Maynard. 1983. "Keynes as an Investor." *Economic Articles and Cor-respondence, Investment and Editorial. Collected Writings*, Vol. XXVIII. London: Macmillan.

Minard, Lawrence. 1979. "Wave of the Past? Or Wave of the Future?" *Forbes*, October, 45–52.

Minsky, Hyman P. 1982. *Can "It" Happen Again? Essays on Instability and Finance*. New York: M.E. Sharpe.

Minsky, Hyman P. 1986. *Stabilizing an Unstable Economy*. New Haven: Yale University Press.

Moggridge, D.E., ed. 1983. "Keynes as an Investor." *Economic Articles and Cor-respondence, Investment and Editorial. Collected Writings*, Vol. XXVIII. London: Macmillan.

Rothbard, Murray N. [1963] 1983a. *America's Great Depression*, 4th ed. New York: Richardson and Snyder.

Skidelsky, Robert. 1983. *John Maynard Keynes: Hopes Betrayed, 1883–1920*. New York: Viking Press.

Somary, Felix. [1960] 1986. *The Raven of Zurich*. London: C. Hurst.

15 WHO PREDICTED THE 1929 CRASH?

"Prediction is the acid test for any explanation of events and their relationships."

—E. C. Harwood[1]

Determining who did and who did not predict the stock market crash of 1929 and the subsequent depression is not just an exercise in curiosity. Rather, it suggests a great deal about the strengths and weaknesses of an economist's theories on how the world works. Such a study may also be extremely useful in discriminating between financial theories in vogue today. The ability to predict an event or new trend is the acid test of any hypothesis. As Milton Friedman argues, "theory is to be judged by its predictive power . . . the only relevant test of the *validity* of a hypothesis is comparison of its predictions with experience."[2]

In reviewing the attitudes of economists, bankers, brokers, financial advisors, and politicians in the 1920s, I have come to the conclusion that the mainstream schools of orthodox economics almost universally miscalculated the financial events that occurred in late 1929 and the economic debacle that followed. Only a handful of economists and financial observers—many of whom were considered by

---

Reprinted from *The Meaning of Ludwig von Mises*, ed. by Jeffrey M. Herbener (Kluwer Academic Publishers, 1993), 247–283. I wish to thank Milton Friedman, Richard M. Ebeling, Bettina Bien Greaves, the late William W. Bartley, III, and Murray N. Rothbard for providing helpful comments and additional sources of information. Any conclusions and opinions expressed herein are strictly my own.

1. E. C. Harwood, *Cause and Control of the Business Cycle* (Great Barrington, Mass.: American Institute of Economic Research, 1957), 63.

2. Milton Friedman, "The Methodology of Positive Economics," *Essays in Positive Economics* (Chicago: University of Chicago Press, 1953), 8–9.

the establishment to be unorthodox "cranks"—forecast the massive deflationary forces that rocked the foundation of the economic and political world.[3]

The Significance of the Crisis

Without question, the stock market crash in October, 1929, was a monumental event. Although most politicians, academic economists, and Wall Street experts felt that the collapse in the securities markets was an isolated event at the time, today most economic historians feel differently, convinced that it was a principal turning point in pushing the world economy into an ever-deepening abyss.

Galbraith notes, "This, the day of the Great Stock Market Crash, remains in the social memory after a full fifty years. And for good reason. After that day, life for millions was not again the same."[4] Investment writer Donald J. Hoppe concurs. "The stock market crash of October, 1929, is one of those unique dramatic landmarks, such as the assassination of Julius Caesar, the landing of Columbus or the Battle of Waterloo, that historians find so convenient for marking the major turning points in the destiny of man."[5]

---

3. Curiously, three econometricians from Harvard and Yale recently absolve their academic ancestors of any grievous sin in not anticipating the Great Depression by arguing that the crash and depression were "unforecastable." See Kathryn M. Dominguez, Ray C. Fair, and Matthew D. Shapiro, "Forecasting the Depression: Harvard Versus Yale," *American Economic Review* (September 1988). Dominguez et al. found that not only did the Harvard Economic Service as well as Yale's Irving Fisher fail to anticipate the crash and depression, but also their own modern econometric model could not predict the events of 1929–1933 either. "Our results imply that the Harvard and Yale forecasters cannot necessarily be faulted for remaining optimistic after the Crash. Their continued optimism is consistent with our conclusion based on time-series methods that the Depression was not forecastable" (605).

On the contrary, the correct conclusion to draw from Dominguez's article is not that the depression was unpredictable, but that the economics establishment has been using the wrong forecasting model! Harvard and Yale did not "tie" in the forecasting game, as the apologists claim; they both lost. In short, their methodology of forecasting depressions has been and remains seriously flawed. It is a tragedy that orthodox economists have not found a reliable theory of depressions, and that sophisticated time-series models have been unable to improve on the embarrassing record of the Harvard Economic Service and Irving Fisher. There is no reason to exult over a faulty model that expresses optimism in the face of the worst economic cataclysm in modern times.

4. John Kenneth Galbraith, *The Great Crash, 1929* (1954; Boston: Houghton Mifflin, 1979), xi; new introduction.

5. Donald J. Hoppe, *How to Invest in Gold Stocks and Avoid the Pitfalls* (New Rochelle, N.Y.: Arlington House, 1972), 99. Another financial writer, James Dines, argues that "the stock market 'discounts' the future, so that when people refer to '1929,' they mean not so much the market crash of that year, but the Great Depression, which the barometric stock market forecasted for 1932" (James Dines. *The Invisible Crash* [New York: Random House, 1975], 23).

Irving Fisher and the "New Era" Advocates

First, let us review the optimistic views of historical figures who were devastatingly wrong about the 1929 crash and ensuing economic crisis. The most famous American economist, Yale professor Irving Fisher, belongs in this category. Fisher built a reputation as the foremost monetary theorist and advocate of the "quantity theory of money." Even today, he is hailed by some to be one of America's best economists.[6]

Based on his contemporary theoretical works, *The Nature of Capital and Income and The Purchasing Power of Money*, Fisher firmly believed in the long-run neutrality of money, signifying that an increase in the money supply would result in a proportional increase in prices without causing any long-term ill-effects. While he did refer to "maladjustments" and "overinvestments" that might occur in specific lines of production, Fisher regarded them as points of short-term disequilibrium, caused mostly by institutional factors (contracts, customs, legal restrictions, etc.), which would eventually work themselves out.[7]

Fisher's emphasis on long-term monetary stability and his tragic failure to see the coming onslaught were evident throughout the 1920s. He was a principal advocate of the "New Era" optimism of the Roaring Twenties, one of the upbeat apostles of a "new and better world." In the mid-1920s, he suggested that the "so-called business cycle" no longer had any essential basis in the economic system.[8] He favored the inflationary expansion of credit by the Federal Reserve in the 1920s, as long as prices remained relatively stable, and in fact had a great deal of faith in the Federal Reserve system, expecting that it could stabilize the economy if a crisis arose.

Price stabilization was Fisher's principal monetary goal. He became a leading advocate of the "stable money" movement, having organized in May 1931, the Stable Money League, later to become the Stable

6. Mark Blaug calls Fisher "One of the greatest, if not the greatest, and certainly one of the most colourful American economists" (*Who's Who in Economics*, Mark Blaug, ed., 2nd ed. [Cambridge, Mass.: MIT Press, 1986], 273).

7. Irving Fisher, *The Nature of Capital and Income* (1906; 1912; Augustus M. Kelley, 1965); *The Purchasing Power of Money*, 2nd ed. (1911; 1916; 1922; New York: Augustus M. Kelley, 1963), 184–85, passim. Perhaps a remark by Lord Keynes might appropriately apply to Fisher's long-run equilibrium approach to monetary phenomenon: "Economists set themselves too easy, too useless a task if in tempestuous seasons they can only tell us that when the storm is long past the ocean is flat again" (John Maynard Keynes, *A Tract on Monetary Reform* [London: Macmillan, 1923], 80).

8. Irving Fisher, "Our Unstable Dollar and the So-Called Business Cycle," *Journal of the American Statistical Association* (June 20, 1925): 179–202.

Money Association. Other prominent members of the stabilization association were economists Alvin Hansen, Arthur C. Pigou, Ralph G. Hawtrey, Knut Wicksell, Gustav Cassel, and John Maynard Keynes.[9]

The idea was not so much to stabilize the growth of the money supply, but to stabilize prices, particularly wholesale and consumer prices. According to Fisher and other price-stabilization advocates, if consumer prices remained relatively stable, everything was all right. But if prices began to sag, threatening deflation, the Fed should intervene and expand credit. In fact, wholesale and consumer prices in the United States were remarkably stable, and even declined slightly during the 1920s. Thus the monetarists thought everything was fine. They were thrown off-guard by this apparent price stability of the twenties. They failed to see the mischievous effects the Fed's expansionary policy would have in the latter half of the 1920s and dismissed the warning signs of economic trouble in such areas of the Florida real estate boom and the

Dow Jones Industrial Average, 1920–1933

Figure 1

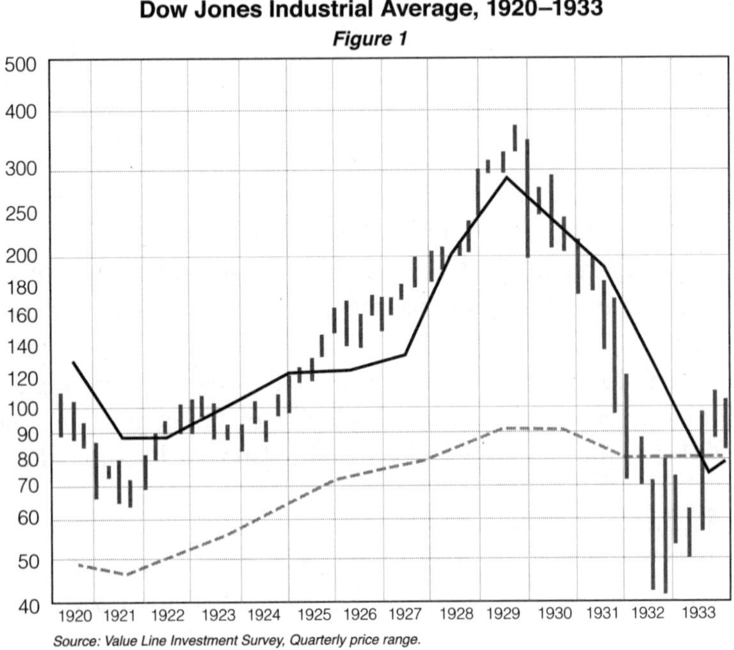

Source: Value Line Investment Survey, Quarterly price range.

9. A short review of the price stabilization movement is found in Murray N. Rothbard, *America's Great Depression*, 4th ed. (1963; New York: Richardson & Synder, 1983), 153–64.

stock market euphoria.[10]

In the latter half of the 1920s, Fisher became the chief oracle of the stock market boom. His excessive optimism was personal as well as ideological, since besides being a professor, he was a millionaire businessman and major investor on Wall Street.

Fisher saw the booming stock market as a reflection of the "New Era" of permanent prosperity in America. He denied any "orgy of speculation," even though the Dow Jones Industrial Average had climbed from 103 in 1922 to an all-time high of 381 on Sept. 3, 1929, more than tripling in seven years *(see Figure 1)*. When, on Sept. 5, 1929, the less-influential financial advisor Roger W. Babson warned investors of an

---

10. Milton Friedman, today's most famous monetarist, denies that the Federal Reserve was the engine of inflation in the 1920s, or that the 1920s was inflationary at all. "By 1923, wholesale prices had recovered only a sixth of their 1920–21 decline. From then until 1929, they fell on the average of 1 percent per year . . . The stock of money, too, failed to rise and even fell slightly during most of the expansion . . ." He concludes: "Far from being an inflationary decade, the twenties were the reverse. And the Reserve System, far from being an engine of inflation, very likely kept the money stock from rising as much as it would have if gold movements had been allowed to exert their full influence" (Milton Friedman and Anna J. Schwartz, A Monetary History of the United States 1867–1960 [Princeton: Princeton University Press, 1963], 298). Friedman calls the 1920s the "high tide" of the Federal Reserve System and makes a sharp distinction between the general economy and the stock market and real estate bubbles (291–92). He offers no explanation for the precipitous decline in the stock market. His principal concern is the sharp decline in the money stock between 1929 and 1933. See ibid., 299–300.

However, Anna J. Schwartz, in a separate article, suggests a probable relationship between the restrictive monetary policy beginning in late 1928 and the stock market crash. But she still insists that Fisher was right in believing that stock prices in 1929 were not generally overvalued. "Had high employment and economic growth continued, prices in the stock market could have been maintained" (Schwartz, "Understanding 1929–1933," Money in Historical Perspective [Chicago: University of Chicago Press, 1987], 130). Originally appeared in The Great Depression Revisited, Karl Brunner, ed. (Boston: Martinus Nijhoff, 1981), 5–48.

To support her thesis, Schwartz cites an article by Gerald Sirkin, professor of economics at the City University of New York. Based on seemingly reasonable price-earnings ratios for most stocks in 1929, Sirkin concludes that overall stock prices in 1929 "hardly present a picture of a 'speculative orgy'" (Sirkin, 'The Stock Market of 1929 Revisited: A Note," Business History Review 49 no. 2 [Summer 1975]: 223–31). This is a classic example of the ivory-tower world of academia run amuck.

As any experienced security analyst knows, price-earnings ratios can be a highly misleading indicator of speculative activity. In fact, by their very nature, price-earnings ratios severely underestimate the degree of stock market speculation because both prices and earnings tend to rise during a boom. Granted, pie ratios rise overall in a bull market as a result of rising earnings expectations. But higher future earnings were illusory for a variety of reasons. Sirkin fails to realize, for example, that from 1926 to 1929, industrial production advanced only 8.1 percent and commodity prices fell 4.7%, while common stock prices rose 93%! See Schroeder Boulton, "Inflation and the Stock Market," in H. Parker Willis and John M. Chapman, The Economics of Inflation (New York: Columbia University Press, 1935, 311). According to the Standard Statistics Common Stock Average, a well-diversified holding of U. S. stocks would have more than trebled in value from 1924 to 1929. How Sirkin could consider such an increase in stock prices "not speculative" is beyond me. Whenever stock prices rise consistently faster than industrial output in general, a stock market "correction" is inevitable. Clearly, the easy-credit policies of the Fed in the 1920s went primarily into stocks, real estate, and other capital-intensive markets rather than other areas of the economy, creating an imbalance that hardly reflected itself in price-earnings ratios. Thus, "speculative orgy" is a proper description of the 1929 stock market.

impending crash, Fisher refuted Babson, saying, "There may be a recession in stock prices, but not anything in the nature of a crash."[11]

For nearly two months, Fisher appeared to be right. While the market did not reach new highs, neither did it fall sharply. On October 15th, less than two weeks before the crash, Fisher opined, "I expect to see the stock market a good deal higher than it is today, within a few months."[12] The next day, he made the soon-to-be-immortal prediction that "stock prices have reached what looks like a permanently high plateau."[13]

On Monday, October 21, 1929, he suggested that "even in the present high market, the price of stocks have not yet caught up with their real values." Any drop in stock prices "was a shaking-out of the lunatic fringe that attempts to speculate on margin . . . ."[14] Finally, on October 22nd, two days before Black Thursday, Fisher stated, "in my opinion, current predictions of heavy reaction affecting the general level of securities find little if any foundation in fact."[15]

But Fisher was unrepentant after the unexpected collapse of stock prices between late October and December. By mid-December, he had written a new book, *The Stock Market Crash—And After*, a bold attempt to reestablish optimism in the nation. He rationalized, "I had stated my opinion in September, preceding the panic, that the market had reached its peak, as proved to be the case. I also expressed the view that the recession would not be in the nature of a serious crash, in which I was mistaken. I also predicted that the new plateau of stock prices would survive any recession. This has proven true."[16]

Unfortunately, Fisher was wrong again. Despite his faith in Hoover's program to stem the tide, the Dow industrials fell an additional 200 points before bottoming out in 1932 around 40! His own portfolio was practically wiped out by the extended Wall Street crash. To end the depression in the early thirties, Professor Fisher advocated reflation,

11. *New York Herald-Tribune*, Sept. 6 1929. For an account of the Babson-Fisher feud, see Robert T. Patterson, *The Great Boom and Panic*, 1921–1929 (Chicago: Henry Regnery, 1965), 89–90. Several weeks later, on Oct. 16 1929, Fisher said, "I do not feel that there will soon, if ever, be a fifty or sixty point break below present levels, such as Mr. Babson has predicted."

12. Gordon Thomas and Max Morgan-Witts, *The Day the Bubble Burst* (New York: Penguin Books, 1979), 324.

13. Edward Angly, compiler, *Oh Yeah?* (New York: Viking Press, 1931), 38. *New York Times*, October 16, 1929.

14. Thomas and Morgan-Witts, *The Day the Bubble Burst*, 343.

15. Patereon, *The Great Boom and Panic*, 29.

16. Irving Fisher, *The Stock Market Crash—And After* (New York: Macmillan, 1930). His introduction is dated December 15, 1929.

devaluation, and abandoning the gold standard. Welcoming Franklin Delano Roosevelt's decision to act in 1933, he felt the bottom had been reached and he could finally stave off bankruptcy.[17]

Clearly, Fisher's monetary ideology and theory of price stabilization proved to be fatally flawed in the critical stages of a world economic crisis. His macroeconomic vision concealed basic financial facts that should have raised serious question marks about the soundness of the economic system. For instance, wasn't he concerned about the fact that the call rate on stock margin loans reached 15–20 percent in 1929, while the discount rate remained at 6 percent? Such a discrepancy should ring alarm bells to any seasoned speculator. Surely he must have sensed danger. Yet, typical of many financial advisors blinded by a pet theory, he could not see what now appears to be obvious. Monetarists such as Fisher who focus exclusively on general commodity prices as an indication of inflation instead of Federal Reserve credit policies are bound to be disappointed in their ability to predict the future of economic events.

Mitchell and "New Era" Optimism

Fisher was not alone among members of the economic profession in his failure to predict the crash. Another representative of the "New Era" thesis was Wesley C. Mitchell, the uncontested authority on business cycles in the 1920s. Mitchell was not only an economics professor at Columbia but also was director of the National Bureau of Economic Research in New York, thus embodying the spirit of academic, business, and government collaboration. He was a classic example of an economist who, with all his erudite credentials and objective analysis, should have been able to foresee the impending crisis. Yet he did not.[18]

Ironically, only several months before the critical turn of events in 1929, Mitchell wrote an essay in a National Bureau report that historian William E. Stoneman calls "the definitive document of moderate

17. For a review of Fisher's career, see Irving Norton Fisher, *My Father Irving Fisher* (New York: Comet Press, 1956), especially 242–65.

18. Perhaps the reason for Mitchell's failure to recognize the forthcoming crisis was that he was essentially an empiricist, not a theoretical economist. As Stoneman states, "Originally inspired by Veblen, Mitchell had soon been drawn into a purely empirical and quantitative approach to economics" (William E. Stoneman, *A History of the Economic Analysis of the Great Depression in America* [New York: Garland Publishing, 1979], 20). Without a theoretical underpinning, it is virtually impossible to reach any conclusions about the future based solely on past economic data. Cf. Milton Friedman. "Wesley C. Mitchell as an Economic Theorist," *Journal of Political Economy* (December 1950); and Arthur F. Burns, ed. *Wesley Clair Mitchell, The Economic Scientist* (New York: National Bureau of Economic Research, 1952), 237–82.

New Era economics."[19] Mitchell's essay was a final review of the 1920s economy, prepared for the President's Conference on Unemployment, which was chaired by Herbert Hoover and included leaders in finance, labor, science, and education. The report of the committee set the tone of the study: "Acceleration rather than structural change is the key to an understanding of our recent economic developments .... Our situation is fortunate, our momentum is remarkable."[20]

Although Mitchell's heart was with the "New Era" euphoria, he refrained from saying that the business cycle was a thing of the past, noting that "all is not well." He foresaw that "the pace will slacken presently" and the signs of prosperity were "wearing thin."[21] Nevertheless, while expressing some misgivings about pockets of economic and price weakness in the economy, he endorsed the high-wage, high-consumption character of the country. Since there was little evidence of an "unhealthy boom," it would be unlikely that there would be any "violent relapse." He saw few signs of overbuilding and overspeculation.[22]

Another case for "New Era" confidence in the U.S. economy was expressed by the Harvard Economic Society. Although not particularly bullish, the Harvard Economic Society predicted a correction in the market, but "no business depression." After the crash, the economic society stated that "despite its severity, we believe that the slump in stock prices will prove an intermediate movement and not the precursor of a business depression such as would entail prolonged further liquidation."[23]

The Misinterpretation of Keynes

Other well-known economists also missed the sudden decline in

19. Stoneman, *A History of the Economic Analysis*, 20.

20. "Report of the Committee," *Recent Economic Changes in the United States* (New York: McGraw-Hill, 1929), ix, xxii. In the introduction, Edwin F. Gay, professor of economic history at Harvard, states: 'The strength and stability of our financial structure, both governmental and commercial, is of modern growth" (11).

21. Wesley C. Mitchell, "A Review," *Recent Economic Changes in the United States* (New York: McGraw-Hill, 1929), 909–10.

22. Ibid., 890–94, 909–10. Another economist who had a bright outlook on the stock market and the economy was Professor Charles Dice of Ohio State, who claimed in his book, *New Levels in the Stock Market*, that stock prices were only "registering the tremendous changes that were in progress." See Robert Sobel, *Panic on Wall Street* (New York: Macmillan, 1968), 368.

23. Frederick Lewis Allen, *Only Yesterday* (New York: Harper & Row, 1931), 323. However, not everyone at Harvard was unconcerned. According to one report, Dean Wallace Donham and professor of investment banking Clinton P. Biddle warned students to get out of the market in early October, 1929. See Tom Shachtman. *The Day America Crashed* (New York: G. P. Putnam's, 1979), 98.

the markets and the economic crisis in 1929. R. G. Hawtrey, Britain's leading monetarist and cycle analyst, was convinced by 1926 that if credit could be controlled, the "trade cycle" could be banished forever.[24]

British economist John Maynard Keynes shared Fisher's optimism about America's Federal Reserve expansionary policy. He was generally preoccupied with the British economic malaise that began several years before the depression in the United States. Keynes had correctly predicted the disastrous results of Britain's return to the gold standard at an overvalued sterling exchange rate in 1925, but he had no such luck in prognosticating the economy across the Atlantic. He hailed the management of the dollar by the Federal Reserve Board from 1923 to 1928 as a "triumph" for central bank management.[25] He remained unconcerned about the huge rise in stock prices on Wall Street. In fact, in 1927, he met with Swiss banker Felix Somary and was anxious to buy stocks. When Somary expressed pessimism about the future of securities prices, Keynes responded with the prediction, "We will not have any more crashes in our time."[26]

In late 1928, Oswald T. Falk, one of the members of the board of the National Mutual Life Insurance Company, of which Keynes was chairman, was alarmed at the "dangerous inflation" in the United States, suggesting that the company liquidate most of its American holdings. But Keynes wrote two papers disagreeing with Falk. In the second paper dated September 1, 1928, entitled "Is There Inflation in the United States?," he reviewed data on the cost of living and business credit and concluded that there was "nothing which can be called inflation yet in sight."

Referring to both real estate and stock values in the United States, Keynes added: "I conclude that it would be premature today to assert the existence of overinvestment . . . . I should be inclined, therefore, to predict that stocks would not slump severely (i.e., below the recent low level) unless the market was discounting a business depression." Such would not be probable since the Federal Reserve Board "will do all in

---

24. R. G. Hawtrey. "The Trade Cycle," reprinted in *Readings in Business Cycle Theory* (Philadelphia: American Economic Association, 1944), 333–49. Originally published in 1926 in a Dutch journal.

25. Colleague D. H. Robertson concurred in 1929 that "a monetary policy consciously aimed at keeping the general price level approximately stable . . . has apparently been followed with some success by the Federal Reserve Board in the United States since 1922" (Robertson, "The Trade Cycle," *Encyclopedia Britannica*, 14th ed. [1929] 22:354).

26. For an account of the conversation between Keynes and Somary, see Felix Somary, *The Raven of Zurich* (1960; London: C. Hurst, 1986), 146–47.

its power to avoid a business depression."[27] By the time he had completed his *Treatise on Money* in 1930, however, he admitted he had been misled by stable price indices in the 1920s, and that a "profit inflation" had developed in 1928.[28]

The Political Environment in 1929

Back in the United States, the Coolidge and Hoover administrations also failed to foresee trouble ahead. When Coolidge left office in March 1928, he continued the "New Era" optimism, calling American prosperity "absolutely sound" and stocks "cheap at current prices."[29] Herbert Hoover was not as enthusiastic about the cheap credit policies of the Federal Reserve as Coolidge and Treasury Secretary Andrew Mellon were, particularly in stimulating the stock market. He opposed Benjamin Strong, Governor of the Federal Reserve of New York, who since 1924 had encouraged lower interest rates and easy credit in the United States through open-market operations in order to boost domestic prices and alleviate Britain's overvalued exchange rate.

Under the leadership of Strong and the New York Fed, the Federal Reserve Board had gradually reduced the discount rate, the interest charged to members to borrow money from the central bank, from 6½ percent in 1921 to below 4 percent by August 1927. *(See Figure 2).* Only in late 1928 did Strong belatedly fret about the "terrible speculation" going on in the United States, and by then it was too late. He died and was incapable of turning the tide.

By the spring of 1929, the Federal Reserve Board became alarmed over the caprices of Wall Street and the lending of funds for stock purchases. It issued a warning to member banks not to lend money for stock purchases, eventually raised the discount rate, and stopped net sales of government bonds on the open market. The full impact of this anti-inflation policy wasn't felt until October.

Despite these growing concerns, Hoover continued to make highly favorable public statements about the soundness of the economy. Years

27. John Maynard Keynes, *The Collected Writings of John Maynard Keynes*, vol. 13 (London: Macmillan, 1973), 52–59. Also see Charles H. Hession, *John Maynard Keynes* (New York: Macmillan, 1984), 238–39.
28. John Maynard Keynes, *A Treatise on Money*, vol. 2 (New York: Harcourt, Brace and Co., 1930), 190; see 190–98. Keynes lost three-fourths of his net worth during 1929. See Donald Muggeridge, "Keynes As an Investor," in *The Collected Writings of John Maynard Keynes*, vol. 12 (London: Macmillan, 1973).
29. Herbert Hoover. *Memoirs of Herbert Hoover: The Great Depression, 1929–1941* (New York: Macmillan, 1952), 16.

later, in his memoirs, Hoover said he was misled by members of the Federal Reserve, who told him, "We shall have no more financial panics . . . . Panics are impossible . . . unthinkable."[30] Soon the raging stock market became known as the "Hoover bull market," which Hoover did nothing to discourage, at least publicly. Treasury Secretary Mellon continued to allay fears that the market was moving too far too fast. "There is no cause for worry. The high tide of prosperity will continue," he said in September 1928.[31]

Discount Rate
Federal Reserve Bank of New York, 1921–1929
Figure 2

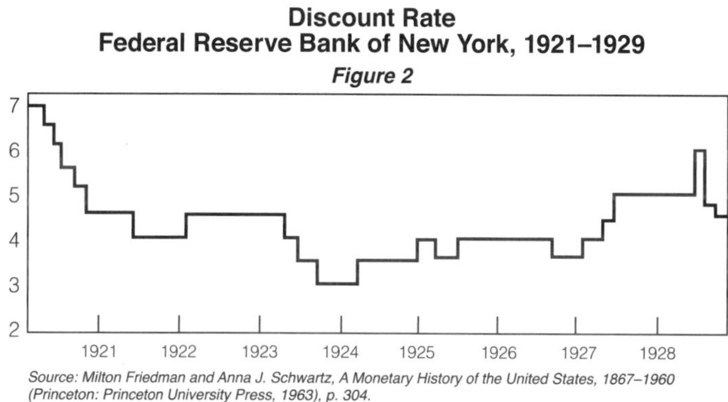

Source: Milton Friedman and Anna J. Schwartz, A Monetary History of the United States, 1867–1960 (Princeton: Princeton University Press, 1963), p. 304.

The day after Black Thursday, when the market dropped 100 points, Hoover announced to the nation, "The fundamental business of the country, that is the production and distribution of commodities, is on a sound and prosperous basis."[32] Several months later, in March 1930, he spoke optimistically. "All the evidence indicates that the worst effects of the crash will have passed within sixty days."[33] Unfortunately, Hoover had his head in a cloud.

---

30. Ibid., 7.
31. Galbraith, *The Great Crash*, 1929, 15. Galbraith condones the phony enthusiasm of government pronouncements as a harmless "ritual which, in our society, is thought to be a great value for influencing the course of the business cycle. By affirming solemnly that prosperity will continue, it is believed, one can help insure that prosperity will in fact continue" (16). On the other hand, perhaps if Hoover had spoken out earlier against the "South Sea Bubble" on Wall Street (Hoover's phrase used in his memoirs, not in 1929), perhaps the public would not have jumped in frantically as they did in late 1929, only to be massacred and financially destroyed. Perhaps the best thing that can be said about political predictions is that, in the words of de Jouvenal, "the man with the least foresight is . . . the man in the seat of power" (Bertrand de Jouvenel, *The Art of Conjecture* [New York: Basic Books, 1957J, 151).
32. Thomas and Morgan-Witts, *The Day the Bubble Burst*, 376.
33. Donald J. Hoppe, *How to Invest in Gold Stocks*, 100.

The Financial Bulls

There were, of course, an exceedingly large group of bankers, brokers, and financial writers who saw no dangers on Wall Street even weeks before the crunch and plunged into the market with reckless abandon. Speculators included the Fisher brothers of Detroit, wheat magnet Arthur W. Cutten (known as the "Great Bull"), and Charles E, Mitchell, president of National City Bank of New York. Mitchell, as late as September 15, 1929, spoke favorably. "The markets generally are now in a healthy state."[34]

Financial journals such as *The Wall Street Journal* and *Barron's* were late in foreseeing the stock market decline and frequently belittled the market "bears," such as Roger Babson. William P. Hamilton, editor of *The Wall Street Journal* until late 1929, was a follower of the Dow theory, based on the technical investment approach of Charles H. Dow, the cofounder of the journal. Based on Dow's work, Hamilton wrote *The Stock Market Barometer* and argued that when two lines (the Dow industrials and the rails) broke above the equilibrium "line," it was an indication that the market was bullish. When the two lines broke below their market average, it was a bearish sign.

Throughout the 1920s, Hamilton and *The Wall Street Journal* were essentially optimistic as the trendlines moved upward. In October 1927, in the midst of the bull market, Hamilton editorialized that, based on the Dow theory, "The stock market is saying, in so many words, that the business outlook is good and likely to continue . . . ."[35] *The Wall Street Journal* remained confident up to the time of the crash, a typical attitude of market technicians. Hamilton debunked Babson's September 5th warning of a collapse.

But, suddenly, on October 25th—a day after Black Thursday—Hamilton flashed a warning signal in a journal editorial, "Turn of the Tide." He was 52 days and 80 points late from the top, but he recommended selling before the market dropped another 150 points. However, by early November, Hamilton had switched attitudes again, especially after John D. Rockefeller, by then an octogenarian, announced bravely,

34. John Brooks, *Once in Golconda* (New York: Harper & Row, 1969), 112. Mitchell appears to have ignored warnings made by economists at his own bank. A report by the National City Bank of New York stated on April 18, 1929, "If the rate of credit increase rises above the rate of business growth, we have a condition of inflation which manifests itself in rising prices in some departments of the business structure, overconfidence, excessive speculation, and an eventual crash."

35. Editorial, *Wall Street Journal*, October 3, 1927.

"There is nothing in the business situation to warrant the destruction of values that has taken place in the past week, and my son and I have for some days past been purchasing sound common stocks."[36] Hamilton editorialized in *The Wall Street Journal*: "The sun is shining again, and we will go on record as saying some good stocks are cheap. We say good stocks are cheap because John D. Rockefeller said it first. Only the foolish will combat John D.'s judgment."[37]

Stock-market fundamentalists, who relied on earnings and other vital statistics to predict the future of individual companies, did not necessarily fare any better in the stock market crash than the Dow theorists and other technicians did. Benjamin Graham, author of the Wall Street bible, *Security Analysis*, did not escape. "Graham's clients suffered in the Crash like everybody else. But he managed to keep them solvent, and over the next several decades, he consistently compiled a creditable investment record."[38]

One of the biggest promoters of the stock market and easy credit was William Crapo Durant, president of General Motors. When the Fed warned member banks not to divert funds to stockbrokers for margin in February 1929, Durant strongly opposed this measure, and in a secret meeting in Washington, tried to persuade Hoover and the Fed to return to easy money policies. When they refused, Durant clandestinely unloaded billions of dollars in GM stock and other securities. He was able to do this without causing a market panic by having former GM officer John J. Raskob, who had recently become chairman of the Democratic Party, travel around the country promoting GM and the stock market! In a well-publicized interview in the August 1929, issue of *Ladies Home Journal*, entitled, "Everybody Ought to Be Rich," Raskob suggested that if a person invested only $15 per week in stocks, he could accumulate $80,000 or more in 20 years.

However, in the end, Durant's scheme failed. While he largely escaped the October crash, he got back into the market prematurely in 1930 and was wiped out. By 1936, he declared bankruptcy.[39]

The only other principal character in the "see no evil" play of the twenties was John Moody, president of Moody's Investor Service and

36. *New York Times*, October 31, 1929. Quoted in Thomas and Morgan-Witts, *The Day the Bubble Burst*, 402.
37. "Broad Street Gossip," *Wall Street Journal* (1 November 1929), 2.
38. David Dreman, *The New Contrarian Investment Strategy* (New York: Random House, 1982), 43.
39. For a full account of Durant's devious maneuvers, see Dana L. Thomas, *The Plungers and The Peacocks* (New York: G. P. Putnam's, 1967), 189–92, 214–15.

publisher of *Moody's Bond Ratings*. Although his firm had suggested caution in January 1929, by May, he envisioned an America geared for a future without precedent. "The lessons taught by the crude financial errors of the speculative corporate period, extending from 1898 down into the war and through the deflation of 1920–21, had been well learned by government and financial interests all over the country."[40]

How ironic that the man who rated the safety of the corporate and government bonds could be rated so low for accuracy, especially after having lived through the Panic of 1907! In stark contrast, the Standard Statistics Company and Poor's *Weekly Business and Investment Letter* were both extremely cautious in late 1929.[41]

"Sound Money" Economists As Dissenters

The number of bearish economists, bankers, and financial writers who actually predicted a stock market crash and economic depression were few and far between in the 1920s.

Among American economists, the only group to raise serious concerns over the inflationary twenties were from the old-fashioned "sound money" banking school. Two eminent economists representing this "hard-money" tradition were Benjamin M. Anderson, the chief economist at Chase National Bank, and H. Parker Willis, professor of banking at Columbia University and editor of the *Journal of Commerce*. Both economists were highly critical of Irving Fisher and the quantity theory of money. They shared the "Austrian" microeconomic approach toward economic events and emphasized the "real" distortions caused by bank credit expansion, especially in the stock market and real estate.

As the editor of *The Chase Economic Bulletin*, Benjamin Anderson frequently attacked the Fed-induced inflation of the 1920s and the policy of commodity price stabilization, calling it "wrong and dangerous."[42] He blamed rising interest rates in the late 1920s on the earlier efforts by the Federal Reserve to maintain artificially low interest rates. In particular, he said that "we touched the match to the powder keg" and "turned

40. *The Literary Digest*, May 26, 1928.

41. Allen, *Only Yesterday*, 322.

42. Benjamin M. Anderson, "Commodity Price Stabilization a False Goal of Central Bank Policy," *The Chase Economic Bulletin* 9 (3): 4. A summary of Anderson's reflections on the 1929–1933 economic crisis is found in his excellent work, *Economics and the Public Welfare: A Financial and Economic History of the United States, 1914–1946* (1949; Indianapolis, Ind.: Liberty Press, 1979), esp. 144–50, 182–230.

loose the incalculable psychological force of speculative contagion" in August, 1927 when the Fed reduced the discount rate to 3½ percent.[43]

He attacked Swedish economist Gustav Cassel for suggesting that the United States did not release enough credit in 1925–27 because commodity prices continued to decline.[44] After the October 1929, massacre, Anderson said the cause of the trouble was "excessive cheap money and unlimited bank credit available for capital uses and speculation" in 1922–28. As to where the market was headed, he stated, "I am not a prophet .... I do not know what the stock market is going to do." But he discounted the possibility of a depression. "A business crisis today is absolutely precluded." He called for a mild slowdown only.[45]

Like Anderson, Willis rejected a strict quantity theory of money. "Rising prices are by no means universally identical with inflation ... [The] mechanism of inflation is not uniform."[46] For Willis, inflation induces an imbalance between production and consumption. "Inflation helps speculation by creating unsettled speculative conditions."[47]

Mises and Hayek as Economic Forecasters

In Europe, the only group of economists to predict a market collapse and worldwide depression were the Viennese economists, Ludwig von Mises and Friedrich A. Hayek. It was their prediction of a forthcoming economic collapse in the 1920s that created an intense interest in their economic theories in the early 1930s, especially in England.

Mises was an economic advisor to the Austrian Chamber of Commerce when he wrote his definitive *The Theory of Money and Credit* in 1912. Based on the monetary theories of Knut Wicksell, Mises argued that the forced lowering of interest rates by central banks inevitably creates an artificial boom, especially in the capital-goods industries, which cannot last. Moreover, Mises stated that the gold standard, even though weakened by the central banks, would eventually force individual nations to give up their inflationary policies and go through a bust. He was critical of Fisher's price-index stabilization scheme, which "could not in

43. Ibid., and "The Financial Situation," *The Chase Economic Bulletin* 9 (6): 4.

44. See Gustav Cassel, *Post-War Monetary Stabilization* (New York: Columbia University Press, 1928), 92–93.

45. Anderson, "The Financial Situation" *The Chase Economic Bulletin* 9, (6): 4, 13–14.

46. H. Parker Willis, "Some Conclusions: The Nature and Effect of Inflation," in H. Parker Willis and John M. Chapman, *The Economics of Inflation* (New York: Columbia University Press, 1935), 207–08.

47. Ibid., 216.

any way ameliorate the social consequences of variations in the value of money."[48] The bust was inevitable whether consumer prices increased or not. As Mises later explained in his magnum opus, *Human Action*, "The crash was the necessary outcome of the attempts to lower the rate of interest by credit expansion."[49]

As early as 1924, Mises told his colleagues in Vienna that an economic collapse was coming. The depression would be worldwide because practically every country was on a gold standard with a central bank that was inflating after the Great War. Fritz Machlup recalls Mises "gift of prophecy":

> As his assistant in the university seminar which met every Wednesday afternoon, I usually accompanied him home. On these walks we would pass through a passage of the Kreditanstalt in Vienna. From 1924, every Wednesday afternoon as we walked through the passage for pedestrians he said: That will be a big smash. Mind you, this was from 1924 onwards; yet in 1931, when the crash finally came, I still held some shares of the Kreditanstalt, which of course had become completely worthless.[50]

There is more to this story. In the summer of 1929, Mises was offered a high position at Credit Anstalt, which at the time was one of the largest banks in Europe. His future wife, Margit, was ecstatic, but Mises surprised her when he said he decided not to accept the offer. "Why not?" she asked. His response shocked her: "A great crash is coming," he said, "and I don't want my name in any way connected with it."[51] After the United States market collapsed several months later, world trade suffered and in May 1931, Credit Anstalt went bankrupt which, more than any other event, extended the depression throughout Europe.

48. Ludwig von Mises, *The Theory of Money and Credit*, 2nd ed, (1934; Irvington-on-Hudson, N.Y.: Foundation for Economic Education, 1971), 402.

49. Ludwig von Mises, *Human Action*, 3rd rev. ed. (Chicago: Henry Regnery, 1966), 853.

50. Fritz Machlup, "Tribute to Mises" (The Mont Pelerin Society, September 13, 1974), 12. Machlup also said that Mises predicted as early as 1927 that the end of freedom in Central Europe was coming and suggested that free-market economists would be forced to leave Europe. The threat of Hitler in the 1930s resulted in the fact that by 1938, according to Machlup, "most of us had acted upon the master's advice and had taken the first chance we got to leave our native country in good time" (13).

51. Margit von Mises, *My Years with Ludwig von Mises*, 2nd ed. (Spring Mills, Penn.: Libertarian Press, 1984), 23.

After the depression was in full swing, Mises commented on his prediction in an introduction to the English translation of *The Theory of Money and Credit*:

> From 1926 to 1929 the attention of the world was chiefly focused upon the question of American prosperity. As in all previous booms brought about by expansion of credit, it was then believed that the prosperity would last forever, and the warnings of the economists were disregarded. The turn of the tide in 1929 and the subsequent severe economic crisis were not a surprise for economists; they had foreseen them, even if they had not been able to predict the exact date of their occurrence.[52]

Mises' student, Friedrich A. Hayek, also expected an economic crisis, specifically in the United States. His timing appeared to be a little more precise than Mises'. As director of the Austrian Institute of Economic Research, Hayek published several pessimistic articles in the institute's monthly reports in 1929. Referring to this prediction in an interview in 1975, Hayek stated:

> I was one of the only ones to predict what was going to happen. In early 1929, when I made this forecast, I was living in Europe which was then going through a period of depression. I said that there [would be] no hope of a recovery in Europe until interest rates fell, and interest rates would not fall until the American boom collapses, which I said was likely to happen within the next few months.[53]

Hayek explained the theoretical underpinnings for his outlook in the late 1920s:

> What made me expect this, of course, is one of my main theoretical beliefs that you cannot indefinitely maintain an

52. Ludwig von Mises, "Preface to English Edition," *The Theory of Money and Credit*, H.E. Batson, trans. (Indianapolis, Ind.: Liberty Fund, 1980), 14–15. Written in June, 1934.

53. Interview with F. A. Hayek, *Gold & Silver Newsletter* (Newport Beach, Calif.: Monex International, June 1975). Hayek's report appeared in *Monatsberichte des Osterreichischen Instituts für Konjunkturforschung* (1929). Lionel Robbins refers to Hayek's prediction of the depression in America in the Foreword to Hayek's *Prices and Production*, 1st ed. (London: George Routledge & Sons, 1931), xii.

> inflationary boom. Such a boom creates all kinds of artificial jobs that might keep going for a fairly long time but sooner or later must collapse. Also, I was convinced after 1927, when the Federal Reserve made an attempt to stave off a collapse by credit expansion, the boom had become a typically inflationary one.
>
> So in early 1929 there was every sign that the boom was going to break down. I knew by then that the Americans could not prolong this sort of expansion indefinitely, and as soon as the Federal Reserve was no longer willing to feed it by more inflation, the thing would collapse.
>
> In addition, you must remember that at the time the Federal Reserve was not only unwilling but was *unable* to continue the expansion because the gold standard set a limit to the possible expansion. Under the gold standard, therefore, an inflationary boom could not last very long.[54]

The Austrian economists were able to forecast the economic debacle, particularly in the United States, because they looked beyond general price indices and stable macroeconomic phenomenon such as wage levels and consumer spending. They focused on the micro foundations of the economy, and how artificially low interest rates and credit expansion encouraged "a dangerous stock market and real estate boom."[55] In sharp contrast to the orthodox economists in the 1920s, the Austrians did not consider real estate and the stock market as isolated factors in the economy. As Rothbard indicates, both securities and real estate are titles to capital and are an integral reflection of the excessive expansion of the capital-goods industries in an inflationary boom.[56] Hence, an economic depression would necessarily include the decline in real estate and securities values.

As Hayek indicates, the Austrian economists in the 1920s were mindful of changes in the money supply figures in the United States. They

---

54. "Interview with Hayek, *Gold & Silver Newsletter*, June 1975.

55. Murray N. Rothbard, "The New Deal and the International Monetary System," in *The Great Depression and New Deal Monetary Policy* (San Francisco: Cato Institute, 1980), 85. Rothbard's article originally appeared in *Watershed of Empire: Essays on New Deal Foreign Policy*, Leonard P. Liggio and James J. Martin, eds. (Colorado Springs: Ralph Myles, 1976).

56. Rothbard, *America's Great Depression*, 75, 324, n. 24. Benjamin M. Anderson also emphasized the speculative mania in stocks and real estate. He pointed out that the bull market in real estate was not just in Florida, but in Manhattan and other areas of the country. Anderson, *Economics and the Public Welfare*, 186–87, 204.

Growth Rate of Total Money Supply United States, 1921–1929

Figure 3

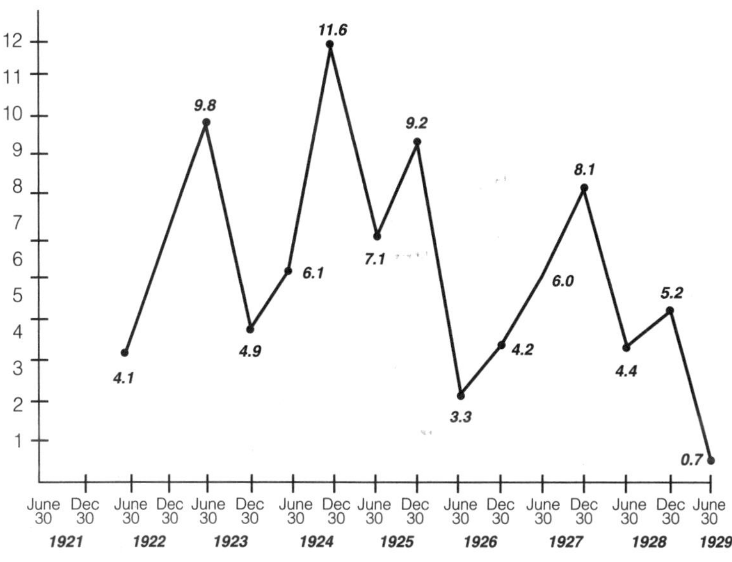

Source: Murray N. Rothbard, America's Great Depression (San Francisco: Cato Institute, 1980), Table 1, p. 88.

knew that a financial break was not far away when the monetary engine slowed down, or stopped *(see Figure 3).* As Rothbard summarizes:

> The inflation of the 1920s was actually over by the end of 1928. The total money supply on December 31, 1928, was $73 billion. On June 29, 1929, it was $73.26 billion, a rise of only 0.7 percent per annum. Thus, the monetary inflation was virtually completed by the end of 1928. From that time onward, the money supply remained level, rising only negligibly. And therefore, from that time onward, a depression to adjust the economy was inevitable. Since few Americans were familiar with the "Austrian" theory of the trade cycle, few realized what was going to happen.[57]

Swiss Banker Felix Somary

Another little-known Austrian economist and Swiss banker, Felix Somary, was prophetically pessimistic prior to the depression. In fact,

57. Ibid., 147.

according to contemporaries, Somary prophesized the stock market crash, remained gloomy throughout the depression era, and foresaw the second world war as an inevitable consequence of the peace treaties after 1918.[58] Somary grew up in Vienna, studied economics under Böhm-Bawerk, and knew fellow students Joseph Schumpeter, Ludwig von Mises, and Otto Bauer. Like Mises, Somary was a defender of the free market and the gold standard and a critic of socialism and governments inflationary policies. In 1901, he won the seminar prize for writing an article defending the inevitability of depressions. "How often in my later life have I again had to defend the thesis of major depressions and their inevitability, even in Socialist states, where they merely take another form."[59]

Somary found his brand of "hard-money" economics useful as a Swiss banker, money manager, and diplomat. In September 1926, Somary delivered a speech at the University of Vienna, predicting that the economic upswing and stock market boom that was just in its infancy "must end with the bankruptcy of governments and the destruction of banks."[60]

He rejected the commonly held view by mainstream economists at the time that commodity prices were stable and therefore no inflationary crisis could arise. Yet inflation was apparent in securities prices. In September 1928, he spoke before a group of economists and stressed the large disparity between loan rates and the yield on stocks, which he regarded as an "unmistakable symptom of a crash."[61] His speech was not well-received. "Here among my acquaintance were representatives of at least a dozen economic theories, but not one of them had an inkling of the nearness of the greatest crash of our generation."[62]

Somary recommended selling shares as early as 1926, thus missing out on a large part of the bull market on Wall Street. Many of his clients left him. In the summer 1929, he noted:

> For three years I had advised against share purchases, but many clients had not followed that advice; now was the time to extricate them from their shareholdings, as soon as possible. My

58. Felix Somary, *The Raven of Zurich: The Memoirs of Felix Somary*, A. J. Sherman, trans. (New York: St. Martin's Press, 1986), 272–92.
59. Ibid., 14.
60. Ibid., 281.
61. Ibid., 153.
62. Ibid.

telephone call saved many large amounts and in several cases, a client's entire fortune.[63]

Somary remained gloomy after the crash. In expectation of a banking panic in Europe, Britain going off the gold standard, and a worldwide depression, in early 1931 he withdrew all of the assets of Blankart & Cie., the Swiss bank he managed, on deposit with banks in England, Germany, and Italy.[64] But in June 1932, he turned cautiously optimistic and published a small pamphlet entitled *Turning Point?*, suggesting that the worldwide depression had possibly bottomed out.[65] From all accounts, Somary was remarkably prescient until a few years before his death. In a lecture given at Harvard University, he warned that the government's cheap money policies would soon result in a new depression and economic catastrophe. The date was April 1956.[66]

Babson and the Cassandras on Wall Street

A few notable financial figures became increasingly apprehensive about the stock market and the industrial boom in the late 1920s. No doubt the most famous doomsayer was Roger W. Babson, an investment counselor from Boston who had an extensive career in politics, church work, education, and science. To many, he was considered a mystical crank who tried to apply the laws of physics (Newton's Law of Action and Reaction) to economics and finance. Actually, Babson's combined use of trendlines in the "Babsoncharts" and division of business cycles into four distinct periods (improvement, prosperity, decline, and depression) is not that different from those used by many respected chartists and cycle analysts today. But back in the 1920s, the use of such technical analysis was just beginning.

Nevertheless, Babson's fundamentals were basically sound. After determining which phase of the business cycle the country was in, he would review old volumes of the *Commercial and Financial Chronicle* to get a sense of what to expect. He had a healthy suspicion of market booms, which he knew could end swiftly after witnessing the 1907 panic and the Florida real estate bust in 1927–28.

63. Ibid., 157.
64. Ibid., 162.
65. Ibid., 166.
66. Ibid., 293–302.

Starting as early as September 1926, he became bearish on the stock market. (The Dow Industrials was only around 160 and would move another 200 points before topping out!) Babson admitted that his most serious mistake was in being premature in his pronouncements. His famous call on September 5, 1929, when he told listeners to sell stocks and buy gold, was not the first time he had predicted a crash. He stated so in his well-publicized speech before the Annual National Business Conference: "I still repeat what I said at this time last year and the year before; namely, that sooner or later a crash is coming which will take the leading stocks and cause a decline of from 60 to 80 points in the Dow Jones barometer."[67]

In his autobiography, Babson confessed:

> Although I gave a very pessimistic address immediately preceding the collapse in September 1929, yet I had been giving similar warnings for about eighteen months. Although a study of newspaper files shows that the Babson Organization was given almost exclusive credit for forecasting the great depression of 1929–35, yet it should be emphasized that we thought the break would come before it did. In the same way we thought the upward turn would come before it did in 1932.[68]

Babson expected a rapid business recovery starting in September 1930—again years before it happened. Perhaps he was relying on the quick recovery made from the 1907 panic. History does not always repeat itself!

Harwood: Another New England Voice in the Wilderness

Fellow New Englander E. C. Harwood was another voice in the wilderness who forecast dire consequences of unsound monetary practices.

---

67. *New York Herald-Tribune*, September 6, 1929. Babson, known as the "Gloomy Gus of the financial soothsayer community," lost his credibility for crying wolf too often. "Babson had been wrong for such a long time that few could take him seriously, as he pontificated from a point hundreds of miles away from the nerve center of Wall Street" (Tom Shachtman, *The Day America Crashed* [New York: G. P. Putnam's, 19791, 99).

68. Roger W. Babson, *Actions and Reactions: An Autobiography of Roger W. Babson*, 2nd ed. (New York: HarperCollins, 1950), 267. See also Earl L. Smith, *Yankee Genius: A Biography of Roger W. Babson* (New York: Harper & Brothers, 1954), 262–70. According to *The Wall Street Journal* (September 6, 1929), Babson had predicted a crash in the stock market as early as September 11, 1926.

Based in Great Barrington, Mass., he founded the American Institute for Economic Research, an independent investment advisory service and publisher of economic and financial studies. Harwood was a strong advocate of the gold standard and believed that bank credit inflation was responsible for business malinvestments and financial fluctuations.

In addition to writing for his own publications, Harwood wrote regularly for *The Annalist*, a financial and economic weekly published by the *New York Times*. Noting the growing net export of gold from the United States in 1927, he concluded that the credit expansion by the Federal Reserve had to come to an end soon. In March 1928, he compared the expanding credit to a swollen shoe:

> To return to the credit "shoe," we are in this position: the foot has swelled; there are numerous "bunions"; the Federal Reserve is tightening the "lacing"; and there is a fair probability that the "shoe" itself will shrink materially. Therefore, we should not be surprised if a pinching sensation develops in the not far distant future.[69]

Several years later, Harwood noted that the publication of his article was timely—bond prices reached their high in March 1928. On January 25, 1929, he wrote in *The Annalist* that the banks were "overloaned" and that only the Federal Reserve could forestall a collapse. In a follow-up article on February 15th, he warned about the "grave dangers" in security speculation. "In the absence of any outside check, the situation is similar to the famous tulip speculation which occurred in the Netherlands, or even to the ill-fated Florida land boom . . . . [T]he current speculation in, and price inflation of, capital goods as represented by securities is far more dangerous than commodity speculation."[70]

Finally, on August 2, 1929, Harwood concluded that "the time may not be far distant when the country will realize, in the light of a 'cold gray morning after' that it has just been on another credit-splurging

69. E. C. Harwood, "The Probable Consequences to Our Credit Structure of Continued Gold Exports," *The Annalist* (March 23, 1928). This and other articles by Harwood are summarized in his *Cause and Control of the Business Cycle*, 5th ed. (1932; Great Barrington, Mass.: American Institute for Economic Research, 1957), 63–66.

70. E. C. Harwood, "Speculation in Securities vs. Commodity Speculation," *The Annalist* (February 15, 1929).

spree."[71] Moreover, once inflationary forces took hold in the post-1929 era, Harwood did not expect a quick return to prosperity.

Joe Kennedy: A Lone Wolf Operator

Probably the most successful speculator in the 1929–33 period was Joe Kennedy. He seemed to have the ideal temperament for speculating —"a passion for facts, a complete lack of sentiment, a marvelous sense of timing," said a confidante.[72]

According to various accounts, Kennedy stayed in the market until late 1928, when he sold most of his RKO "A" stock and options, netting several million dollars. He spent the 1928–29 winter at his second home in Palm Beach, Fla., which he had purchased at a bargain price after the Florida real estate slump. Kennedy decided not to reinvest in 1929 but to stay in cash. "Only a fool holds out for the top dollar," he once said.[73] In the summer of 1929, when he saw that shoeshine boys were talking about the stock market, it reaffirmed his decision to stay out. "Then and there, so ran his recollection, he decided that a market anyone could play, and a shoeshine boy could predict, was no market for him."[74]

Kennedy also allegedly sold short during the long market descent in the early 1930s and made more than $1 million. Then he reentered Wall Street on the long side in early 1933, six months after the market had bottomed.[75]

The Story of Jesse Livermore

What about Jesse Livermore, the speculator king and "the Great Bear" of Wall Street? He made his name by shorting stocks in the Panic of 1907. But, despite his reputation as a perennial short seller, he was a frequent buyer in the 1920s. He occasionally dabbled on the short side of the market in 1924 and shorted the market more frequently as the bull market matured. Knowing that Babson was going to deliver an alarmist speech on an otherwise dull market day in September 1929,

71. E. C. Harwood, "Deterioration of the American Bank Portfolio," *The Annalist* (August 2, 1929).
72. Richard J. Whalen, *The Founding Father: The Story of Joseph P. Kennedy* (New York: New American Library, 1964), 66.
73. Ibid., 104, based on an interview with Oscar Haussermann in Boston on October 10, 1962.
74. Ibid., 105.
75. Ibid., 107, 132.

he loaded up on the short side, and profited handsomely when the "Babson Break" forced a sharp dip in the market.

Quoted in the *New York Times* on October 21st, he pointed out fundamental defects in the market: "What has happened . . . is the inevitable result of continuous rank manipulation of many stock issues to prices many times their actual worth based upon real earnings and yield returns . . . . If anyone will take the trouble to analyze the prices of . . . stocks . . . they must look at them as selling at ridiculously high prices."[76] Responding to Professor Fisher's rosy outlook, Livermore exclaimed, "What can a professor know about speculation or stock markets? Did he ever trade on margin? Does he have a single cent in any of these bubbles he talks are cheap?"[77]

In terms of his public announcements, Livermore appeared to join the ranks of market dissenters. Unfortunately, he was of two minds during the crash and did not follow his own advice! According to biographer Paul Sarnoff, Livermore had a habit of trading both sides of the market during the 1920s, and was both short and long in 1929–30. Sarnoff concludes, "Even though Livermore had won millions on the short side of the market, he had actually lost about six million in his long position! Incredibly enough, Livermore's losses just about balanced any gains he may have made."[78]

The Two Faces of Bernard Baruch

The legendary Bernard Baruch said in his autobiography that he warned his friends right before the crash that he was selling out and for them to follow suit. He added, "Several times in 1928, in fact, I sold, feeling that a break was imminent, only to have the market continue upward."[79] He also allegedly sold stocks short in the spring of 1930, to make up for stocks he still held, and bought some gold stocks as a hedge.

76. *New York Times*, October 21, 1929. See also Tom Shachtman, *The Day America Crashed*, 57.
77. Thomas and Morgan-Witts, *The Day the Bubble Burst*, 336. Of course, Irving Fisher was heavily invested in the market—he even borrowed money from the banks to buy new venture stocks and increase his position in Remington Rand, his primary stock holding. Remington declined from $28 to $1 during the long bear market. As one New Yorker commented, "Gosh, he's supposed to know all the answers, and look how he got burned!" (quoted in I. N. Fisher, *My Father Irving Fisher*, 262–63).
78. Paul Sarnoff, *Jesse Livermore, Speculator-King* (Palisades Park, N.J.: Investors Press, 1967), 90. Contrary to rumor, Livermore did not kill himself after the stock market crash. He committed suicide in 1940, not 1930.
79. Bernard M. Baruch, *My Own Story* (New York: Henry Holt, 1957), 244.

Certainly, Bernard Baruch did not suffer outwardly from the 1929–33 depression; he continued to travel abroad, support relatives, and make charitable and political contributions. But outward signs can be deceptive, and autobiographies are notoriously tainted. In actuality, while Baruch did get in on the ground floor of the stock market in 1924, he did not use the elevator to come down from its penthouse in 1929. He got caught up in the "industrial renaissance" optimism of the twenties. In June 1929, he prophesied a new era of peace, understanding, and international cooperation.[80] A recent study of his brokerage records, tax returns, and other financial dealings resulted in a revisionist portrait of the Wall Street guru:

> The weight of the evidence supports the conclusion that he didn't sell out in time. A thoroughgoing industrial-renaissance optimist, he underestimated the gravity of the situation for months following the Crash and sold stocks only belatedly (so belatedly that his 1929 tax return showed a stock-trading profit: he hadn't taken his losses yet). On the other hand, he also managed to stay out of "the Cleaners." He was not over-extended on margin, and he resisted the temptation to buy stocks heavily before the liquidation had run its course. Before the devaluation of the dollar, he had the presence of mind to buy gold and gold-mining shares. He was not the Bernard Baruch of legend, but that was the only standard by which he can be said to have failed.[81]

Other Pessimistic Forecasts

A few financial editors realized early that the mad speculation on Wall Street would eventually end in a catastrophic plunge. Alexander Dana Noyes, financial editor of the *New York Times*, was highly critical of the speculative mania. In a November 21, 1928, editorial he stated that,

> the stock market speculation has reached an exceedingly dangerous stage . . . . [T]he recent action of the stock market,

80. James Grant, *Bernard Baruch: The Adventures of a Wall Street Legend* (New York: Simon & Schuster, 1983), 243 and 223–53.
81. Ibid., 233–34.

> supplemented by yesterday's wild extravagances, should emphasize the belief that this sort of thing cannot possibly be continued much longer . . . .[82]

By September 1929, Noyes was making comparisons between the panic of 1907 and 1929, although he expressed the hope that the new Federal Reserve could stabilize the situation. After the crash hit, Noyes suggested that the general public was caught off guard because, unlike in previous panics, there were no warning signs of a major business or bank failure in 1929. "The end of the great speculation came at the moment when the whole community seemed to have convinced itself that the end would never come."[83]

Paul M. Warburg, prominent New York banker and a founder of the Federal Reserve System who previously encouraged an "easy-money" policy, attacked the "orgies of unrestrained speculation" in the March 9, 1929, issue of *Commercial and Financial Chronicle*, pointing out that high stock prices were "quite unrelated to respective increases in plant, property, or earning power." He predicted that unless the speculative binge ended, it would "bring about a general depression involving the entire country."[84]

The Commercial and Financial Chronicle generally took a sober view of the financial situation in the late 1920s. In early 1929, president and editor Jacob Seibert editorialized that the "financial debauchery" of the late twenties was due to easy credit Fed policy.[85] He suggested that the Fed's warning of excessive stock speculation in February 1929, was "altogether right" but too late to stem the tide.[86]

However, after the crash, which he blamed on the Fed, he felt that the underlying economic conditions were now "sound."[87]

---

82. *New York Times*, November 21, 1928. Quoted in Patterson, *The Great Boom and Panic*, 57–58.

83. Dana L. Thomas, *The Plungers and The Peacocks*, 194. *Dun's Review & Modern Industry* reflected the confident atmosphere by business in 1929: "Nothing has occurred to indicate that widespread recession is under way . . . . " (October 5, 1929).

84. *Commercial and Financial Chronicle* (March 9, 1929), 1444. Quoted in Patterson, *The Great Boom and Panic*, 73. Regarding Warburg's critical role in promoting the Fed's policy of easy credit and low interest rates, see Rothbard, *America's Great Depression*, 117–20.

85. *The Commercial and Financial Chronicle*, March 9, 1929, 1443.

86. Ibid., March 30, 1929, 1968–69.

87. Ibid., October 26, 1929, 2577.

Summary: THE UNEASY CASE FOR FORECASTING

Forecasting may be, like government, a necessary evil. To make consistent profits, whether in business or investments, one must have an accurate expectation of what the future holds. In the case of the boom-bust business cycle of the roaring twenties and the depressed thirties, making the right prediction at the right time was critical. As Bertrand de Jouvenel says, "A forecast is never so useful as when it warns men of a crisis."[88] Those who failed to see the coming onslaught enjoyed the fruits of the boom while it lasted, but were destroyed financially when the unexpected bust hit. On the other hand, the handful of sober analysts who correctly prophesied the crisis avoided much of the economic pain and may even have profited from it.

But timing is a critical element in the art of forecasting. It does little good to predict a future event if you are too early—or too late. Roger Babson is a good example. Suppose an investor had followed his advice and bought blue-chip stocks in 1924, when the Dow Jones Industrial Average was near the ground floor at 100. If the investor had responded to Babson's warning of a slump, suppose he sold in late 1927, when the Dow Jones Averages hit 200. His investment would have doubled, not a bad three-year return. But he would have missed the next 180 points on the upside from 1927 until late 1929.

When the crash finally hit, his faith in Babson was renewed. But then, in September 1930, upon Babson's forecast of a "rapid business recovery," the investor would have repurchased, thinking this would be the turning point. The Dow was then back at 200, the same price it was when Babson recommended selling in late 1927! Unfortunately, the Dow continued to slump another 150 points in the next two years. Such a marked decline would be sufficient to wipe out any profits earned in the 1920s. Conclusion: Babson's "too early-too late" advisory service turned out to be far more costly than expected.

MISES AND THE SELF-CONTRADICTION OF FORECASTING

If a conservative investor followed Mises's prediction of a "big smash" as early as 1924, he would not have participated in either the boom or the bust, assuming he had the willpower not to stay out amidst

88. Bertrand de Jouvenel, *The Art of Conjecture*, 126.

the cries of optimism from others year after year.[89] Despite his own "gift of prophecy," Mises was undoubtedly the most outspokenly antagonist toward the virtues of forecasting among Austrian economists. Mises was well aware of the desire of businessmen and investors to know the precise time to act. While he recognized the inevitable results of inflation, price controls, and other forms of government intervention, he was adamant that no one can predict a specific date when an event or crisis will occur, "The economist knows that such a boom must result in a depression. But he does not and cannot know when the crisis will appear . . . . There are no rules according to which the duration of the boom or the following depression can be computed."[90]

Mises warned businessmen and investors that there is no such thing as "quantitative economics," and therefore "forecasts about the course of economic affairs cannot be considered as scientific." He debunked the use of "charts and curves," which refer to the past, not the future. "If the future were merely a continuation of the trends that prevailed in the past, it would not be uncertain and we would not be in need of any forecasting."[91]

Mises ends his discussion by drawing the insightful conclusion that accurate forecasting by the vast majority of businessmen and investors is *a priori* impossible and self-contradictory! "The very fact that people are putting faith in the forecast of a crash results in the annulment of the prediction: it *instantly* produces the crash," The *only* way accurate information about a future economic debacle could be helpful to the speculator is if "he *alone* has it while all other people are still *bullish*"[92] Babson practically says the same thing: "The making of forecasts tends to defeat their accuracy."[93] That is, *if they* are followed—and, of course, Babson's was largely ignored until the very end.

Mises' profound insight explains why the 1929 crash and ensuing economic contraction were unexpected by almost everyone, especially the establishment. Only the so-called monetary "cranks" and unorthodox investors—a lonely minority—could effectively predict the crash. In short, Mises' theory of forecasting is highly subjective, based on the

89. Mises was apparently not interested in investing. He once told his fiancé, "If you want a rich man, don't marry me. I am not interested in earning money. I am *writing* about money but will never have much of my own" (Margit von Mises, *My Years with Ludwig von Mises*, 24).

90. Mises, *Human Action*, 870–71.

91. Mises, "The Plight of Business Forecasting," *National Review* (April 4, 1956), 18.

92. Ibid.

93. Babson, *Actions and Reactions*, 267.

public's expectations of the future. In many ways, it is remarkably akin to a contrarian style of investing—i.e., to go against the expectations of the general public—although Mises would undoubtedly reject the more extreme form of contrarianism, such as "the majority is always wrong."[94]

Humphrey B. Neill's classic work, *The Art of Contrary Thinking*, appears to adopt a nearly complete Misesian framework. Here are some samples:

> When everyone thinks alike, everyone is likely to be wrong . . . . The contrary theory is a way of thinking . . . more of an *antidote* to general forecasting than a system *for* forecasting. In a word, it is a thinking tool, not a crystal ball . . . . One can interpret charts almost any way he wishes . . . there is *no* known method *of timing* events or trends . . . it is wiser to be early than to be late . . . a contrary opinion is usually ahead of time . . . . If the habit of contrary thinking does no more than to teach us to develop our own resources—*and to like to be alone occasionally*—it would be worthwhile . . . . So it is that economists may see their published predictions go wrong, whereas if they had kept them secret, the forecasts might well have worked out with extraordinary accuracy . . . . The nonconformist . . . cares little for precise "tops" or "bottoms"—he doesn't try to measure the exact magnitude of the ups and downs because he knows there is no reliable yardstick.[95]

Mises and Hayek were able to predict the 1929–33 crisis many years before it took effect. It took a long time because the public did not know of their prognostication or of their brand of economics. If the general public and the opinion-makers had all been followers of Mises and Hayek, the crash would have occurred sooner—or not at all (since the Federal Reserve might have stopped inflating sooner, and the stock market would never have reached its lofty levels).

But few people knew of the Austrians or paid any attention to the doomsayers. Hayek knew that the collapse was imminent once the Federal Reserve stopped inflating in late 1928 and said so in an *obscure* publication—it was not the front page of the *New York Times*. Nor did

94. For a critique of contrary investing and other forecasting methods from a Misesian point of view, see Harry Browne, *Why the Best-Laid Investment Plans Usually Go Wrong* (New York: William Morrow, 1987).
95. Humphrey B. Neill, *The Art of Contrary Thinking*, 4th ed. (1954; Caldwell, Idaho: Caxton Printers, 1980).

the gloom-and-doomers, such as Babson and Harwood, get much publicity until the near end. Once the fundamental economic factors are in place—such as the halting of monetary growth or the raising of the discount rate—the time it takes for the trend to change is often a matter of public psychology: When does the public begin to sense a change?

For Mises, "it is not our task to examine this problem," but for the speculator, it is a critical determinant.[96] Humphrey Neill emphasized, "It seems to me that the long history of economic forecasting clearly demonstrates that psychology is the missing key."[97] Contrary investing is a fashionable psychological tool for forecasting these days, but it is practically difficult to implement, as many professional "contrarians" have discovered. And, of course, if everyone says, "We are all contrarians now," it is plainly self-contradictory. The simple idea of "buying when everyone is selling" or vice versa is easier said than done—it works only during *extreme* overbought or oversold situations, as Neill points out. "The public is right *during* the trends but wrong at both ends!"[98]

Nevertheless, as long as those who understand the inner workings of the economy remain outside the mainstream of public opinion, a rational program for accurate forecasting is possible. Hayek and Harwood demonstrated this to be the case in the late 1920s. They did not speak in generalities but focused on specific factors in the market to indicate that a top was imminent: the net export of gold, the end of monetary expansion by late 1928, the raising of the discount rate in summer 1929, and the general public's frenzied interest in Wall Street in late 1929, as reflected in the high call rates on margin loans. No one, of course, was able to predict the exact date, but it became possible to say, "within the next few months" something drastic must happen. Like the birth of a child, you know the approximate time but not the precise day or hour.

Recently, especially after the inflationary blow off in the late 1970s, the public's perspective of monetary trends changed. "We are all monetarists now!" is the rally cry. It seems that everyone watches the money supply—it's front page news. In this sense, Mises may be right, and the markets react to monetary changes much more quickly. The forecaster must recognize when change is in the air and general expectations alter.

96. Mises, "The Plight of Business Forecasting," 17.

97. Neill, *The Art of Contrary Thinking*, 98.

98. Ibid., 44.

It used to be that the monetary view of economic events was largely ignored or unknown by the public at large. Thus, in the 1920s, it was relatively easy for an Austrian economist or "sound money" analyst to predict a catastrophic depression like the thirties. It was not difficult in the age of inflation and Keynesianism in the 1960s and 1970s for a handful of nontraditional monetary economists or hard-money writers to forecast higher gold prices and the dollar devaluation.

What are the prospects of a 1929-style crash when books making such predictions are on the *New York Times* bestseller list? Financial advisor Joseph Granville writes of the "reincarnation of Roger Babson in our time."[99] But what happens when there are dozens of outspoken Roger Babsons appearing on network talk shows, all predicting an economic apocalypse in the near future?

We have hardly reached the point yet where economists are saying, "We are all Austrians now!" but more and more followers of Mises and Hayek are appearing almost unexpectedly around the country. I doubt, however, if any of them will win one of Keynes' beauty contests. The political views of the Austrians and hard-money advisors will never be popular. But that is not to say that their economic analysis will be ignored. Therefore, it may be more difficult to predict the future collapse of Western civilization. Under the circumstances, we might well be reminded of Mises' hypothesis that events will not happen as we expect. If everyone reads Professor Batra's alarmist tract, *The Depression of 1990*, and follows his advice, the "crash" may well come a lot sooner than 1990, if Mises is right.[100] Then, we may all concur with Sir Isaac Newton, who said, "I can calculate the motions of heavenly bodies, but not the madness of people."[101]

---

99. Joseph Granville, *The Warning: The Coming Great Crash in the Stock Market* (New York: Freundlich Books, 1985), 304–10.

100. Ravi Batra, *The Great Depression of 1990* (New York: Simon & Schuster, 1987). Batra, a pessimistic determinist, violates all of the principles of forecasting—setting a specific date, relying on past cycles to predict the future (cycles that Batra admits do not always repeat themselves), etc. He recommends that to avoid the crisis, the government should impose a wealth tax and rescind the Reagan cuts on marginal tax rates. Indeed, such actions might well cause a depression. Incidentally, a stock market crash did in fact occur on October 19,1987, only two days after this paper was delivered at the Mises seminar in New York.

101. Quoted in Richard E. Band, *Contrary Investing* (New York: McGraw Hill, 1985), 15.

16 FINANCIAL ECONOMICS

The Austrian school of economics has only recently begun to publish articles and books about the raging debates in finance theory. Are stock prices predictable? Can investors beat the market? Is it possible for an investor to minimize risk and maximize return on his investment portfolio? What is the role of government in the securities industry? Let us consider how Austrian economic theory can provide insights into these issues.

Are Stock Prices Predictable?

There is no consensus today on the question of whether economic or financial events are forecastable. Many Wall Street practitioners, technical analysts, and financial gurus are convinced that they can predict the future prices of stocks and other financial assets. They rely on a variety of tools, including economic theories, econometric models, company fundamentals, technical chart patterns, and complicated mathematical systems, to determine the direction of markets.

Many technical chartists see each financial market as some kind of a living organism, destined like lemmings to repeat the same instinctive behavior over and over again. Other analysts, steeped in engineering, mathematics, computer science, or the natural sciences, see the market in an entirely mechanistic way, like the movement of the stars and planets. To them, the stock market is just a complicated numbers-crunching puzzle.

At the other end of the spectrum are the academic "random walkers"

Reprinted from *The Edgar Companion to Austrian Economics*, ed. by Peter J. Boettke (Edward Elgar Publishers, 1994), 231–243.

who deny that anyone on Wall Street has a crystal ball. These theoreticians of finance, including Harry Markowitz, Fischer Black, Merton Miller, William Sharpe, and Paul Samuelson, assert that prices of financial assets are completely unpredictable, at least in the short term. Their saint is Louis Bachelier, a nineteenth-century French mathematician, who stated, "The mathematical expectation of the speculator is zero."

In other words, at any given instant, the probabilities are 50 percent that stock prices will rise and 50 percent that they will fall. Bachelier also claimed that stock prices vary according to the square root of time, which bears a remarkable resemblance to molecules randomly colliding in space. This phenomenon, known as Brownian motion, came to be called "random walk" in the literature of finance (Bernstein 1992). The random walk theory asserts that stock prices are essentially random, that "'short-term' changes in stock prices cannot be predicted. Investment advisory services, earnings predictions, and complicated chart patterns are useless" (Malkiel 1990, 24).

Market Analysis and Human Action

Austrian economic theory can shed light on this never-ending debate between these two polar positions. The world of finance often appears as a sophisticated game of numbers and chart patterns, but Austrians stress that behind the mathematics and geometry are thousands of buy-and-sell transactions between individuals. In short, the financial markets represent human action.

According to Austrians, human action is fundamentally distinct from nature. Unlike animals, plants and inorganic matter, human beings possess free will and free choice. People adopt values and employ means to achieve specific ends to improve their condition. They are always evaluating their situation, changing their mind, acquiring new skills, learning from their mistakes, and sometimes overreacting. In short, human beings are neither machines nor lemmings. As such, unlike the events in nature, human action is not completely predictable. Economics, the science of human action, is inherently subjective. It is qualitative, not quantitative (Mises 1966).

In applying this dualistic epistemology, Austrians refer to any misapplication of the physical sciences to economics and finance as "scientism" (Hayek 1942). A natural scientist can predict with considerable precision the outcome of a chemical or physical experiment. But an economist will not be able to make a similar prediction about the prices and output of next year's wheat harvest. He may be able to say with some authority that prices will fall if the expected harvest is double the previous year's output, assuming other factors remain unchanged. But he may have considerable difficulty in accurately forecasting *how much and when* the price of wheat will fall.

Predicting the direction of interest rates is an even more arduous task. An increase in the supply of money may not necessarily result in a reduction in interest rates. Rates may actually rise and bond prices fall if inflationary expectations are strong enough. The outcome is uncertain, because an increase in the money supply does not simply shift the supply curve for loanable funds but may shift the demand curve as well. In any case, it is extremely difficult to forecast the direction of interest rates, let alone the magnitude of change.

The actions and emotions of people, not things, influence events and price action in the economy and the financial markets and therefore cannot be precisely measured. Sir Isaac Newton summed it up best when he said, "I can calculate the motions of heavenly bodies, but not the madness of people." Investors should be wary of any financial adviser or economist who predicts exact dates, sets precise price targets, or attempts seriously to answer the question, "What will the Dow Jones Industrial Average be on December 31st?" All such efforts are guesswork. The future of human activity is always uncertain to some extent: There are no constant numerical relations in human action, and therefore there are no coefficients that can be included in this law that are not simply arbitrary and erroneous (Rothbard 1980, x).

Austrian economists are also suspicious of technical trading systems that rely on cycles, trends or other mechanical devices linked to historical data. They take the warning, "past performance is no guarantee of future performance" very seriously. Unreliable financial theories include the Kondratieff cycle theory, the Elliott wave theory, the Dow theory, and the gold-silver ratio. These forecasting systems depend on an objective standard that is inconsistent with subjective expectations (Browne 1987).

Austrians in the Middle

Austrian theory does not suggest, however, that market action is completely unpredictable. If a choice is made *(Figure 1)* between one extreme, those who say the market is totally predictable, and the other extreme, those who say that the market is totally unpredictable, the Austrians fall somewhere in between (Garrison,1984).

Figure 1

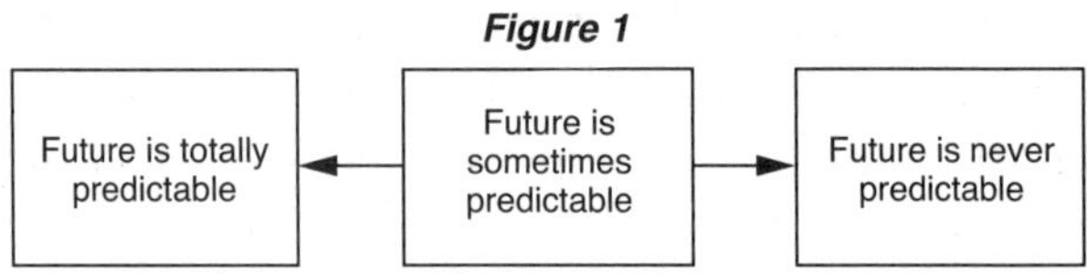

Prices of stocks and other financial assets can be predicted with some degree of accuracy because the actions of the market are always nonrandom. All financial events and prices are linked to human decision making. There is always a cause-and-effect relationship in the financial marketplace. By properly understanding and assessing the policies of a nation and the behavior of the market players, an analyst can get a sense of where the market is headed. This is where the role of the economist *qua* entrepreneur comes into play. However, because of the complex set of variables that operate in the marketplace, it is impossible to be precise about the future of market behavior. There is *always* uncertainty.

How Important Is the Stock Market?

Austrians reject the view held by many mainstream economists that the stock market has little or nothing to do with the economy and that economists can safely ignore the machinations of Wall Street. It is unfortunate that neoclassical economics has become "the economics of capitalism without capitalists, capital assets and financial markets" (Minsky 1986, 120). The stock market cannot be divorced from the industrial system; while it occasionally becomes overvalued or undervalued, it "tends to reflect the 'real' developments in the business world" (Rothbard 1983, 75). Nor is Wall Street a gigantic casino, as Keynes alleged. A share or stock is not a lottery ticket; it is partial ownership in a company (Skousen 1992b). The stock market is a major source of capital in a nation, a concept easily forgotten in a world of day trading, telephone switching, butterfly spreads, and the OEX.

In the long run, the profitability of individual companies determines the performance of the stock market and, in a profound way, reflects the robustness of a nation's economy. A nation's economic and political policies have tremendous influence on the direction of the markets. Stock prices will tend to perform best in countries that provide a stable legal system, enforce property rights, impose low taxes on investment assets, minimize commercial regulations, and provide the broadest degree of freedom in the production, distribution, and consumption of goods and services. Wise investors will find the best investment opportunities in the most stable and free economies, in which stock exchanges are well developed, and will avoid investing in countries with a high degree of socialism and government intervention.

In addition, investors can gain or lose as a result of changes in tax rates, money supply, regulations, and other forms of government policy. Such shifts in economic policy can dramatically affect the value of stocks, bonds, real estate, and other financial assets. The investor who better understands the significance of these changes will profit the most. For example, in the late 1960s, it became apparent to a few astute investors that Western governments could not maintain their policies of fixed exchange rates and an official gold price of $35 per ounce. Investors who recognized early the effects of inflation on the financial markets profited handsomely (Skousen 1988).

Short-Term Forecasting

But what about the movement in stock prices from day to day or week to week? While the short-term behavior of prices is much more difficult to predict, there are guidelines to watch for. In studying financial history, investment analysts may recognize patterns of market psychology. For example, at the bottom of a long bear market, the public frequently appears pessimistic. Contrarians and value-seeking investors look for these "sold-out" conditions to buy.

At the top, the public is frequently overly enthusiastic, and intelligent speculators look for opportunities to sell. Speculators and analysts often rely on price patterns, volume figures, and other technical data to assess the psychological attitudes of the general public to determine tops and bottoms of markets. Thus, some forms of technical analysis may be valuable to the market forecaster as long they reflect "human nature" and the psychology of investors.

In addition, financial forecasters can profit immensely if most other analysts and investors misread or misunderstand the fundamental inner workings of the economy, the markets, and the effects of government policy, or use an inappropriate trading system. Naive and misguided investors can create a lot of "noise" in the marketplace, giving wise investors an opportunity to get in early before the public realizes it has misread the situation. As the old Wall Street adage says, "In the land of the blind, the one-eyed man is king."

For example, in the 1980s, Europe established an exchange rate mechanism (ERM) between major currencies. After a decade, it became apparent to many currency traders and international bankers that the ERM, as all forms of price controls, could not last, despite the efforts of central banks. Strong currencies such as the German mark were undervalued and weak currencies such as the British pound were overvalued. Speculators who took advantage of the situation profited handsomely when the ERM collapsed in September 1992. The public, who had little understanding of the economics underlying the ERM, lost out.

Another example: In the early 1970s most investors continued to hold bonds in the face of an easy money policy. Meanwhile, shrewd bondholders sold their position in anticipation of rising price inflation and an eventual fall in bond prices. The general public, not recognizing how the inflation transmission mechanism worked, lost out when price inflation surfaced and bond prices fell. Thus, the market rewards those investors who understand sound economics and punishes those who do not. However, forecasters must not assume that market psychology always remains the same. In a very real sense, each financial event is unique. The stock market action of 1987–90 was not a repeat of 1929–33. Both began with a crash but performed quite differently afterward. There are always new factors involved in each financial event, many of which are difficult to anticipate.

Moreover, as rational expectations theory notes, the public can learn from its mistakes and become more knowledgeable about the economy and the markets. The next time the government adopts an easy money policy, the public, remembering the past, may react right away and sell bonds, reducing the profit opportunities for nimble speculators. Finally, because the factors affecting the market vary over time, it is difficult to predict when the trend will change. For instance, after a long bear market, an investor may not know whether a price rise is the beginning of a bull market or just a bear market rally. Such entrepreneurial decision making is more of an art than a science.

Modern Portfolio Theory

Modern portfolio theory (MPT) is an academic approach developed by professors of finance to assist individuals and institutions in measuring risk and in selecting a portfolio that maximizes their return, given the level of risk they wish to take. Three financial economists—Harry Markowitz, Merton Miller, and William Sharpe—received the Nobel Prize in economics in 1990 for their efforts to quantify risk in stock and portfolio selection. These finance professors have reached three main conclusions: (1) rates of return are related directly to investment risk; (2) investors should not try to beat the market; and (3) investors should diversify their portfolios as much as possible. What can Austrian economics say about these assertions?

First, MPT states that, to induce an investor to bear more risk, the expected return must be higher. Return is related to risk. Wildcatters will not drill for oil if all they can hope for is a return equal to a bank savings account. Investors will not buy growth stocks if the expected return is no greater than blue-chip stocks that pay high dividends. Clearly, this assertion is based on common sense. However, mainstream methods of measuring risk and uncertainty in the market are often suspect. Beta is considered the most useful gauge to measure risk against expected return. Beta is a statistic created to estimate a stock's volatility beyond the general ups and downs of the whole market. By measuring a stock's volatility relative to the entire market, beta is intended to estimate systematic risk relative to general market cycles.

The capital asset pricing model (CAPM) is a technique designed to help investors select securities with expected rates of return that match the risk investors wish to take. In order to achieve higher rates of return, CAPM calls for investors to select a broad portfolio of high-beta stocks. Initial studies showed that over the long run, the rate of return is higher for investments with high-beta coefficients. However, recent studies have raised serious doubts about CAPM and the usefulness of beta coefficients in estimating risks. Some studies indicate that the low-beta stocks have at times outperformed high-beta stocks. (Malkiel 1990, 238–63).

Austrian economic theory raises doubts about the CAPM as a reliable model for stock selection. There is no guarantee that companies whose stocks have been traditionally volatile will offer a higher rate of return in the next bull market, or that low-beta stocks will underperform the market. The underlying assumption behind CAPM is that beta coefficients are relatively constant throughout market cycles, a violation of the principle that history never quite repeats itself. There is no reason why a stock's beta cannot change radically over time, as the result of modifications in company management, the product line, or customer demand.

Risk and the Structure of Production: an Austrian Contribution

Finance professors dissatisfied with beta and the CAPM have searched for alternative theories. The arbitrage price theory (APT), developed by Stephen A. Ross, is a popular alternative method of measuring systematic risk in various sectors of the securities market according to changes in inflation, the yield curve and the business cycle. Austrian economics suggests that further advances could be made along the lines of what might be called an "intertemporal pricing model" (IPM). IPM disaggregates stocks into sectors according to their place along the intertemporal transformation process. The model predicts that stock prices will tend to be more volatile in industries located in the earlier stages of processing and less volatile in industries located in the final stages of consumption.

According to IPM, the time structure of production and consumption pervades the entire economy and the financial markets. The Austrian theory of the business cycle asserts that changes in the money supply, interest rates, and government policy affect the structure of the economy and the financial markets systematically (Rothbard 1983). When the government artificially lowers interest rates and expands the money supply, it creates an artificial boom in the capital goods industries and in capital assets.

Industries engaged in the early stages of production tend to expand more rapidly than industries engaged in the later stages of production. Unfinished higher order goods have a longer period of production, are more capital intensive, and are more interest rate sensitive than most lower-order consumer goods. Equally, when real interest rates rise and the economy contracts, the capital goods industries tend to shrink more rapidly than the consumer goods industries.

We can see this phenomenon using the aggregate production structure (APS) of an economy, shown in Figure 2, below. APS measures the annual gross output of all stages of production, from natural resources to final consumer goods. The vertical axis measures the time it takes for goods and services to be produced, from the earliest raw commodity stage to the final consumer stage, while the horizontal axis measures the gross output or revenue of each stage of production.

Figure 2

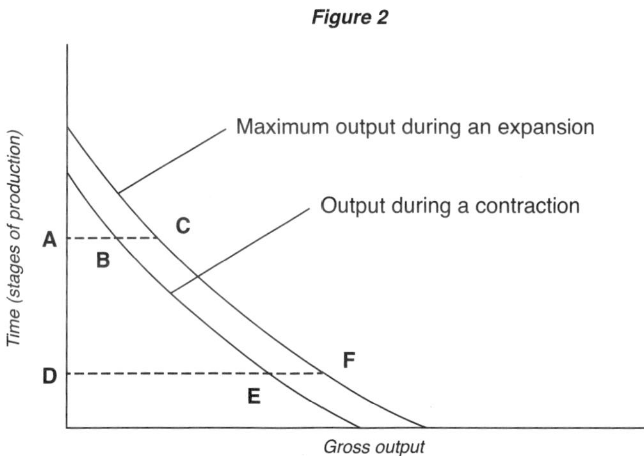

The APS illustrated in Figure 2 demonstrates what happens to the economy during the business cycle. Throughout the cycle, the early stages (capital goods industries) tend to expand and contract on a magnitude much greater than that experienced by the later stages (consumer goods industries). Note that *BC/AC* is substantially smaller than *EF/DF*. Historical studies confirm that output, prices, employment, and inventories in capital goods industries tend to be more volatile than those in consumer goods industries (Skousen 1990).

This Austrian insight can be applied to the securities market. The IPM explains why the stock prices of mining, manufacturing, and other early-stage companies tend to be more volatile than those of retail and other consumer-oriented firms. Prices of mining stocks usually fluctuate more than those of utilities or grocery store companies. Even within industries, the stage of processing to which a publicly traded company belongs matters a great deal. Prices of junior oil stocks, which engage in early stage exploration and development, tend to fluctuate more than those of major oil companies that sell fuel at the pump.

The IPM can also explain apparent exceptions to this phenomenon. For example, car and residential housing stocks are considered retail stocks, yet they are cyclical in nature. This is because cars and housing are durable goods that take years to be used up. Therefore, car and housing stocks are just as sensitive to changes in interest rates as are mining and natural resource stocks. According to IPM, stock volatility is a function of the total period of production and consumption (Skousen 1990).

Can Investors Beat the Market?

The second principal debate in finance is whether individuals are smart enough to outperform the stock market averages consistently. Proponents of the efficient market theory (EMT) assert that it is next to impossible to beat the market over the long term. According to the strong version of EMT, the stock market is so efficient that all new information is quickly discounted in the financial markets: No one can outperform the market except by occasional luck.

Proponents point to numerous studies indicating that most professional money managers, stockbrokers, and investment advisers are unable to beat the averages or to perform better than a randomly selected portfolio of stocks. Nor can security analysts accurately predict earnings by major corporations over a one-year or five-year period (Malkiel 1990). Since bull and bear markets are unforecastable, the EMT proponents recommend buying a large portfolio of stocks (or a stock index fund) and holding for the long term. Trading is considered counterproductive, not only because of transaction costs and taxes but also because it cannot improve upon the averages.

Proponents of EMT raise serious doubts about the possibility of either a "high return/low risk" or a "low return/high risk" investment. Figure 3 demonstrates the possibilities.

Line *AB* represents the average risk-reward ratio of various investments. As return increases, so does the risk. Point C represents an undervalued situation, that is, a higher return compared to other investments with similar risk (high return/low risk). According to the EMT, this condition cannot last because investors will recognize the advantage of this investment and rush out to buy it, thus driving up the price. The risk stays the same, but

Figure 3

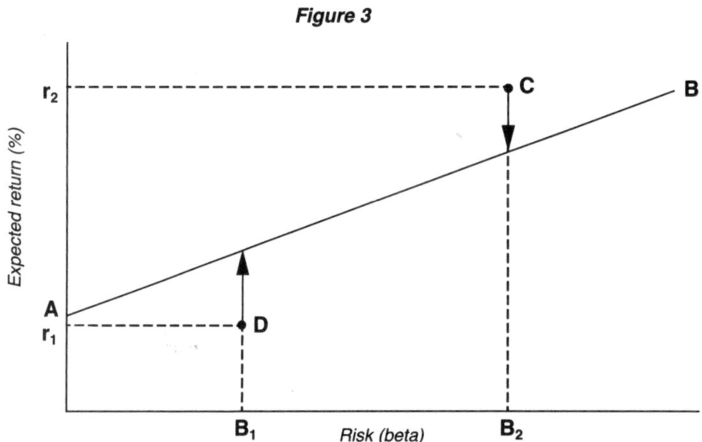

the higher price reduces the return for new buyers, thus bringing the risk-reward ratio into line with other investments. The same principle applies to point D, an overvalued investment (low return/high risk). Investors, recognizing the situation, will sell the investment. The risk remains the same, but the lower price makes the asset more appealing and the return higher, thus bringing the risk-reward ratio into line with other investments.

Once again, the Austrians take a middle ground between those who say that the market is always and everywhere efficient, and those who say that the market is always in a state of irrational disequilibrium. The market is neither perfect nor broken. The truth lies somewhere in between (Garrison 1984). While containing much truth, the EMT does not tell the whole story. In some ways, the strong version of EMT is the perfect competition model of the financial markets (Skousen 1991). The primary objection to EMT is that it assumes that the entrepreneur qua arbitrager always moves the markets rapidly and immediately toward equilibrium. It denies that the entrepreneur can create new disequilibrium conditions or that disequilibrium conditions last long enough for investors to make consistent above-average returns.

According to Austrians, the entrepreneur is the central figure in the economic system. The investor qua entrepreneur has the uncanny ability to see things that other analysts do not see, to find temporarily undervalued stocks and to get out of overvalued investments. The fact that many money managers have been able to outwit other market participants for decades (Arnold Bernhard and his Value Line Investment Survey, John Templeton and his Templeton Funds, Peter Lynch and his Magellan

Fund, Warren Buffett and his Berkshire Hathaway Partnership, as well as many commodity traders) is proof that superior speculators do exist.

In the above illustration, Austrians would ask: *Who* are the first investors to discover point C (undervalued) and buy and point D (overvalued) and sell? These alert entrepreneurs are able to profit by acting before everyone else. MPT fails to explain how undervalued (high return/low risk) and overvalued (low return/high risk) situations arise in the first place. Clearly, a more complete theory of finance must explain how above-average profitable opportunities arise and not simply how they disappear.

Austrian economics may offer a more dynamic theory of investment markets. Schumpeter emphasizes how entrepreneurs upset the supply or demand factors and create an above-average investment opportunity as the market shifts *away* from equilibrium conditions (Schumpeter 1950). Kirzner suggests that alert entrepreneurs discover an above-average investment and through competitive bidding, move *toward* equilibrium conditions (Kirzner 1973). Oskar Morgenstern, an Austrian economist who later worked closely with John von Neumann and Clive Granger on the theory of games and finance, concludes that entrepreneurs are so successful in moving prices rapidly toward equilibrium that markets can be regarded as highly efficient. In fact, Morgenstern was a firm believer in the EMT and the random movement of stock prices (Granger and Morgenstern 1970). While Morgenstern considered himself a follower of Menger and Böhm-Bawerk, his spectral analysis of stock prices clearly falls outside the Austrian middle ground.

EMT is, of course, not without merit. Clearly, everyone cannot beat the market because everyone is the market. For the same reason, it is impossible for everyone to get out at the top or get in at the bottom. Accurate forecasting by the vast majority of businessmen and investors is a priori self-contradictory. Suppose, for example, that everyone expects a crash. The result will be a crash *before* the time everyone expects it: "The very fact that people are putting faith in the forecast of a crash results in the annulment of the prediction: it instantly produces the crash" (Mises 1956). What is left out of the EMT equation is the role of a few investors who have the unique capacity to act in a way opposite to the rest of the public.

While it is impossible for the vast majority of investors to outperform the market, to get out at the top, or get in at the bottom, a small minority of speculators can consistently outperform everyone else. These superior forecasters have a better understanding of market psychology and the way the economy really works; therefore, they are able to stay ahead of all the others. But they tend to be loners (Neill 1980). Of course, there are no guarantees that a top-performing money manager or adviser will stay ahead of the pack. Human nature is such that it is easy to fall from the top. Many shrewd money managers have discovered undervalued gems in one year, only to be disappointed in the next.

Is There an Ideal Investment Portfolio?

MPT supporters maintain that broad diversification reduces risk and increases the overall return in an investment portfolio. The more diversified the portfolio, the less volatile the return will be and the better the chance of profiting from unexpected market advances. According to their research, it is better to buy stocks across several industries, not just within an industry; better to buy a stock index fund rather than a dozen stocks; better to buy a broad mix of stocks, bonds, and money market funds than just stocks; and, finally, better to buy stock, bonds, real estate, gold, and other liquid investments both here and abroad. According to MPT, an internationally diversified mixed asset portfolio is the ideal low-risk portfolio.

Once again, however, the MPT process of selecting an ideal portfolio relies on past performance rather than sound economic analysis to make its case. For instance, in the early 1980s, many professors of finance recommended that institutions add real estate to their portfolios because it had a long record of rising prices and showed very little volatility. As a result, institutions invested billions of dollars in commercial and residential property, only to see real estate prices fall sharply in value as the economy and government policies shifted in the 1980s.

The Role of Government

Does government have a legitimate role in protecting investors against bad investment decisions and potential fraud? What should the role of government be in regulating the securities industry? Federal and state securities regulations began in earnest in the 1930s and 1940s, following the 1929 stock market crash. Supporters of regulation alleged that securities fraud and manipulations by syndicates and pools were widespread during the Roaring Twenties. Congress passed a series of laws requiring the registration of publicly traded companies, the licensing of brokers and investment advisers, the imposition of criminal and civil penalties on a variety of "fraudulent" securities activities, and the establishment of the Securities and Exchange Commission (SEC). States also passed "blue sky" laws requiring similar measures at a state level. Later, the Commodities Futures Trading Commission (CFTC) was created to regulate futures markets.

However, it is important to point out that the New York Stock Exchange and major brokerage houses had already begun to take measures prior to the Security Act of 1933 to eliminate fraud and stock manipulation. Milton Friedman and other free-market advocates have long emphasized the importance of private industry in providing methods of monitoring and controlling ethical standards in industry and commerce (Friedman 1962). There is no reason why stringent ethical standards cannot be established by stock exchanges, brokerage houses, the National Association of Securities Dealers, and publicly traded corporations. Furthermore, the financial media play an important role in educating the investment public and exposing fraud, abuse, insider trading, and other inappropriate activities.

Even when those in the financial industry deem government rules and regulations necessary, the industry should consider the high costs of regulation, both apparent and hidden. For example, federal and state registration expenses are so high that many small-growth companies find it prohibitive to take their companies public in the United States. State regulators impose burdensome regulations and sometimes limit the types of investments available to individual investors. The existence of the SEC and state regulatory agencies also creates a false sense of security, giving the impression that brokers, investment advisers, and mutual funds are less likely to defraud investors or lead them astray (Skousen 1992a).

Summary

According to the Austrian school, the financial markets reflect the actions and emotions of individual investors and institutional managers. As such, the stock market represents their assessment of the future. Austrians believe that the securities markets will perform best when enlightened individuals are given the freedom to make their own investment decisions. Bureaucratic restrictions, burdensome regulations, and high tax rates will tend to stifle the financial markets.

Stock prices, as all prices in the market economy, are determined by human decision making, and therefore are never random. Austrians rely primarily on fundamental analysis, including political and economic factors, to determine future prices of investments, and they use technical analysis only to the extent that it represents the psychology of investors. However, because investors can change their mind and are constantly acquiring new information, it is difficult to predict the future of stock prices. Austrians emphasize the unique ability of the entrepreneur in forecasting and profiting in the competitive marketplace and are critical of academic theories that ignore the role of risk-taking entrepreneurs in the investment markets and their ability to predict the future and earn above-average returns.

Bibliography

Bernstein, Peter L. *Capital Ideas: The Improbable Origins of Modern Wall Street*. New York: Free Press, 1992.

Browne, Harry. *Why the Best-Laid Investment Plans Usually Go Wrong*. New York: William Morrow, 1987.

Friedman, Milton. *Capitalism and Freedom*. Chicago: University of Chicago Press, 1962.

Garrison, Roger W. 1984. "Time and Money: The Universals of Macroeconomic Thinking," *Journal of Macroeconomics*, spring.

Granger, Clive W.J. and Oskar Morgenstern. *Predictability of Stock Market Prices*. Lexington, Mass.: Heath Lexington, 1970.

Hayek, Friedrich A. 1942. "Scientism and the study of society", *Economica*, IX, 35, August.

Kirzner, Israel M. *Competition and Entrepreneurship*. Chicago: University of Chicago Press, 1973.

Malkiel, Burton G. *A Random Walk Down Wall Street*. 5th ed., New York: W. W. Norton, 1990 [1973].

Norton. Minsky, Hyman P. *Stabilizing an Unstable Economy*. New Haven, Conn.: Yale University Press, 1986.

Mises, Ludwig von. "The Plight of Business Forecasting", *National Review*, April 4, 1956.

Mises, Ludwig von. *Human Action*. 3rd ed.. Chicago: Regnery, 1966 [1949].

Neill, Humphrey B. *The Art of Contrary Thinking*. 4th ed.. Caldwell, Idaho: Caxton Printers, 1980 [1954].

Rothbard, Murray N. "Foreword," in James B. Ramsey, *Economic Forecasting—Models or Markets?* San Francisco: Cato Institute, 1980.

Rothbard, Murray N. *America's Great Depression*. 4th ed.. New York: Richardson and Snyder, 1983 [1963].

Schumpeter, Joseph A. *Capitalism, Socialism and Democracy*. 3rd ed. New York: Harper & Row, 1950 [1942].

Skousen, Mark. "Murray Rothbard As Investment Advisor." In Walter Block and Llewellyn

H. Rockwell, Jr. (eds) *Man, Economy, and Liberty: Essays in Honor of Murray N. Rothbard*. Auburn, Ala.: The Ludwig von Mises Institute, 1988, 151–74.

Skousen, Mark. *The Structure of Production*, New York: New York University Press, 1990.

Skousen, Mark. "The Economist As Investment Advisor." *Economics on Trial*. Homewood, Ill: Business One Irwin, 1991, 255–73.

Skousen, Mark. *The Investors Bible: Mark Skousen's Principles of Investment*. Potomac, Maryland: Phillips Publishing, 1992a.

Skousen, Mark. "Keynes As a Speculator: A Critique of Keynesian Investment Theory." In Mark Skousen (ed.) *Dissent on Keynes*. New York: Praeger, 1992b, 161–9.

Skousen, Mark. "Who Predicted the 1929 Crash?" In Jeffrey M. Herbener (ed.) *The Meaning of Ludwig von Mises*. Auburn, Ala.: The Ludwig von Mises Institute, 1993, 247–83.

17 A TALE OF TWO DOLLARS

"Government is the only agency that can take a valuable commodity like paper, slap some ink on it, and make it totally worthless."

—Ludwig von Mises

"No state shall . . . coin money; emit bills of credit; make anything but gold and silver coins a tender in the payment of debts . . . . "

—U.S. Constitution, Article I, Section 10

"Too many people miss the silver lining because they're expecting gold."

—Maurice Setter (English football player)

"What woman, having ten pieces of silver, if she loses one piece, does not light a candle and sweep the house, and seek diligently til she find it? And when she found it, she called her friends and neighbors together, saying, 'Rejoice with me; for I have found the piece which I have lost.'"

—Luke 15:8–9

A Tale of Two Dollars

The following graph shows the value of two types of dollars issued by the United State government as legal tender.

Reprinted by permission of Investment Rarities, Inc., 7850 Metro Parkway, Minneapolis, Minnesota 55425, 1-800-328-1860.

In 1960, both types of dollars were equally valued at $1.

However, their fate over the next 50 years is entirely different. See Figure 1 below.

As you can see, Dollar #1 has seen its purchasing power gradually deteriorate, so that after 50 years, it is worth only $0.10.

Dollar #2 has done just the opposite. In 50 years, its value has gradually risen and is now worth 18 times its original $1 value.

What's the difference?

Dollar #1 is the paper dollar, the Federal Reserve Note, the irredeemable paper money that we use in everyday transactions.

Dollar #2 is the American Eagle one-ounce silver dollar issued annually by the United States Mint. The price of silver has been volatile, but the long-term trend is up dramatically. In 1960, one ounce of silver was worth approximately $1. Today, the American eagle silver dollar, which contains one ounce of pure silver, is worth approximately $18.

Thus, the silver dollar has increased 18 fold in 50 years, or an average compounded rate of 6 percent per year.

A similar study can be done between the $20 Federal Reserve Note and the $20 double-eagle gold coin minted between 1850 and 1933. They were both equal to $20, until the United States went off the gold standard in 1933. Since then, the $20 paper money has lost 95 percent of its value, while the $20 gold coin is worth more than $1,000.

Why the difference?

Figure 1
Real Value (CPI adjusted)—Five-Year Price Average

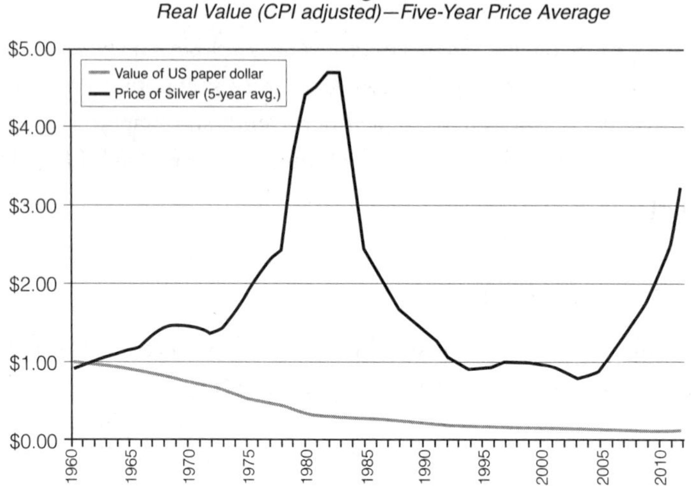

The Dangers of a Fiat Money Standard

As an economist, I can answer that with one word: Discipline. Or lack of discipline!

When a country goes off the gold and silver standard, there's a tendency by the government to print too many dollars. Monetary authorities lack the discipline to limit the growth of the money supply. Congress has too many pressures to spend more than it taxes and runs deficits. And the Federal Reserve indirectly finances these deficits.

Minting new dollar bills is easy and inexpensive. It costs only a few pennies to print a dollar bill for $1, $5, $10, $20, or $100.

Since 1960, paper money currency in circulation has increased from $32 billion to $913.5 billion. That's a 7 percent annual compounded rate, more than double the annual real growth rate of the economy.

When too much money is chasing too few goods, the result is price inflation and the loss of purchasing power. Not surprisingly, the paper dollar or Federal Reserve Note has gradually lost value since going off the hard-money standard.

As a woman said at the New Orleans conference in November 1974: "My grandfather took the first [paper] dollar he ever made put it in a frame he bought with a dime. Now the frame is worth a dollar and the dollar is worth a dime."

Despite all the talk of "fighting inflation," the fact of the matter is that the government isn't very enthusiastic about controlling prices; it's too much of a temptation to inflate the money supply under a fiat money standard.

To understand this tale of two dollars, one paper and the other silver, let's take a short survey of how it all came about.

The Benefits of the Classical Gold Standard

In the nineteenth century, the major industrial powers of the world desired a stable international currency for trade and adopted the international gold standard. Some countries, such as the United States, adopted both a gold standard and a silver standard (known as "bimetalism").

Under the international gold standard, the American dollar, the British pound, and other currencies were defined in terms of ounces of gold. For example, in 1900, under Queen Victoria, the British defined the pound sterling as ¼ troy ounce of gold. Meanwhile, under President

McKinley, the United States defined the American dollar as 1/20 of a troy ounce of gold. Thus, the exchange rate between the British pound and the U.S. dollar was fixed: a British pound was equal to $5.

The classic international gold standard—where all the major currencies were linked to one another in terms of gold—lasted from 1815 until 1914, when World War I broke out.

The gold standard had many benefits. As Murray N. Rothbard states:

> We can look back upon the "classical" gold standard, the Western world of the nineteenth and early twentieth centuries, as the literal and metaphorical Golden Age .... The international gold standard meant that the benefits of having one money medium were extended throughout the world. One of the reasons for the growth and prosperity of the United States has been the fact that we have enjoyed one money throughout the large areas of the country .... One money facilitates freedom of trade, investment, and travel throughout the trading and monetary area, with the consequent growth of specialization and the international division of labor (*What Has Government Done to Our Money?*, 4th ed., 1990, 91–92).

Milton Friedman and Anna Schwartz wrote the following about the classic gold standard:

> The blind, undersigned, and quasi-automatic working of the gold standard turned out to produce a greater measure of predictability and regularity—perhaps because its discipline was impersonal and inescapable—than did deliberate and conscious control exercised within institutional arrangements intended to promote stability (*A Monetary History of the United States, 1867–1960*, 1963, 10).

The United States Also Adopted the Silver Standard

But before gold became the principal monetary metal, the world, including the United States, had a long tradition in using silver coins for its commercial transactions and people's banking and savings needs.

Silver coins were the most common currency among the Greeks, the Romans, and the British. The British pound was, in fact, the pound sterling, referring to sterling silver.

The dollar originated with the Spanish dollar. The Spanish dollar *(see below)* originated from a high-quality one-ounce silver coin produced by a Bohemian count in Joachim's Valley in Germany. These were reputable coins known for their uniformity and fineness. The Spanish called them "thalers"; in colonial America, they became "dollars." The Spanish dollars were reales and cut into eight parts, or "pieces of eight," and thus "two bits" was a colloquial term in the nineteenth and twentieth century to designate a quarter of a U. S. dollar.

Figure 2: Spanish silver dollar
Silver 8 real coin of Charles III of Spain

The Story of the American Silver Dollar

The United States Mint (located in Philadelphia, New Orleans, Denver, Carson City, and San Francisco) began making its own silver dollars in 1794 and has continued on and off ever since then.

The U.S. Mint has produced millions of silver dollars, especially the Seated Liberty dollars (1836–73), the Morgan silver dollars (1878–1904, 1921), and the Peace dollars (1921–1935).

Figure 3
Morgan silver dollars (left) and Peace silver dollars (right)

Each silver dollar contains 0.773 troy ounces of silver and are strikingly beautifully designed.

Unfortunately, a large percentage of silver dollars have been melted down for a variety of reasons. Approximately only 17 percent of the Morgan silver dollars remain after the U.S. Mint melted down 270 million silver dollars in 1918.

Paper Versus Hard Money

The Founding Fathers, especially Thomas Jefferson, were suspicious of paper money after suffering from runaway inflation during the American Revolution. The colonists' money, the Continental, lost more than 90 percent of its value during the revolution. "Not worth a Continental" was a common phrase.

The Founders inserted this clause in the U.S. Constitution in Article 1, Section 10: "No state shall . . . coin money; emit bills of credit; make anything but gold and silver coins a tender in the payment of debts . . . ."

However, it was not long before the convenience of paper money and banknotes became commonplace. These various forms of paper currency were either (a) promises to pay gold or silver on demand, or (b) warehouse receipts of gold or silver on deposit with the banks.

The U.S. government issued its own notes backed by gold and silver and, during the Civil War, issued notes backed solely by the good faith and credit of the United States without any specie backing. These notes were called "greenbacks" because they were printed in green.

Figure 4
$20 gold certificate

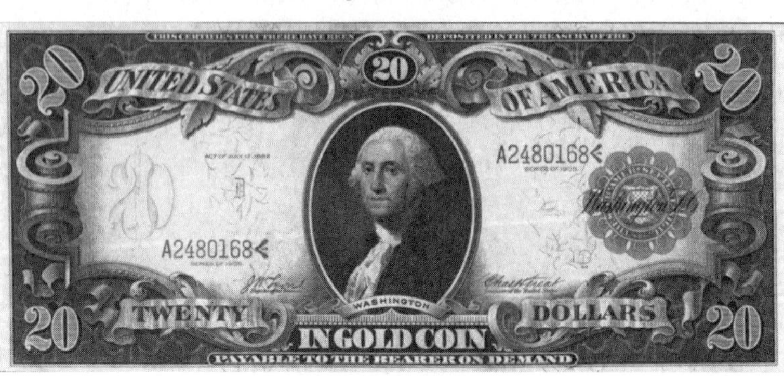

The U.S. Mint Issues Gold and Silver Certificates

After the Civil War, the U.S. went back on the gold and silver standard and began issuing two kinds of currency: the gold certificate and the silver certificate.

The gold certificate was a warehouse receipt and a contract between the U.S. Treasury and the owner of the certificate. The Treasury issued it between 1882 and 1933. *(See image to the left.)*

The front of each gold certificate stated in bold lettering:

"This certificates that there has been deposited in the Treasury of the United States of America TWENTY DOLLARS IN GOLD COIN payable to the bearer on demand."

That meant that for every $20 gold certificate the government issued, the U.S. Treasury had to have on hand a $20 gold coin, such as the Saint-Gaudens double eagle. *(See below.)*

People consider the Saint-Gaudens double eagle one of the most beautiful coins ever minted, and I highly recommend buying them.

Figure 5
Saint-Gaudens double eagle U.S gold coin

The Silver Certificate and Silver Dollars

The United States was also on a silver standard from 1878 until 1933. When a nation is on both a gold and silver standard, it is known as "bimetalism."

As with the gold certificate, the U.S. Treasury issued the silver certificate, backed by silver dollars and served as a contract between the U.S. government and its citizens.

Each silver certificate stated: "This certificates that there has been deposited in the Treasury of the United States of America ONE SILVER DOLLAR payable to the bearer on demand."

Figure 6
$1 silver dollar certificates

That meant that for every $1 silver certificate the government issued, the U.S. Treasury had to have on hand a silver dollar (such as a Morgan or Peace dollar shown in Figure 3) to pay anyone who demanded it.

The Meaning of Honest Money: My Fight With Milton Friedman

The gold and silver certificate program was an excellent sound money program because it severely limited the ability of the government to print money. Under a gold and silver certificate program, the only way the government could issue more paper currency (gold and silver certificates) was to mint more gold coins and silver dollars—an extremely expensive proposition.

Historically, inflation was not a problem when the US and the world was on a gold and silver standard.

In the late 1990s, I had dinner with a group of friends that included Milton Friedman, the great free-market economist and monetary authority. We were both speakers at the famous New Orleans Gold Conference run by gold bug Jim Blanchard. During the dinner at Commander's Palace, Milton turned to me and asked, "Why are gold bugs so passionate about gold and silver?"

I pulled out from my pocket a gold certificate and read him the contract between the government and its citizens. I said, "We're passionate about gold and silver because it represents HONEST MONEY. Under a gold and silver standard, paper currency is a legally binding contract between government and citizen that assured the public that its money would be not lose its purchasing power."

I went on to say, "So, what kind of contract exists today between the government and its citizens? Milton, do you have a $20 bill?" He reached into his pocket and handed over a $20 bill. "See, the contract has completely disappeared. Now it says only 'Federal Reserve Note.' And the Fed doesn't even pay interest!" Then I paused and said, "Milton, this $20 bill isn't worth the paper it's printed on."

And I tore it up! I ripped up Milton Friedman's $20 Federal Reserve Note into a half-dozen pieces.

Suddenly, the atmosphere changed. Milton turned to me and angrily said, "Mark, you had no right to destroy my property!" His wife Rose, who was with us, chimed in, "Yes, Mark, you shouldn't have done that. That was Milton's private property." My friends Gary North and Van Simmons stared in horror and didn't say a word. Milton's voice rose, and other dinner guests looked over at us and could see emotions rising. At this point, I worried that my relationship with the Friedmans was quickly ending that very night. Finally, I said, "Well, I suppose you want your money back?"

Milton and Rose insisted heartily. So I reached into my pocket and pulled out a $20 Saint-Gaudens double eagle gold coin! I handed the gold coin to Milton and said, "Okay, here's your $20!"

He looked startled and stared at the gold coin. I thought he would be pleased, but I was wrong. Suddenly, he handed it back to me. "I don't want it!"

I gulped, struggling for words. "But Milton, it's a gift. Here, take it. It's a $20 gold coin, worth a lot more than a $20 Federal Reserve Note."

"No," he repeated emphatically. "I don't want it."

After an agonizing pregnant pause, I finally figured out a solution. Setting the gold coin aside, I reached into my pocket, pulled out a fresh new $20 paper note, and handed it to him. "There, okay, will this help?"

He calmed down and took the $20 bill, and things quieted down. Finally, I gathered up some courage and brought out the gold coin again. "Look," as I handed it over to him again. "Look at the date." He examined the coin again. "Oh, 1912—my birth year!" he laughed haltingly. Rose looked on and smiled.

I explained that the entire evening was a setup, an opportunity for me to give him a Saint-Gaudens double eagle gold coin minted in the year he was born. The coin was in a PCGS certificated plastic container with the words, "To the Golden Milton Friedman." I told Milton and

Rose that my friend across the table, Van Simmons, was a coin dealer and had gone to great lengths to find a 1912 double eagle, which was rare. Van added that it had been FedExed overnight from Switzerland and arrived only an hour before dinner. I think only then did the Friedmans recognize what was going on. The next morning they came up and thanked me for the coin and my gesture of appreciation.

Throughout the evening, Gary North—a well-known economic historian and gold bug—said nothing. But in the morning, he came up to me at the conference and said something profound. "Mark, I've thought all night about what happened at dinner at Commander's Palace. You and I have an ideology of gold. And Milton has an ideology of paper money. Mark, last night you attacked his ideology!"

It was quite an unforgettable evening, that's for sure.

The Decline and Fall of the Hard-Money Standard, 1914–1971

Tragically, the forces of inflation and deception overcame the demands for honest money. The gold and silver standard gradually fell apart after the establishment of the Federal Reserve System, America's central bank, in December 1913.

In 1914, with the start of the World War I, the Bureau of Printing and Engraving (an arm of the U.S. Treasury) started printing Federal Reserve Notes. Like the "greenbacks" issued during the Civil War, the Federal Reserve Notes were issued without any backing by gold or silver. They were made legal tender for all debts, public and private, so that individuals and businesses could not demand that payment for goods and services be made in gold or silver coins or gold or silver certificates.

Notes normally pay interest, but Federal Reserve Notes never did.

Instead of being printed in gold, the Federal Reserve Notes were printed in green.

In 1933, President Franklin Delano Roosevelt took the United States off the gold standard. He devalued the dollar (from $20 per ounce to $35 per ounce) and forced Americans to turn in their gold coins to the Treasury. No more gold coins or silver dollars were minted, although smaller coins (half dollars, quarters, dimes, nickels, and copper pennies) and paper currency were produced.

The gold certificate program ended entirely, but the silver certificate program continued—for a while. Americans could continue to save, spend, and trade silver dollars and paper currency (both silver certificates and Federal Reserve Notes circulated in the economy).

The transition was subtle. First, the U.S. Treasury changed the contract on the silver certificates. Instead of "one silver dollar," the contract read, "This certifies that the Treasury of the United States will pay the bearer on demand ONE DOLLAR IN SILVER."

"One dollar in silver" is not the same as "one silver dollar."

The Great Silver Shortage of 1964–65

As the U.S. continued to inflate the currency and the money supply during and after World War II, the price of silver gradually rose. Since silver dollars contain 0.77 ounces of silver, if the price of silver exceeded $1.29, the silver metal in the silver dollar would be worth more than a dollar. Speculators could melt the silver dollar and get more than $1 for their efforts.

And that's exactly what happened in the mid-1960s. As Figure 1 (the first graph) shows, the price of silver was around $1 in 1960, but by 1964, it has risen above $1.29. Throughout the 1950s, silver dollars regularly circulated, but by the early 1960s, investors started hoarding silver dollars, and then half dollars, quarters, and dimes—all 90 percent silver—started disappearing.

The U.S. Mint was forced to dramatically increase its production of coins, and by 1965, threw in the towel and removed all of the silver content from quarters and dimes (replacing them with nickel and other metals).

During this time, the hard-money movement began, and investors started buying and storing bags of "junk" silver (referring to silver dollars, halves, quarters, and dimes minted prior to 1965). Millions of these coins were also melted down into bullion.

In 1968, the U.S. Treasury ended the silver certificate program entirely, and American citizens could no longer turn in their certificates for silver.

1971: Going off the Gold Standard and Entering the Wilderness Years

During this time, the last vestiges of the international gold standard ended. Under FDR, Americans could no longer own gold, but foreigners could still buy gold from the U.S. Treasury at $35 per ounce. But because of the inflationary policies of the U.S. government, gold started rising above $35 per ounce by the late 1960s, and more and more foreigners, especially the French government, bought gold from the "gold window" at the Treasury.

On August 15, 1971, President Richard Nixon announced that he was closing the gold window and the Treasury would no longer sell gold to foreigners for $35 per ounce. Nixon ended the Breton Woods Agreement that fixed exchange rates between currencies. He also announced his infamous 90-day freeze on prices, wages, and rents in the United States.

It was not a good day for honest money or financial freedom. The period from 1966 until 1986 was the wilderness years for U.S. gold and silver. The U.S. Mint gradually removed silver entirely from its coinage and later even copper from its pennies. The coins they did produce, such as the Eisenhower dollar and the Kennedy half dollar, never did circulate, and subsequent coins, the Susan B. Anthony dollar and the Sacagawea dollar, have never caught on.

If you want to give a gold or silver coin with mint dates between 1966 and 1986, you will need to find a foreign gold or silver coin.

The Modern Era of Fiat Money

With the end of the silver certificate program, and the closing of the gold window, the only currency in commercial use was Federal Reserve Notes, the legal tender greenbacks that were no longer redeemable in gold or silver. Today, we call it the "fiat" money standard, meaning that Federal Reserve Notes are legal tender, and individuals and businesses are required to accept the government currency for all transactions and payment of debts and taxes. The term "fiat" is Latin, meaning "let it be done." "Fiat" money is not backed by any commodity, only by the "full faith and credit" of the United States.

All countries today have "fiat" money systems, although some countries like Switzerland still require that its treasuries keep on reserve a certain percentage of gold or silver. All major nations and the International Monetary Fund (IMF) hold millions of ounces of gold in reserve, and they often add or subtract from their hoard by buying and selling gold from each other or from private sources. Recent net buyers of gold have included China and India.

Figure 7
The Federal Reserve Note today

The United States Treasury still owns approximately 150 million ounces of gold, held at Fort Knox, Tenn., and at the New York Federal Reserve in downtown Manhattan. Some critics dispute whether the U.S. owns this much gold and have demanded an audit.

The Return of Legal Tender Gold and Silver Coins Under President Reagan

When gold was legalized in the United States in 1975, Americans could invest in precious metals by buying in either (a) older coins such, as the Saint-Gaudens double eagle gold coins and the Morgan or Peace silver dollars, (b) bags of "junk" silver (pre-1965 halves, quarters, or dimes), or (c) foreign bullion coins, especially the South African Krugerrand, a one-ounce gold coin.

Investing in convenient one-ounce bullion coins like the Krugerrand were so popular by 1985, President Ronald Reagan—a long-time believer in sound money—signed into law the Gold Bullion Act that instructed the U.S. Mint to produce gold and silver bullion coins in convenient sizes to match the popularity of the Krugerrand.

Since then, the U.S. Mint has produced millions of American eagle gold bullion coins and silver bullion coins. The gold eagle is a legal tender gold coin that has a nominal value of $50. Coins are available in 1, ½, ¼, and 1/10 ounces.

Since 1997, the U.S. Mint has also made available a platinum bullion coin with the same dimensions.

Return of the Silver Dollar

The silver bullion coin is unique. It is a legal tender coin that has a nominal value of $1 and contains exactly one troy ounce of silver bullion. Thus, it is about 10 percent larger than the old Morgan and Peace silver dollars. See figure below.

The new silver dollar has several features worth noting:

1. The front has a beautiful rendition of Miss Liberty, the mintage year, the words "Liberty" and "In God We Trust," and a spectacular rising sun (Ben Franklin's image of America's rising fortunes).
2. The obverse has the words "United States of America;" the official insignia of the United States, an Eagle with arrows (military strength) and the olive leaf (peace); 13 stars representing the original 13 colonies.

The new silver dollar is a striking coin of tremendous beauty, and it belongs in every investor's portfolio.

Why Silver Is a Good Long-Term Investment

I recommend silver as a long-term investment, and the new silver dollars are a great way to accumulate and transfer wealth, among other things.

Silver is unique, in that it is both an industrial and monetary metal. Its price is far more volatile than gold's. When the economy is weak, silver is likely to trade more like a base metal, for which supply and demand have a greater impact.

But silver is money . . . just as gold is money. It is not just another commodity. There is also a strong monetary demand for silver. Asians (especially India) have had a strong cultural affinity for hoarding silver. In the United States, silver has served as the foundation of its monetary system for more than two centuries. Today the U.S. Mint produces more than 20 million silver bullion coins per year.

While silver has been volatile, the long-term return on silver is significant—around 6 percent per year in compounded return, as Figure 1 indicates. That's more than enough to maintain its hedge against price and monetary inflation.

Ten Creative Ways to Use Your Silver Coins

Over the years, I've discovered a wide use for silver coins. Here are ten great ways:

1. Create a "buried treasure" with your silver. Store silver dollars along with your gold and other valuables in a safe deposit box, or a home safe. They make a great long-term hedge against inflation. The silver bullion coins come conveniently in rolls of 20 coins.

Or you can be a little more creative with ways to safely and privately hide away your hard assets. For example, Jim Cook of Investment Rarities sold thousands of "midnight gardeners," large heavy-duty pipe containers that can hold a large number of gold and silver coins and other valuables. (Just be sure to remember and write down where you buried the midnight gardeners, or you may find yourself losing a fortune. It happens all too often.)

2. Use a silver dollar as a good luck piece and keep it in your pocket or purse at all times. Take it out from time to time and feel the coin in your hand. Admire its beauty and its many messages of inspiration and patriotism. Look at the words "In God We Trust" and admire the fine workmanship of a bygone era when we enjoyed sound money in today's unstable world. Keeping that coin in your pocket will keep you well grounded in sound economics.

I have some misgivings about the way investors use silver coins.

They are a good long-term investment, and that's why the vast majority of silver dollars, both old and new—which includes probably more than 500,000 Morgan and Peace silver dollars and 200,000 American eagle silver dollars—are stored away in some vault, and most investors squirrel away their silver in private vaults, never to see the light of day or the eye of an admirer.

Today, it's popular to grade silver dollars and package them in Professional Coin Grading Service's (PCGS) or other professional grading services' plastic containers, then hide them away in safe deposit boxes or safes. The only time you see these rare beauties is at coin shows or investment conferences.

I'd like to change that. For many years, I've been showing friends and acquaintances the rare beauty of silver and gold coins, giving them away as gifts, and encouraging others to do so.

Most importantly, if we are ever going to return to a hard-money system, we need to spread the message. What better way to do it than to circulate silver dollars?

In short, it's not enough to invest in and store silver dollars; it's time to circulate them. Here are several suggestions.

3. Buy silver as decorative art or jewelry. I know collectors who have bought sculptures, such as Frederick Remington's *Bronco Buster*, all in solid silver. If you buy at the right price, it can be an excellent investment. Silver necklaces, bracelets, and earrings are also popular and, again, if purchased at a reasonable price, can be good deals.

In 1999, Jim Blanchard, founder of the New Orleans conference and a long-time friend, died. In honor of his life and friendship, I gave his wife Lesia a 1943 Walking Liberty silver half-dollar coin in brilliant uncirculated condition. Why 1943? That was the year he was born. Why a half-dollar Walking Liberty? Because from the age of 17, he was paralyzed from the waist down. Why the Liberty silver coin? Because he was a devote believer in the cause of freedom and sound money. Lesia had it made into a necklace that she wears today.

4. Offer silver dollars to employees on special occasions or holidays, or to show your appreciation for a job well done. Make sure that the mint date is current, so that when employees look at the date, they will be reminded of what they did when you gave them a silver dollar. I know presidents of companies who have given every employee a silver dollar during the holidays and at other special times.

5. Silver dollars make great tips for an extraordinary job by a bell hop, clerk, waiter, or tour guide. They almost always recognize a silver dollar and will cherish it forever.

Sometimes a manager won't normally take a tip, so I get around it by the following technique: After they do a good deed for me, I pull out a silver dollar from my pocket and say, "Have you ever seen one of these?"

Usually they will say, "It's a silver dollar."

In response, I say, "It's yours. Thanks for helping me out." And I hand them the coin. They never refuse it.

And they will always remember you.

In fact, for the past twenty years, a bell hop has worked at the New Orleans Hilton Hotel, where the annual New Orleans Investment Conference is held (founded by Jim Blanchard). His name is John. Twenty years ago, I gave him a silver dollar for helping with my bags. I came back a year later, and when I arrived at the Hilton, he was there to greet me, "Welcome back, Mr. Skousen!"

I've given him a silver dollar every year.

6. Offer a silver dollar as a marketing incentive. At FreedomFest, my annual show in Las Vegas, we always offer a newly minted silver dollar to the first 100 people who sign up. It really works. At the conference, I tell everyone to get a silver dollar as a symbol of FreedomFest, and then I encourage them to go the exhibit hall, track down one of the many coin dealers at the conference, and buy a silver dollar or a bunch of them. The coin dealers love it, and it's a good deal for attendees too.

During presidential election years, I would give away silver dimes at the MoneyShows in Orlando, Las Vegas, and San Francisco. (Shades of John D. Rockefeller, who was famous for giving out dimes to visitors and children. See photo below.) As a marketing tool to attract people to our booth, I announced to the large audience that we would give anyone who came to our booth a genuine pre-1965 silver dime. Hundreds showed up to get their dime.

I gave them two choices. I said, "If you are a Democrat or member of the Green Party, we offer you the Roosevelt dime," with FDR's image on it. "If you are a Republican or Libertarian, we offer you a Lady Liberty dime," because of the image of Lady Liberty (also called the "Mercury" dime).

Interestingly, we ran out of Lady Liberty dimes. Most attendees of the MoneyShows turned out to be conservatives and libertarians.

7. Give silver dollars to siblings, relatives, children, and grandchildren when you visit them or for special occasions. Silver dollars make great gifts for birthdays, graduations, baptisms, Bar Mitzvah, becoming an Eagle Scout, going on a mission, anniversaries, or any other achievement. They will love them and remember you.

I recommend you give silver dollars that your friends and relatives can feel in their hands. I know it is popular to have coins graded, certified, and preserved in a hard plastic container, such as those the PCGS offers, but I think it's valuable for people to actually feel the coins in their hands like our ancestors did in the early twentieth century. Certified coins are an excellent idea for rare or collectible coins, but they usually aren't necessary for common-dated coins and bullion coins.

8. Use the silver dollar as a fun game. One game is called "spin the silver dollar." See who can spin the silver dollar for the longest time until it comes to rest. The record is 25 seconds, held by my son Tim. It's best to spin the coin on a very hard surface.

Another fun game is "buried treasure." Every youngster has dreamed of finding a buried treasure of gold and silver doubloons on a deserted island. How many times have you seen people using metal detectors at the beach to find long-lost coins?

William F. Buckley tells the story of when he buried a treasure chest of silver and gold coins on an island for his son, Christopher, and his friends to find. He left them a map, and Christopher and his friends had to sail to the island and find the buried treasure chest. Unfortunately, right after Buckley buried the treasury, a hurricane came through the Northeast and so changed the landscape of the island that they never could find the buried treasure.

9. Use silver dollars as an estate planning tool. Silver privately purchased from coin dealers or coin shows are a great way to build financial assets that can easily be transferred during your lifetime to friends and colleagues without paying an estate tax. Just be sure you give under the gift exemption rules.

10. Use the silver dollar as a teaching tool. As a professor and lecturer, I use the silver dollar frequently as an object lesson or visual aid.

In the early 1980s, silver had soared briefly to more than $30 per ounce. At the New Orleans conference, I announced to the audience of several thousand that one of my recommended coin dealers was offering each attendee the opportunity to buy a silver dime for a $1 bill. It sound-ed crazy on the surface that anyone would pay a dollar for a dime, but literally hundreds lined up to do so. Why? At the time a silver dime was worth $1.20. It demonstrated of how little value a dollar bill has become.

When I teach the story of money in college or in a lecture, I ask a student to take out four quarters and drop them on the table. It makes a tingling sound. Then I drop a silver dollar on the table, and it makes a loud thump, or a ringing sound. The difference is like night and day between today's token coins and yesterday's solid silver. We talk about how our money, like our culture and our values, has declined over time.

It reminds me of a book in my library called *Roman History From Coins*, by Michael Grant (Cambridge University Press, 1958). Not surprisingly, Roman coins mirror the rise, decline, and fall of the Roman Empire. At first, the Romans put images of animals and plants on its coins, followed by Roman gods, then dead heroes, and finally living rulers, such as Caesar.

After passing around a gold certificate and a silver certificate, followed by a double eagle gold coin and Morgan silver dollar, I ask a student to show me a dollar bill, a Federal Reserve Note.

I ask the student, "Where is the contract between the government and the holder of the dollar bill?"

If he remembers his history, the student answers, "There isn't any. It says 'Federal Reserve Note.'"

"That's correct," I respond. "And the Federal Reserve Note doesn't even pay interest. This dollar bill isn't worth the paper it's printed on."

And then I proceed to tear up the student's $1 bill. Everybody in the classroom is shocked that I would destroy this student's property.

After teaching them a lesson in sound money, I then turn back to the student and say, "I destroyed your property. Do you want your $1 back?"

If he says, "Yes, please," I reach into my pocket and hand him a silver dollar. "Here's your dollar back!" By that time, every student in the class is green with envy that they didn't get to participate in this experiment in monetary economics.

Giving Away Silver Dollars With Unique Dates

On other occasions, I use the old Morgan silver dollars to illustrate the difference between Keynesians, Marxists, and Austrian economists.

When I was teaching at Rollins College in Winter Park, Fla., one of my colleagues in the economics department was a radical Marxist. I was visiting one day in his office and pulled out an old silver dollar and said, "Erich, I'd like to give you this silver dollar as an expression of our friendship, but only on one condition. You have to name the economist who died in the year this coin was minted."

He smiled and was delighted to meet the challenge. He looked at the coin and the date, "1883."

"Oh, that's easy," he said, "It's Karl Marx!"

I responded quickly, "That's right. Don't ever forget it. He's dead!"

But the Marxist professor was quick on his feet. He retorted, "Yes, you're right, Karl Marx is dead. But I'M ALIVE!"

Indeed, he is right. Sorry to say, Marxism is still alive and well on many campuses in the world.

For Keynesians, I ask a slightly different question. For example, recently I had dinner with Lord Robert Skidelsky, who has written a three-volume definitive biography of John Maynard Keynes. I asked him, "Can you identify the economist who was born in the year this coin was minted?"

Of course, he answered, looking at the 1883 date: "Keynes."

The fun part came afterwards. I asked him if he knew which economist died in 1883 .... He said he wasn't sure, but thought it was Marx.

"Right again," I said. "And don't forget it. Marx died and was reincarnated into Keynes!"

He was not amused by this suggestion.

For economists and political thinkers with a free-market bent, I offer them a Morgan silver dollar with a slightly different date. I present them with a coin dated 1881. It's an unusual date because it's a palindrome, that is, it is the same number whether you read it upside down or backwards. So it's a unique date for a famous economist.

I ask, "Can you name the economist who was born on the date this coin was minted?"

I actually asked this question to George W. Bush in 2000 when he was running for president. He came close. He said, "Hayek?", referring to Friedrich A. Hayek, the great Austrian economist who was born in 1899.

He was close. "It's Ludwig von Mises, the father of the new Austrian school." But I gave him the coin anyway—my only contribution to his campaign. Maybe he carried this lucky coin on him and that's why he won the 2000 election by a handful of votes.

As they say, in every cloud, there's a silver lining.

The Austrian School of Economics: Pro-Gold and Pro-Silver

The Austrian school of economics is the strongest defender of gold and silver as monetary metals and support a return to the classical gold standard. Most other schools of thought, including the Keynesians and monetarists, are against returning to the gold standard, which they regard as the "barbarous relic."

I encourage everyone reading this booklet to learn more about the Austrian school by reading the works of Ludwig von Mises, Friedman Hayek, Murray Rothbard, Henry Hazlitt, and many others. (Several of my books highlight the Austrian school, including *The Making of Modern Economics*; *Vienna and Chicago, Friends or Foes?*; and *Economic Logic*.)

Use Those Paper Dollars to Buy Silver Dollars

Once you have decided to invest in silver and gold, what's the next step? What should you do? And what should you not do?

First and foremost, cash in those Federal Reserve Notes, which lose value year after year, and invest in hard assets that are a good hedge against inflation. I recommend you invest a portion of your investment assets, 10–15 percent depending on economic conditions, in gold and silver. Here are some choices:

- In your brokerage accounts or individual retirement accounts (IRAs), add gold and silver bullion in the form of exchange-traded funds (ETFs), such as SPDR Gold Trust (GLD), which holds gold bullion, and iShares Silver Trust (SLV), which holds silver bullion.
- Buy American eagle silver bullion coins from the U.S. Mint or reputable dealer, and store them safely at home or in a safe deposit box. Consider buying them in rolls of 20. Silver bullion coins are also available in other countries, such as Canada and Australia. It's best to buy coins minted in the country where you reside for maximum recognition and liquidity. If you live in the United States, buy American eagles. If you live

in Canada, buy Canadian maple leafs. And so forth.
- Buy common dated collectible coins in uncirculated condition, such as the Morgan and Peace silver dollars, and pre-1965 silver dimes, quarters, and halves. I also recommend Walking Liberty (1916–47) half dollars, Franklin half dollars (1948–63), and the Kennedy half dollar (1964).

I also recommend a variety of common dated gold coins in uncirculated condition, such as the Saint-Gaudens double eagle gold coin (1850–1933).

Avoid entirely the oversized Eisenhower dollars (1971–78), Susan B. Anthony dollars, and Sacagawea dollars, which have no silver content and are generally unpopular with collectors. They are not likely to hold their value against inflation in the long run.

Where to Buy Silver and Gold Coins

You can buy silver and gold coins from several sources:

1. Order through reputable coin dealers with a long-standing tradition of consumer satisfaction. You can buy coins in person at local coin shops or from national coin dealers by calling their 800 number. A majority of states charge sales taxes on coin purchases, so most investors buy bullion coins through the mail.

Note that there is a bid-asked spread between the price you pay and the price you sell your coins. Plus you will pay a commission to the coin dealer.

You should be very careful in selecting a coin dealer, because the industry has seen many dealers come and go over the years. Many coin dealers who have advertised heavily end up going out of business or committing fraud, leaving customers holding the bag.

If you would like my current list of recommended coin dealers, please email me at editor@markskousen.com, and I'll be glad to send you the list.

Even among reputable dealers, prices do vary, so I urge you to shop around and see which dealer offers the best deal.

2. Attend coin shows. Major cities have one or two coin shows every year, and this is an excellent opportunity to become educated in silver and gold, and the variety of products offered for sale. You might go the first time without much cash or a checking account, because I guarantee you will be tempted to buy.

Caveat Emptor: Dos and Don'ts

Buying silver on margin or futures contracts is not recommended, except for the sophisticated investor. Futures and options trading is too risky for the conservative investor. Your best approach is to buy silver coins with cash, store them, and profit in the long run.

As Jim Cook states, "Owning physical silver is a more modest, conservative, and humble way to go. Fortunately, this humble approach offers the greatest opportunity for gains and the least risk. By purchasing actual physical silver, and taking it into your possession, you put yourself in the best position to capitalize on a rise in the silver price. By owning it outright, you are far more likely to continue holding for the time period necessary to maximize profits."

What about silver in your IRA (individual retirement account)? Custodial accounts are available for storing physical gold and silver in your IRA, but a more convenient way to do it is by buying exchange-traded funds (ETFs) in gold bullion (symbol GLD) and silver bullion (symbol SLV).

I'd also be very careful about storing your precious metals with a dealer. Better to store them yourself at home, a bank safe deposit box, or with a reputable independent institution (such as the Perth Mint in Australia). Over the years, I've read of numerous cases in which investors stored their hard assets with coin companies that run into trouble or engaged in fraud. Don't let it happen to you. Take possession of your gold and silver coins as much as possible, and store them securely. Theft is a serious problem when it comes to precious metals. Thieves love to discover bullion and coins in people's homes because they are nonidentifiable.

Silver bars in troy ounces (from one ounce to 400 ounce bars) are available, and are especially popular in Europe, but I prefer more recognizable legal tender silver coins issued by various national mints around the world.

Nor am I a fan of buying privately minted silver or gold coins. You often overpay for these coins or medallions. You may have a hard time selling them in the secondary market or on eBay. Why bother, when you can buy coins produced and certified by the U.S. Mint and coins that have a ready market.

Finally, don't use U.S. gold and silver coins to minimize taxes. Several investors have sold assets at the face value of gold and silver coins to minimize capital gains taxes, based on the fact that these coins are still legal tender. However, the IRS has challenged these tax strategies and the federal courts have routinely supported the IRS's position. Result? You end up paying back taxes, interest, and penalties.

Summary: Gresham's Law at Work

We have learned in these pages that the U.S. government issues two legal tender dollars—the paper dollar Federal Reserve Note and the American eagle silver dollar.

Fifty years ago, the paper dollar and the silver dollar circulated together, one interchangeable with the other. But then the silver content of the silver dollar became worth more than $1, and gradually the silver dollar disappeared, leaving Federal Reserve Notes as the only circulating currency.

This disappearing act is an example of Gresham's law. It is named after Sir Thomas Gresham (1519–79), who coined the phrase, "Bad money drives out good."

In this modern case, the bad money, Federal Reserve Notes, drove the good money, silver dollars, out of circulation.

Since 1960, the circulating bad money has lost 90 percent of its value, while the uncirculating good money has increased seventeen fold.

And let there be no mistake about it. Paper money issued by the state is bad money and should be replaced by silver and gold dollars, the good money.

If all of you who read this booklet follow my advice and invest in good money, and encourage your friends, neighbors, and associates to turn their paper money into silver and gold, we may well return to a sound monetary system.

Recommended Reading

Theodore Butler, *Silver in the New Era* (Investment Rarities, 2005).

James R. Cook, *The Silver Lining* (Investment Rarities, 2007).

Michael Grant, *Roman History From Coins* (Cambridge University Press, 1958). Great little book of 110 pages, illustrated, on how you can learn the history of ancient Rome through the images and values of Roman coins.

William F. Rickenbacker, *Wooden Nickels, Or, the Decline and Fall of Silver Coins* (Arlington House, 1966). The story of the great silver shortage of 1964–65.

Murray N. Rothbard, *What Has Government Done to Our Money?* (Ludwig von Mises Institute, 1990). Reveals the mysteries of money like no other book.

Mark Skousen, *Economics of a Pure Gold Standard* (Foundation for Economic Education, 2010, fourth edition). The history of gold and silver as money. It compares the gold standard with free banking, fractional reserve banking, monetarism, and central banking.

Jerome F. Smith, *Silver Profits in the Eighties* (Books in Focus, 1982). An update of the classic work, "Silver Profits in the Seventies."

James Turk and John Rubino, *The Collapse of the Dollar and How to Profit from It: Make a Fortune by Investing in Gold and Other Hard Assets* (Broadway Business, 2008).

PART III

Austrian Economics:
Newsletters, Books, and Services

A AUSTRIAN ECONOMICS: NEWSLETTERS, BOOKS, AND SERVICES

I hope these chapters (plus the additional articles) have given you a better sense of what Austrian economics is all about and why many financial writers rely on its theories. If you to subscribe to financial newsletters and other services that rely on Austrian economics, consider the following:

Applied Austrian School Economics Ltd., managed by Dr. Frank Shostak, based in Tel Aviv, Israel. He offers a weekly report. For more information, go to www.aaseconomics.com.

Profitable Investing, edited by Richard Band. Richard is a long-time friend who writes a monthly newsletter, with weekly updates. Like me, he tends to be more optimistic in his outlook for the economy and the stock market. He often relies on Austrian economics in his analysis of the macro economy. For more information, go to www.rband.com.

Adrian Day Asset Management is a money management firm managed by Adrian Day, another long-time friend and investment writer. Adrian emphasizes value investing on a global basis, especially in mining companies. He has an excellent track record. He states, "Austrian economics infuses my entire thought process." For more information, go to www.adriandayassetmanagement.com.

The Wellington Letter, edited by Bert Dohmen. Bert writes a monthly newsletter, and offers additional services. Bert is another long-time friend who has been more bearish in recent years. He was one of the few analysts to anticipate in the 2008 financial crisis. For more information, go to www.dohmencapital.com.

Euro Pacific Capital, a full-service brokerage firm that specializes in foreign stocks and precious metals, managed by Peter Schiff. Schiff is the author of several books that stress Austrian economics. His latest work is *The Real Crash*. He also writes a weekly column for Euro Pacific Capital. For more information, go towww.europac.net.

Capital & Crisis newsletter, edited by Chris Mayer, a former banker, and published by Agora. Chris focuses on value investing: www.capitalandcrisis.agorafinancial.com

The Dollar Vigilante, edited by Jeff Berwick. Jeff offers advice on the effect of a falling dollar: www.dollarvigilante.com

Barnhart Investment Advisory is a Chicago based fee-only investment firm managed by Ted Barnhart. Ted writes a blog called "Austrian School of Investment Thought" at www.barnhart advisory.wordpress.com.

Thomas Aubrey runs *Credit Capital Advisory*, a consulting service based in the UK, which provides "insights into the impact of credit disequilibrium on the financial markets." I recommend his book, *Profiting From Monetary Policy: Investing Through the Business Cycle* (Palgrave Macmillan, 2013). For more information, go to www.creditcapitaladvisory.com, or email info@creditcapitaladvisory.com.

You might also be interested in participating in various social media that focuses on Austrian economics and finance on Yahoo, LinkedIn, Facebook, etc.

My Own Services

Forecasts & Strategies is my monthly investment newsletter, published by Eagle Publishing. Subscribers also receive an updated weekly hotline by email and voice recording every Monday. I've been writing my letter since 1980, when Ronald Reagan was elected president. According to the *Hulbert Financial Digest*, my newsletter has outperformed the market in eight of the past nine years. For more information, go to www.markskousen.com.

Books About Austrian Economics

I've also written several books related to Austrian economics that investors might find useful:

The Structure of Production (New York University Press, 1990, updated with a new introduction in 2007) makes the case for a new model of the economy, developed from an Austrian perspective. It is an academic book for advanced students, but the latter half of the book is particularly useful to investors who want to understand the inner workings of the economy, especially why some stocks are inherently more volatile than others.

Rick Rule, a security analyst specializing in natural resource companies, recommends it to all of his clients who want to understand the mining business and how gold stocks relate to the rest of the financial markets.

Economics of a Pure Gold Standard, now in its fourth edition, is published by the Foundation for Economic Education. It makes the case for gold as the best monetary system and discusses gold as a superior inflation hedge since we went off the gold standard in 1971.

Vienna and Chicago, Friends or Foes? Published in 2005 by Capital Press, this book describes the philosophical rivalry between the Austrian and the Chicago schools of free-market economics, especially in four areas in which they have strong disagreements. At the end of each chapter, I conclude who has the upper hand, by either stating "Advantage, Chicago" or "Advantage, Vienna."

Investing in One Lesson. Published in 2007, the one lesson is "Wall Street exaggerates everything: The business of investing is not the same as investing in a business." The lesson is based upon the Austrian insight that economic activity (like the capital markets) further removed from final consumption tends to more volatile.

Happy investing! And remember: A.E.I.O.U.

B BIOGRAPHY

Mark Skousen, Ph. D., is a financial economist, professor, and author with more than 40 years' experience on Wall Street. Since 1980, he has been editor-in-chief of *Forecasts & Strategies*, a monthly investment newsletter that often uses Austrian economics to analyze the economy and the markets (www.markskousen.com).

He has the unique distinction of having worked for the government (CIA), non-profits (president of FEE), and for-profit companies. Currently, he holds the Benjamin Franklin Chair of Management at Grantham University. In 2004–05, he taught economics and finance at Columbia Business School and Columbia University.

Skousen received his Ph. D. in monetary economics in 1977 from George Washington University, where his doctoral dissertation was on "The Economics of a Pure Gold Standard" (later published by the Mises Institute and now the Foundation for Economic Education). He has been an economic analyst for the CIA, a columnist to *Forbes* magazine, chairman of Investment U, and past president of the Foundation for Economic Education (FEE) in New York. He is the editor of his own website, www.mskousen.com, and is the producer of FreedomFest, "the world's largest gathering of free minds," which meets every July in Las Vegas (www.freedomfest.com). He has written for the *Wall Street Journal*, *Forbes*, and the *Christian Science Monitor* and has made regular appearances on CNBC's *Kudlow & Co.* and C-SPAN Book TV.

Several of his works focus on Austrian economics, including *The Structure of Production* (1990, 2007), a macroeconomic model built on the work of Menger, Mises, and Hayek; *Economic Logic* (2000, 2010, 2013), a college-level textbook on Austrian economics; *The Making of Modern Economics* (2001, 2009), which has three chapters on Austrian economists; *Vienna and Chicago, Friends or Foes?* (2005), which contrasts the Austrian and Chicago schools of free-market economics. Skousen has also written for the *Quarterly Journal of Austrian Economics*, and the *Journal of Economic Perspectives*.

Skousen's financial books include *Investing in One Lesson* (2007) and *The Maxims of Wall Street* (2012), the first collection of all the famous Wall Street sayings.

He was recently named one of the top twenty most influential living economists in the world today (www.superscholar.org). In honor of his work in economics, finance, and management, Grantham University renamed its business school, "The Mark Skousen School of Business."

INDEX

A

C

D

E

F

G

H

I

J

K

L

M

N

O

P

S

T

U

V

W

Y

Z